Emo

Thesaurus

Abdullahi Hagar

Other books by Abdullahi Hagar

Sentence Thesaurus
Sentence Starters
Dialogue Tags
Transistional Words & Phrases
Adjective Thesaurus
Adverb Thesaurus
Verb Thesaurus

A

AFFECTION
Definition: A gentle feeling of fondness or liking.
See FONDNESS

Affection came over me.
Affection crossed my face.
Affection fell over me.
Affection filled my eyes.
Affection filled my mind.
Affection flowed around me.
Affection pierced my heart.
Affection saturated my voice.
Affection surged through me.
Affection swept through me.
Affection warred inside me.
Affection washed over me.
Affection washed through me.
Affection welled inside me.
I smiled with affection.
Affection blazed in my eyes.
Affection burned in my eyes.
Affection crept into my voice.
Affection gleamed in my eyes.
Affection radiated from my face.
Affection shimmered in my expression.
Affection shone in my eyes.
Affection shone through my tears.
Affection stirred in my breast.

My chest squeezed with affection.
My chest swelled with affection.
My eyes brimmed with affection.
My eyes darkened with affection.
My eyes filled with affection.
My eyes glowed with affection.
My eyes moistened with affection.
My eyes shimmered with affection.
My eyes shone with affection.
My eyes softened with affection.
My face filled with affection.
My face suffused with affection.
My heart ached with affection.
My heart engorged with affection.
My heart filled with affection.
My heart fluttered with affection.
My heart looked for affection.

My heart overflowed with affection.
My heart soared with affection.
My heart squeezed with affection.
My heart swelled with affection.
My heart swollen with affection.
My heart warmed with affection.
My throat tightened as affection.
My tone filled with affection.
My voice deepened with affection.
My voice throbbed with affection.
I felt a burst of affection.
I felt a flood of affection.
I felt a glow of affection.
I felt a gust of affection.
I felt a pang of affection.
I felt a prick of affection.
I felt a pulse of affection.
I felt a rush of affection.
I felt a surge of affection.
I felt a swell of affection.
I felt a wave of affection.
I felt an undercurrent of affection.
My eyes lit up with affection.
My eyes were full of affection.
My eyes were misty with affection.
My eyes were warm with affection.

My face was soft with affection.
My heart was full of affection.
My heart was heavy with affection.
My voice was full of affection.

AGGRAVATION

Definition: Annoyance or exasperation.
See ANNOYANCE

Aggravation clouded my face.
Aggravation crawled through me.
Aggravation crossed my face.
Aggravation crossed my forehead.
Aggravation entered my expression.
Aggravation entered my voice.
Aggravation filled my face.
Aggravation grated my voice.
Aggravation laced my voice.
Aggravation moved through me.
Aggravation rose in me.
Aggravation sifted through me.
Aggravation washed over me.
Aggravation burned in my gut.
Aggravation crept into my expression.
Aggravation crept into my voice.
Aggravation descended over my features.
Aggravation faded from my expression.
Aggravation flared on my face.
Aggravation flashed across my face.
Aggravation flashed in my eyes.

Aggravation flickered across my face.
Aggravation flickered in my eyes.
Aggravation flickered over my face.
Aggravation passed through my eyes.
Aggravation rang in my words.
Aggravation ripped through my body.
Aggravation scratched at my temper.
Aggravation settled over my face.
Aggravation washed across my face.
My brows lowered in aggravation.
My eyebrows furrowed in aggravation.
My eyes flashed with aggravation.
My eyes flickered with aggravation.
My eyes gleamed with aggravation.
My eyes glowed with aggravation.
My eyes narrowed in aggravation.
My eyes snapped with aggravation.

My eyes went from
aggravation.
My face crawled with
aggravation.
My face tightened with
aggravation.
My face twisted in aggravation.
My face went from
aggravation.
My head jerked in aggravation.
My head throbbed with
aggravation.
My lips crimped with
aggravation.
My lips tightened in
aggravation.
My mouth tightened in
aggravation.
My mouth tightened with
aggravation.
My tone rose with aggravation.
My voice ragged with
aggravation.
My voice rasped with
aggravation.
My voice rose with
aggravation.
My voice strained with
aggravation.
My voice tinged with
aggravation.
My eyes were sharp with
aggravation.
My face grew pinched with
aggravation.
My tone was sharp with
aggravation.

AGITATION

Definition: A state of anxiety or nervous excitement.
See ANXIETY

Agitation ate into me.
Agitation churned inside me.
Agitation clawed at me.
Agitation coursed through me.
Agitation crossed my face.
Agitation edged my voice.
Agitation filled my voice.
Agitation flooded over me.
Agitation knotted my gut.
Agitation knotted my insides.
Agitation knotted my shoulders.
Agitation knotted my stomach.
Agitation laced my voice.
Agitation lined my face.
Agitation pinched my lips.
Agitation pumped my heart.
Agitation ran through me.
Agitation rushed through me.
Agitation scraped my spine.
Agitation slipped from me.
Agitation squeezed my belly.
Agitation swept over me.
Agitation swept through me.
Agitation swirled through me.
Agitation thickened my accent.
Agitation tightened my breath.
Agitation tightened my shoulders.
Agitation tugged at me.
Agitation washed over me.

Agitation washed through me.
Agitation weighed on me.
Agitation went through me.
Agitation wormed through me.
Agitation came into my eyes.
Agitation churned in my gut.
Agitation coursed through my veins.
Agitation crawled up my back.
Agitation crept into my voice.
Agitation crept up my spine.
Agitation etched across my face.
Agitation flickered in my eyes.
Agitation nagged at my mind.
Agitation plucked at my chest.
Agitation pressed against my chest.
Agitation pulsed through my body.
Agitation pumped through my veins.
Agitation roared in my head.
Agitation roiled in my gut.
Agitation rose in my throat.
Agitation skittered down my spine.
Agitation slithered up my spine.
Agitation spilled through my guts.

Agitation sprinted across my eyes.
Agitation swept through my body.
Agitation trembled in my stomach.
Agitation whispered in my gut.
My body hummed with agitation.
My body knotted with agitation.
My chest heaved with agitation.
My eyebrows furrowed in agitation.
My eyes blinked in agitation.
My eyes clouded with agitation.
My eyes widened in agitation.
My face creased in agitation.
My face creased with agitation.
My face flooded with agitation.
My face flushed with agitation.
My face pinched with agitation.
My face twisted with agitation.
My face wisped with agitation.
My head throbbed with agitation.
My jaw worked with agitation.
My mouth puckered with agitation.
My nose quivered with agitation.
My shoulders knotted with agitation.

My stomach clenched in agitation.
My stomach cramped with agitation.
My stomach knotted with agitation.
My voice broken with agitation.
My voice marbled with agitation.
My voice rose in agitation.
My voice shook with agitation.
My voice strained with agitation.
My voice tinged with agitation.
Agitation caused my throat to tighten.
My eyes were bright with agitation.
My face was full of agitation.
My mouth was dry with agitation.
My spine went cold with agitation.
My voice was taut with agitation.
My voice was thin with agitation.

AGONY
Definition: Extreme physical or mental suffering.
See SUFFERING

Agony clapped my hands.
Agony crashed through me.
Agony exploded inside me.
Agony exploded through me.
Agony ignited my nerves.
Agony paralysed my legs.
Agony pierced my body.
Agony pierced my sinuses.
Agony pulsed through me.
Agony ripped through me.
Agony stabbed my side.
I gasped in agony.
I grimaced in agony.
I groaned in agony.
I grunted in agony.
I stiffened in agony.
I writhed in agony.
Agony came over my face.
Agony crawled around my mind.
Agony etched on my face.
Agony exploded in my guts.
Agony flared from my fingertips.
Agony flared in my ribs.
Agony flared up my leg.
Agony froze in my throat.
Agony radiated from my back.
Agony ripped across my face.
Agony ripped through my body.
Agony ripped through my head.

Agony rushed through my body.
Agony seared through my leg.
Agony shrieked from my mouth.
Agony struck my nervous system.
Agony swept through my body.
Agony tore up my spine.
Agony welled into my eyes.
My body contorted in agony.
My body convulsed in agony.
My body creamed in agony.
My body exploded in agony.
My body screamed with agony.
My body shrieked in agony.
My body spasmed in agony.
My body throbbed in agony.
My body writhed in agony.
My ears stabbed with agony.
My eyes closed in agony.
My eyes filled with agony.
My eyes glazed in agony.
My eyes narrowed in agony.
My eyes rolled in agony.
My face clenched in agony.
My face contorted in agony.
My face contorted with agony.
My face etched in agony.
My face lined with agony.
My face twisted in agony.
My face twisted with agony.

My lips tightened in agony.
My nerves screamed in agony.
I bellowed a roar of agony.
I felt a stab of agony.
I gave a cry of agony.
I gave a howl of agony.
I uttered a shout of agony.
My body crumpled up in
agony.
My eyes glowed red with
agony.
My eyes opened wide with
agony.
My eyes were full of agony.
My face screwed up in agony.
My head hung low in agony.
My knees drew up in agony.
My mouth sagged open in
agony.
My voice was hoarse with
agony.

ALARM

Definition: An anxious awareness of danger.
See FEAR

Alarm clawed through me.
Alarm creased my face.
Alarm crossed my face.
Alarm plucked at me.
Alarm pulsed through me.
Alarm rang through me.
Alarm ripped through me.
Alarm shot through me.
Alarm spurred my pulse.
Alarm streaked through me.
Alarm wedged into me.
Alarm widened my eyes.
I flinched in alarm.
I froze with alarm.
I stiffened in alarm.
I swallowed in alarm.
Alarm buzzed in my head.
Alarm came over my face.
Alarm flashed in my eyes.
Alarm flickered in my eyes.
Alarm jingled on my wrist.
Alarm passed across my face.
Alarm probed into my brain.
Alarm raced into my eyes.
Alarm raced through my chest.
Alarm ripped through my gut.
Alarm shot through my eyes.
Alarm sounded in my brain.
Alarm strummed through my
nerves.
Alarm tingled inside my brain.
My body buzzed with alarm.
My body stiffened with alarm.

My body tingled with alarm.
My brows lifted in alarm.
My ears extended in alarm.
My eyes blazed with alarm.
My eyes blinked in alarm.
My eyes rounded in alarm.
My eyes widened in alarm.
My eyes widened with alarm.
My face filled with alarm.
My face flushed with alarm.
My face frozen in alarm.
My head jerked with alarm.
My head turned in alarm.
My heart leapt with alarm.
My heart thumped with alarm.
My mouth opened in alarm.
My voice cracked with alarm.
My voice rose in alarm.
My voice rose with alarm.
I felt a bolt of alarm.
I felt a flare of alarm.
I felt a flood of alarm.
I felt a flutter of alarm.
I felt a pinch of alarm.
I felt a ripple of alarm.
I felt a shock of alarm.
I felt a spark of alarm.
I felt a spike of alarm.
I felt a spurt of alarm.
I felt a stab of alarm.
I felt a sting of alarm.
I felt a stir of alarm.
I felt a surge of alarm.

I felt a thrill of alarm.
I felt a tremor of alarm.
I gave a cry of alarm.
I gave a kick of alarm.
I gave a shudder of alarm.
I gave a squeal of alarm.
My body was taut with alarm.
My eyes opened wide in alarm.
My eyes went wide with alarm.
My eyes were bright with
alarm.
My eyes were full of alarm.
My eyes were huge with alarm.
My eyes were unblinking with
alarm.
My eyes were wide in alarm.
My eyes were wide with alarm.
My head jerked up in alarm.
My spine was rigid in alarm.
My voice cried out with alarm.
My voice rose up in alarm.
My voice shouted out in alarm.
My voice was full of alarm.

AMAZEMENT

Definition: A feeling of great surprise or wonder.
See ASTONISHMENT

Amazement brightened my gaze.
Amazement coloured my voice.
Amazement crept over me.
Amazement crossed my face.
Amazement flared inside me.
Amazement jolted through me.
Amazement lit my eyes.
Amazement lit my face.
Amazement lit my features.
Amazement made me gasp.
Amazement parted my lips.
Amazement rose within me.
Amazement snaked through me.
Amazement twisted my gut.
I grunted in amazement.
Amazement came over my face.
Amazement edged into my voice.
Amazement flashed on my face.
Amazement flickered across my face.
Amazement flickered over my face.
Amazement flitted across my face.
Amazement lit up my face.

Amazement passed across my face.
Amazement passed over my face.
Amazement plastered across my face.
Amazement played across my face.
Amazement reflected in my eyes.
Amazement registered on my face.
Amazement settled on my face.
Amazement settled over my face.
Amazement showed in my eyes.
Amazement sounded in my voice.
My brows arched in amazement.
My brows climbed in amazement.
My brows lifted in amazement.
My brows raised in amazement.
My brows rose in amazement.
My ears flickered in amazement.
My eyebrows arched in amazement.

My eyebrows arched with amazement.
My eyebrows lifted in amazement.
My eyebrows raised in amazement.
My eyebrows rose in amazement.
My eyebrows rose with amazement.
My eyes blinked in amazement.
My eyes blinked with amazement.
My eyes bloomed with amazement.
My eyes brightened with amazement.
My eyes filled with amazement.
My eyes flared in amazement.
My eyes flared with amazement.
My eyes flashed from amazement.
My eyes flashed with amazement.
My eyes flickered with amazement.
My eyes fluttered in amazement.
My eyes opened in amazement.
My eyes popped in amazement.
My eyes popped with amazement.
My eyes rounded in amazement.

My eyes scrunched in amazement.
My eyes shut in amazement.
My eyes stared in amazement.
My eyes twinkled with amazement.
My eyes widened in amazement.
My eyes widened with amazement.
My face altered from amazement.
My face collapsed in amazement.
My face contorted with amazement.
My face frozen in amazement.
My face relaxed with amazement.
My face scrunched in amazement.
My face twisted in amazement.
My face winced in amazement.
My head cocked in amazement.
My head jerked in amazement.
My head shook in amazement.
My head throbbed with amazement.
My jaw dropped in amazement.
My jaw gaped in amazement.
My lips parted in amazement.
My lips rounded in amazement.
My mouth dropped in amazement.

My mouth gaped in amazement.
My mouth opened in amazement.
My mouth parted in amazement.
My skin deepened with amazement.
My voice filled with amazement.
I felt a shiver of amazement.
I felt a tinge of amazement.
I gave a whistle of amazement.
My body was motionless with amazement.
My brows shot up in amazement.
My eyebrows shot up in amazement.
My eyebrows went up in amazement.
My eyes bloomed wide with amazement.
My eyes flew open in amazement.
My eyes grew huge with amazement.
My eyes grew wide with amazement.
My eyes lit up in amazement.
My eyes opened wide in amazement.
My eyes opened wide with amazement.
My eyes shot up in amazement.
My eyes were full of amazement.
My eyes were luminous with amazement.
My eyes were wide in amazement.
My eyes were wide with amazement.
My face lit up in amazement.
My face screwed up in amazement.
My face was alive with amazement.
My face was blank with amazement.
My face was full of amazement.
My face was wide with amazement.
My head was abuzz with amazement.
My head whipped around in amazement.
My mouth dropped open in amazement.
My mouth fell open in amazement.
My mouth hung open in amazement.
My mouth was agape in amazement.
My mouth was wide in amazement.
My voice was soft with amazement.

AMUSEMENT

Definition: The state or experience of finding something funny.

See GLEE

Amusement brightened my eyes.

Amusement crossed my face.

Amusement flooded through me.

Amusement laced my voice.

I grunted with amusement.

I smiled in amusement.

I smiled with amusement.

I snorted with amusement.

Amusement faded from my eyes.

Amusement fell from my face.

Amusement flickered in my eyes.

Amusement ghosted over my features.

Amusement kindled in my gaze.

Amusement lit up my face.

Amusement played on my lips.

Amusement showed on my face.

My ears trembled with amusement.

My eyebrows rose in amusement.

My eyes beamed with amusement.

My eyes brightened with amusement.

My eyes crinkled in amusement.

My eyes crinkled with amusement.

My eyes danced with amusement.

My eyes flared with amusement.

My eyes flashed with amusement.

My eyes gleamed with amusement.

My eyes glinted with amusement.

My eyes glittered in amusement.

My eyes glittered with amusement.

My eyes shimmered with amusement.

My eyes shone with amusement.

My eyes sparkled with amusement.

My eyes twinkled in amusement.

My eyes twinkled with amusement.

My eyes widened in amusement.

My eyes widened with amusement.

My face brightened with amusement.

My face creased in amusement.

My face filled with
amusement.
My head tossed in amusement.
My heart leaped with
amusement.
My lips curled in amusement.
My lips lifted in amusement.
My lips quirked with
amusement.
My lips trembled with
amusement.
My lips twisted with
amusement.
My lips twitched with
amusement.
My mouth curled in
amusement.
My mouth lifted in
amusement.
My mouth perked with
amusement.
My mouth quirked in
amusement.
My mouth tightened with
amusement.
My mouth twisted in
amusement.
My mouth twitched with
amusement.
My tone tinged with
amusement.
My voice filled with
amusement.
My voice laced with
amusement.
My voice tinged with
amusement.

I arched an eyebrow in
amusement.
I gave a snort of amusement.
My eyes were bright with
amusement.
My eyes were full of
amusement.
My eyes were huge with
amusement.
My eyes were wide with
amusement.
My face lit up with
amusement.
My face screwed up in
amusement.
My mouth turned up with
amusement.
My voice was full of
amusement.

ANGER

Definition: A strong feeling of annoyance, displeasure, or hostility.
See ANNOYANCE

Anger battled inside me.
Anger boiled in me.
Anger boiled inside me.
Anger brightened my eyes.
Anger broke within me.
Anger bubbled inside me.
Anger bubbled within me.
Anger built inside me.
Anger burned inside me.
Anger burned through me.
Anger burned within me.
Anger churned inside me.
Anger churned through me.
Anger clenched inside me.
Anger clouded my face.
Anger coiled inside me.
Anger coursed through me.
Anger crept into me.
Anger crossed my brow.
Anger crossed my eyes.
Anger crossed my face.
Anger crowded my throat.
Anger darkened my
complexion.
Anger darkened my eyes.
Anger dimmed my eyes.
Anger emanated from me.
Anger engulfed my body.
Anger entered my voice.
Anger etched my face.
Anger festered inside me.
Anger filled my eyes.
Anger flared in me.

Anger flared inside me.
Anger flared through me.
Anger flashed in me.
Anger flickered in me.
Anger flooded my face.
Anger flooded my soul.
Anger flooded through me.
Anger flushed through me.
Anger grew inside me.
Anger grew within me.
Anger hardened my face.
Anger hardened my insides.
Anger hardened my tone.
Anger hardened my voice.
Anger hardened my words.
Anger heated my blood.
Anger hissed inside me.
Anger knotted my insides.
Anger knotted my stomach.
Anger mottled my face.
Anger mounted inside me.
Anger mushroomed inside me.
Anger opened my eyes.
Anger overpowered my
instinct.
Anger painted my face.
Anger passed over me.
Anger pumped through me.
Anger raced through me.
Anger radiated from me.
Anger railed through me.
Anger ran through me.
Anger reddened my cheeks.

Anger reddened my chief.
Anger reddened my face.
Anger roared in me.
Anger roared through me.
Anger robbed my smile.
Anger rode through me.
Anger roiled inside me.
Anger roiled within me.
Anger rose in me.
Anger rose inside me.
Anger rose within me.
Anger rumbled through me.
Anger rushed through me.
Anger seared my eyes.
Anger seeped through me.
Anger seethed through me.
Anger sharpened my eyes.
Anger sheened my eyes.
Anger shot through me.
Anger slashed my features.
Anger smouldered inside me.
Anger smouldered within me.
Anger sparked inside me.
Anger sparked my adrenaline.
Anger spiked in me.
Anger spiked through me.
Anger spiralled through me.
Anger splintered through me.
Anger stung my eyes.
Anger surged inside me.
Anger surged through me.
Anger swelled inside me.
Anger swept over me.
Anger swirled through me.
Anger swirled within me.
Anger tainted my voice.
Anger tightened my face.
Anger tightened my lips.

Anger tightened my mouth.
Anger tightened my throat.
Anger tinged my voice.
Anger tinged my words.
Anger tore through me.
Anger touched my voice.
Anger trembled through me.
Anger twisted my face.
Anger washed over me.
Anger welled within me.
Anger went through me.
I bellowed in anger.
I blazed with anger.
I burned with anger.
I filled with anger.
I flushed with anger.
I grunted in anger.
I simmered with anger.
I snorted in anger.
I swelled with anger.
Anger blossomed in my chest.
Anger blossomed in my face.
Anger boiled beneath my skin.
Anger boiled in my chest.
Anger boiled in my gut.
Anger boiled in my veins.
Anger braided around my
spine.
Anger bubbled up my throat.
Anger burned in my belly.
Anger burned in my chest.
Anger came into my voice.
Anger chattered in my head.
Anger churned in my gut.
Anger churned through my
belly.
Anger coiled in my belly.

Anger coursed through my veins.
Anger crackled in my eyes.
Anger crept into my tone.
Anger crept into my voice.
Anger dashed across my face.
Anger etched into my face.
Anger expanded in my chest.
Anger expanded in my gut.
Anger exploded through my veins.
Anger festered in my chest.
Anger flared in my breast.
Anger flared in my eyes.
Anger flared in my gaze.
Anger flared on my face.
Anger flashed across my face.
Anger flashed in my expression.
Anger flashed in my eyes.
Anger flashed in my face.
Anger flashed through my mind.
Anger flickered across my face.
Anger flickered in my eyes.
Anger flitted across my expression.
Anger flowed through my veins.
Anger flushed through my face.
Anger glittered in my eyes.
Anger grew in my shoulders.
Anger hummed through my system.
Anger lit up my insides.
Anger lodged in my throat.
Anger made my voice hoarse.

Anger mounted in my voice.
Anger raced across my features.
Anger raged in my eyes.
Anger registered in my eyes.
Anger rippled across my face.
Anger rippled through my body.
Anger roared in my ears.
Anger rose in my gut.
Anger rose in my throat.
Anger rose in my voice.
Anger rose up my neck.
Anger seeped into my body.
Anger seeped into my voice.
Anger seethed in my eyes.
Anger shone in my eyes.
Anger showed on my face.
Anger simmered in my breast.
Anger simmered in my eyes.
Anger sizzled in my eyes.
Anger slammed into my mind.
Anger smouldered in my breast.
Anger smouldered in my eyes.
Anger sparked in my eyes.
Anger surfaced in my tone.
Anger surged through my body.
Anger surged through my veins.
Anger swelled in my chest.
Anger swirled through my insides.
Anger tightened up my face.
Anger tore at my heart.
Anger vibrated in my voice.
Anger washed over my mind.

My blood boiled with anger.
My body quaked with anger.
My body quivered with anger.
My body shook with anger.
My body teemed with anger.
My chest throbbed with anger.
My ears warm with anger.
My eyebrows knitted in anger.
My eyes blazed with anger.
My eyes bulged in anger.
My eyes bulged with anger.
My eyes burned with anger.
My eyes clouded with anger.
My eyes filled with anger.
My eyes fixed with anger.
My eyes flared in anger.
My eyes flared with anger.
My eyes flashed in anger.
My eyes flashed with anger.
My eyes flickered with anger.
My eyes glinted with anger.
My eyes glittered with anger.
My eyes glowed with anger.
My eyes hardened with anger.
My eyes narrowed in anger.
My eyes narrowed with anger.
My eyes shone with anger.
My eyes simmered with anger.
My eyes smouldered with
anger.
My eyes snapped with anger.
My eyes sparkled with anger.
My eyes widened in anger.
My face blackened with anger.
My face blanched with anger.
My face burned with anger.
My face contorted in anger.
My face contorted with anger.

My face creased with anger.
My face darkened in anger.
My face darkened with anger.
My face flared with anger.
My face flashed with anger.
My face flushed in anger.
My face flushed with anger.
My face reddened in anger.
My face reddened with anger.
My face set with anger.
My face strained in anger.
My face tensed with anger.
My face tightened in anger.
My face tightened with anger.
My face twisted in anger.
My face twisted with anger.
My face twitched with anger.
My head sang with anger.
My heart pounded with anger.
My jaw bunched with anger.
My jaw clenched in anger.
My jaw clenched with anger.
My jaw fixed in anger.
My jaw flexed with anger.
My jaw pulsed with anger.
My jaw set in anger.
My jaw squared in anger.
My jaw twitched with anger.
My lips curled with anger.
My lips flattened with anger.
My lips pinched in anger.
My lips pursed in anger.
My lips tightened in anger.
My mouth pinched in anger.
My mouth pinched with
anger.
My mouth pursed in anger.
My mouth thinned in anger.

My mouth tightened in anger.
My neck bulged in anger.
My neck pulsed in anger.
My nose flared with anger.
My skin flushed with anger.
My stomach churned with anger.
My stomach knotted in anger.
My throat tightened with anger.
My tone edged toward anger.
My voice bristled with anger.
My voice cracked with anger.
My voice deepened with anger.
My voice filled with anger.
My voice hardened with anger.
My voice laced with anger.
My voice pitched with anger.
My voice quivered with anger.
My voice raised in anger.
My voice rasped with anger.
My voice rose in anger.
My voice rose with anger.
My voice seethed in anger.
My voice seethed with anger.
My voice shook with anger.
My voice smouldered with anger.
My voice steeped in anger.
My voice stiffened with anger.
My voice tinged with anger.
My voice trembled with anger.
My voice vibrated in anger.
My voice vibrated with anger.
Anger flared red in my vision.
I felt a bit of anger.
I felt a bomb of anger.
I felt a burst of anger.

I felt a chill of anger.
I felt a cloud of anger.
I felt a dart of anger.
I felt a dig of anger.
I felt a dollop of anger.
I felt a flare of anger.
I felt a flash of anger.
I felt a flush of anger.
I felt a groundswell of anger.
I felt a lick of anger.
I felt a mix of anger.
I felt a mixture of anger.
I felt a pang of anger.
I felt a pinch of anger.
I felt a prick of anger.
I felt a pulse of anger.
I felt a punch of anger.
I felt a ripple of anger.
I felt a rise of anger.
I felt a rush of anger.
I felt a shaft of anger.
I felt a spark of anger.
I felt a spray of anger.
I felt a spur of anger.
I felt a spurt of anger.
I felt a stab of anger.
I felt a sting of anger.
I felt a surge of anger.
I felt a swell of anger.
I felt a tinge of anger.
I felt a wave of anger.
I gave a shout of anger.
I gave a sigh of anger.
My ears burned hot from anger.
My eyes glazed over with anger.
My eyes lit up with anger.

My eyes opened wide with
anger.
My eyes rimmed red with
anger.
My eyes turned hot with anger.
My eyes were bright with
anger.
My eyes were dark with anger.
My eyes were fierce with anger.
My eyes were narrow in anger.
My eyes were wide with anger.
My eyes were wild with anger.
My face grew heavy with anger.
My face grew hot with anger.
My face screwed up in anger.
My face turned flush with
anger.
My face turned red with anger.
My face turned rosy with
anger.
My face was fierce with anger.
My face was hot with anger.
My face was livid with anger.
My face was puffy with anger.
My face was red with anger.
My face was ruddy with anger.
My lips were taut with anger.
My neck flushed crimson with
anger.
My skin turned red with anger.
My vision went red with anger.
My voice boomed out in anger.
My voice was full of anger.
My voice was harsh with anger.
My voice was hot with anger.
My voice was taut with anger.
My voice was terse with anger.
My voice was thick with anger.

ANGST

Definition: A feeling of deep anxiety or dread.
See ANXIETY

Angst ate into me.
Angst churned inside me.
Angst clawed at me.
Angst coursed through me.
Angst crossed my face.
Angst filled my voice.
Angst flooded over me.
Angst knotted my gut.
Angst knotted my insides.
Angst knotted my shoulders.
Angst knotted my stomach.
Angst lined my face.
Angst pinched my lips.
Angst pumped my heart.
Angst ran through me.
Angst rushed through me.
Angst scraped my spine.
Angst slipped from me.
Angst squeezed my belly.
Angst swept over me.
Angst swept through me.
Angst swirled through me.
Angst tightened my breath.
Angst tightened my shoulders.
Angst tugged at me.
Angst washed over me.
Angst washed through me.
Angst weighed on me.
Angst went through me.
Angst wormed through me.
Angst came into my eyes.
Angst churned in my gut.

Angst coursed through my veins.
Angst crawled up my back.
Angst crept into my voice.
Angst crept up my spine.
Angst etched across my face.
Angst flickered in my eyes.
Angst nagged at my mind.
Angst plucked at my chest.
Angst pressed against my chest.
Angst pulsed through my body.
Angst pumped through my veins.
Angst roared in my head.
Angst roiled in my gut.
Angst rose in my throat.
Angst slithered up my spine.
Angst spilled through my guts.
Angst sprinted across my eyes.
Angst swept through my body.
Angst trembled in my stomach.
Angst whispered in my gut.
My body hummed with angst.
My eyebrows furrowed in angst.
My eyes clouded with angst.
My eyes widened in angst.
My face creased in angst.
My face creased with angst.
My face flooded with angst.

My face flushed with angst.
My face pinched with angst.
My face twisted with angst.
My face wisped with angst.
My head throbbed with angst.
My jaw worked with angst.
My mouth puckered with angst.
My nose quivered with angst.
My shoulders knotted with angst.
My stomach clenched in angst.
My stomach cramped with angst.
My stomach knotted with angst.
My voice broken with angst.
My voice marbled with angst.
My voice strained with angst.
My voice tinged with angst.
Angst caused my throat to tighten.
I felt a bolt of angst.
I felt a bubble of angst.
I felt a flash of angst.
I felt a knot of angst.
I felt a lot of angst.
I felt a lurch of angst.
I felt a moment of angst.
I felt a pang of angst.
I felt a prick of angst.
I felt a ripple of angst.
I felt a rush of angst.
I felt a sense of angst.
I felt a spasm of angst.
I felt a spurt of angst.
I felt a stab of angst.
I felt a stir of angst.

I felt a sweat of angst.
I felt a tinge of angst.
I felt a tremor of angst.
I felt a tug of angst.
I felt a twinge of angst.
I felt a twist of angst.
I felt a wave of angst.
My face was full of angst.
My mouth was dry with angst.
My spine went cold with angst.
My voice was taut with angst.
My voice was thin with angst.

ANGUISH

Definition: Severe mental or physical pain or suffering.
See AGONY

Anguish clapped my hands.
Anguish clawed at me.
Anguish crashed through me.
Anguish crossed my face.
Anguish darkened my eyes.
Anguish exploded inside me.
Anguish exploded through me.
Anguish filled my body.
Anguish fuelled my voice.
Anguish ignited my nerves.
Anguish lined my face.
Anguish lined my features.
Anguish paralysed my legs.
Anguish pierced my body.
Anguish pierced my sinuses.
Anguish pulsed through me.
Anguish ripped through me.
Anguish robbed my breath.
Anguish sang through me.
Anguish stabbed my side.
Anguish streaked my face.
Anguish swept through me.
Anguish came over my face.
Anguish crawled around my mind.
Anguish etched on my face.
Anguish exploded in my guts.
Anguish flared from my fingertips.
Anguish flared in my ribs.
Anguish flared up my leg.
Anguish flashed in my eyes.
Anguish flickered in my eyes.

Anguish froze in my throat.
Anguish grew in my face.
Anguish radiated from my back.
Anguish ripped across my face.
Anguish ripped through my body.
Anguish ripped through my head.
Anguish rushed through my body.
Anguish sat on my chest.
Anguish seared through my leg.
Anguish shrieked from my mouth.
Anguish struck my nervous system.
Anguish swept through my body.
Anguish tore up my spine.
Anguish washed down my cheeks.
Anguish welled into my eyes.
My body contorted in anguish.
My body convulsed in anguish.
My body creamed in anguish.
My body exploded in anguish.
My body paralyzed with anguish.
My body screamed with anguish.
My body shrieked in anguish.

My body spasmed in anguish.
My body throbbed in anguish.
My body writhed in anguish.
My chest heaved with anguish.
My ears stabbed with anguish.
My eyes closed in anguish.
My eyes filled with anguish.
My eyes glazed in anguish.
My eyes narrowed in anguish.
My eyes rolled in anguish.
My face clenched in anguish.
My face contorted in anguish.
My face contorted with
anguish.
My face crumbled with
anguish.
My face crumpled in anguish.
My face etched in anguish.
My face filled with anguish.
My face lined with anguish.
My face squeezed with
anguish.
My face twisted in anguish.
My face twisted with anguish.
My lips tightened in anguish.
My mouth twisted with
anguish.
My nerves screamed in
anguish.
My voice filled with anguish.
My voice grated with anguish.
My voice twisted in anguish.
My voice vibrated with
anguish.
Anguish lay heavy on my
mind.
I felt a rush of anguish.
I felt a wave of anguish.

My body crumpled up in
anguish.
My eyes glowed red with
anguish.
My eyes opened wide with
anguish.
My eyes were dark with
anguish.
My eyes were full of anguish.
My face screwed up in anguish.
My head hung low in anguish.
My knees drew up in anguish.
My mouth sagged open in
anguish.
My voice was full of anguish.
My voice was hoarse with
anguish.

ANNOYANCE

Definition: The feeling or state of being annoyed.

See IRRITATION

Annoyance clouded my face.
Annoyance crawled through me.
Annoyance crossed my face.
Annoyance crossed my forehead.
Annoyance entered my expression.
Annoyance entered my voice.
Annoyance filled my face.
Annoyance grated my voice.
Annoyance laced my voice.
Annoyance moved through me.
Annoyance rose in me.
Annoyance sifted through me.
Annoyance washed over me.
I exhaled in annoyance.
I frowned with annoyance.
I grunted in annoyance.
I sighed with annoyance.
Annoyance burned in my gut.
Annoyance crept into my expression.
Annoyance crept into my voice.
Annoyance descended over my features.
Annoyance faded from my expression.
Annoyance flared on my face.
Annoyance flashed across my face.

Annoyance flashed in my eyes.
Annoyance flickered across my face.
Annoyance flickered in my eyes.
Annoyance flickered over my face.
Annoyance passed through my eyes.
Annoyance rang in my words.
Annoyance ripped through my body.
Annoyance scratched at my temper.
Annoyance settled over my face.
Annoyance washed across my face.
My brows lowered in annoyance.
My eyebrows furrowed in annoyance.
My eyes flashed with annoyance.
My eyes flickered with annoyance.
My eyes gleamed with annoyance.
My eyes glowed with annoyance.
My eyes narrowed in annoyance.

My eyes snapped with
annoyance.
My eyes went from annoyance.
My face crawled with
annoyance.
My face tightened with
annoyance.
My face twisted in annoyance.
My face went from annoyance.
My head jerked in annoyance.
My head throbbed with
annoyance.
My lips crimped with
annoyance.
My lips tightened in
annoyance.
My mouth tightened in
annoyance.
My mouth tightened with
annoyance.
My tone rose with annoyance.
My voice ragged with
annoyance.
My voice rasped with
annoyance.
My voice rose with annoyance.
My voice strained with
annoyance.
My voice tinged with
annoyance.
I felt a bubble of annoyance.
I felt a flare of annoyance.
I felt a flash of annoyance.
I felt a pang of annoyance.
I felt a prickle of annoyance.
I felt a rush of annoyance.
I felt a spike of annoyance.
I felt a spurt of annoyance.

I felt a stab of annoyance.
I felt a twinge of annoyance.
I gave a shrug of annoyance.
I gave a squawk of annoyance.
My eyes were sharp with
annoyance.
My face grew pinched with
annoyance.

ANXIETY

Definition: A feeling of worry, nervousness, or unease about something with an uncertain outcome.

See WORRY

Anxiety ate into me.
Anxiety churned inside me.
Anxiety clawed at me.
Anxiety coursed through me.
Anxiety crossed my face.
Anxiety filled my voice.
Anxiety flooded over me.
Anxiety knotted my gut.
Anxiety knotted my insides.
Anxiety knotted my shoulders.
Anxiety knotted my stomach.
Anxiety lined my face.
Anxiety pinched my lips.
Anxiety pumped my heart.
Anxiety ran through me.
Anxiety rushed through me.
Anxiety scraped my spine.
Anxiety slipped from me.
Anxiety squeezed my belly.
Anxiety swept over me.
Anxiety swept through me.
Anxiety swirled through me.
Anxiety tightened my breath.
Anxiety tightened my shoulders.
Anxiety tugged at me.
Anxiety washed over me.
Anxiety washed through me.
Anxiety weighed on me.
Anxiety went through me.
Anxiety wormed through me.
Anxiety came into my eyes.

Anxiety churned in my gut.
Anxiety coursed through my veins.
Anxiety crawled up my back.
Anxiety crept into my voice.
Anxiety crept up my spine.
Anxiety etched across my face.
Anxiety flickered in my eyes.
Anxiety nagged at my mind.
Anxiety plucked at my chest.
Anxiety pressed against my chest.
Anxiety pulsed through my body.
Anxiety pumped through my veins.
Anxiety roared in my head.
Anxiety roiled in my gut.
Anxiety rose in my throat.
Anxiety slithered up my spine.
Anxiety spilled through my guts.
Anxiety sprinted across my eyes.
Anxiety swept through my body.
Anxiety trembled in my stomach.
Anxiety whispered in my gut.
My body hummed with anxiety.

My eyebrows furrowed in anxiety.
My eyes clouded with anxiety.
My eyes widened in anxiety.
My face creased in anxiety.
My face creased with anxiety.
My face flooded with anxiety.
My face flushed with anxiety.
My face pinched with anxiety.
My face twisted with anxiety.
My face wisped with anxiety.
My head throbbed with anxiety.
My jaw worked with anxiety.
My mouth puckered with anxiety.
My nose quivered with anxiety.
My shoulders knotted with anxiety.
My stomach clenched in anxiety.
My stomach cramped with anxiety.
My stomach knotted with anxiety.
My voice broken with anxiety.
My voice marbled with anxiety.
My voice strained with anxiety.
My voice tinged with anxiety.
Anxiety caused my throat to tighten.
I felt a bolt of anxiety.
I felt a bubble of anxiety.
I felt a flash of anxiety.
I felt a knot of anxiety.
I felt a lot of anxiety.
I felt a lurch of anxiety.
I felt a moment of anxiety.
I felt a pang of anxiety.
I felt a prick of anxiety.
I felt a ripple of anxiety.
I felt a rush of anxiety.
I felt a sense of anxiety.
I felt a spasm of anxiety.
I felt a spurt of anxiety.
I felt a stab of anxiety.
I felt a stir of anxiety.
I felt a sweat of anxiety.
I felt a tinge of anxiety.
I felt a tremor of anxiety.
I felt a tug of anxiety.
I felt a twinge of anxiety.
I felt a twist of anxiety.
I felt a wave of anxiety.
My face was full of anxiety.
My mouth was dry with anxiety.
My spine went cold with anxiety.
My voice was taut with anxiety.
My voice was thin with anxiety.

APPREHENSION

Definition: Anxiety or fear that something bad or unpleasant will happen.
See ANXIETY

Apprehension ate into me.
Apprehension churned inside me.
Apprehension clawed at me.
Apprehension coursed through me.
Apprehension crossed my face.
Apprehension filled my eyes.
Apprehension filled my voice.
Apprehension flooded over me.
Apprehension grew inside me.
Apprehension knotted my gut.
Apprehension knotted my insides.
Apprehension knotted my shoulders.
Apprehension knotted my stomach.
Apprehension lined my face.
Apprehension pinched my lips.
Apprehension pumped my heart.
Apprehension ran through me.
Apprehension rushed through me.
Apprehension scraped my spine.
Apprehension slipped from me.
Apprehension spiked through me.
Apprehension squeezed my belly.
Apprehension swept over me.
Apprehension swept through me.
Apprehension swirled through me.
Apprehension tightened my breath.
Apprehension tightened my shoulder.
Apprehension tightened my shoulders.
Apprehension tugged at me.
Apprehension washed over me.
Apprehension washed through me.
Apprehension weighed on me.
Apprehension went through me.
Apprehension wormed through me.
Apprehension came into my eyes.
Apprehension churned in my gut.
Apprehension coursed through my veins.

Apprehension crawled up my back.
Apprehension crept into my voice.
Apprehension crept up my spine.
Apprehension darted up my spine.
Apprehension etched across my face.
Apprehension flashed across my mind.
Apprehension flickered in my eyes.
Apprehension nagged at my mind.
Apprehension plucked at my chest.
Apprehension pressed against my chest.
Apprehension pulsed through my body.
Apprehension pumped through my veins.
Apprehension roared in my head.
Apprehension roiled in my gut.
Apprehension rose in my throat.
Apprehension slithered up my spine.
Apprehension spilled through my guts.
Apprehension sprinted across my eyes.
Apprehension swept through my body.

Apprehension tightened in my gut.
Apprehension trembled in my stomach.
Apprehension whispered in my gut.
My body hummed with apprehension.
My body tightened in apprehension.
My eyebrows furrowed in apprehension.
My eyes clouded with apprehension.
My eyes filled with apprehension.
My eyes glinted with apprehension.
My eyes narrowed in apprehension.
My eyes widened in apprehension.
My face creased in apprehension.
My face creased with apprehension.
My face flooded with apprehension.
My face flushed with apprehension.
My face froze in apprehension.
My face pinched with apprehension.
My face strained with apprehension.
My face twisted with apprehension.

My face wisped with apprehension.
My gut tightened with apprehension.
My head throbbed with apprehension.
My jaw worked with apprehension.
My mouth puckered with apprehension.
My nose quivered with apprehension.
My shoulders knotted with apprehension.
My skin prickled with apprehension.
My stomach clenched in apprehension.
My stomach cramped with apprehension.
My stomach knotted with apprehension.
My voice broken with apprehension.
My voice marbled with apprehension.
My voice strained with apprehension.
My voice tinged with apprehension.
Apprehension caused my throat to tighten.
I felt a chill of apprehension.
I felt a flutter of apprehension.
I felt a pang of apprehension.
I felt a prickle of apprehension.
I felt a rush of apprehension.
I felt a sense of apprehension.

I felt a shiver of apprehension.
I felt a sliver of apprehension.
I felt a stab of apprehension.
I felt a thrill of apprehension.
I felt a tinge of apprehension.
I felt a tingle of apprehension.
I felt a touch of apprehension.
I felt a trickle of apprehension.
I felt a twinge of apprehension.
I felt a wave of apprehension.
I swallowed a knot of apprehension.
I swallowed a lump of apprehension.
My eyes were wide with apprehension.
My face was full of apprehension.
My mouth was dry with apprehension.
My spine went cold with apprehension.
My voice was taut with apprehension.
My voice was thin with apprehension.

AROUSAL

Definition: The action or fact of arousing or being aroused.
See PASSION

Arousal boiled inside me.
Arousal bubbled through me.
Arousal caressed my mouth.
Arousal clawed at me.
Arousal clouded my mind.
Arousal coursed through me.
Arousal crowded my chest.
Arousal curled through me.
Arousal darkened my eyes.
Arousal darkened my irises.
Arousal dilated my eyes.
Arousal drifted through me.
Arousal entered my voice.
Arousal exploded inside me.
Arousal exploded within me.
Arousal filled my head.
Arousal flooded through me.
Arousal flowed over me.
Arousal flowed through me.
Arousal fluttered inside me.
Arousal glowed inside me.
Arousal gushed through me.
Arousal heated my blood.
Arousal knifed through me.
Arousal laced my voice.
Arousal licked through me.
Arousal made me melt.
Arousal penetrated my heart.
Arousal poured through me.
Arousal pulsed through me.
Arousal pulsed within me.
Arousal pumped through me.
Arousal radiated from me.

Arousal ravaged my face.
Arousal rippled through me.
Arousal rose from me.
Arousal rose in me.
Arousal shattered within me.
Arousal slammed into me.
Arousal sluiced through me.
Arousal spiralled through me.
Arousal splintered through me.
Arousal surged through me.
Arousal surged within me.
Arousal swelled within me.
Arousal swept through me.
Arousal swirled through me.
Arousal thickened my voice.
Arousal tightened inside me.
Arousal tightened my features.
Arousal wafted through me.
Arousal warmed my insides.
Arousal washed through me.
Arousal went through me.
Arousal banked in my eyes.
Arousal combated in my brain.
Arousal danced in my belly.
Arousal exploded in my chest.
Arousal flamed in my expression.
Arousal flared in my eyes.
Arousal flared in my gaze.
Arousal flashed in my eyes.
Arousal flashed into my eyes.

Arousal flickered in my
expression.
Arousal flickered in my eyes.
Arousal glittered in my eyes.
Arousal nipped at my skin.
Arousal pumped though my
veins.
Arousal swelled inside my
body.
Arousal throbbed against my
belly.
My blood burned with arousal.
My blood heated with arousal.
My body burned with arousal.
My body drugged with arousal.
My body hardened with
arousal.
My body heated with arousal.
My body hummed with
arousal.
My body jangled with arousal.
My body shivered with arousal.
My body stirred with arousal.
My body thrummed with
arousal.
My body twitched with
arousal.
My body unfurled with
arousal.
My body vibrated with arousal.
My ears shut in arousal.
My eyes blazed with arousal.
My eyes danced with arousal.
My eyes darkened with
arousal.
My eyes dilated with arousal.
My eyes filled with arousal.
My eyes flared with arousal.

My eyes flickered with arousal.
My eyes glazed with arousal.
My eyes gleamed with arousal.
My eyes glittered with arousal.
My eyes glowed with arousal.
My eyes hooded with arousal.
My eyes lit with arousal.
My eyes narrowed with
arousal.
My eyes shimmered with
arousal.
My eyes sparkled with arousal.
My face filled with arousal.
My face flushed with arousal.
My face mottled with arousal.
My heart burned with arousal.
My heart swelled with arousal.
My pulse raced with arousal.
My skin blushed with arousal.
My skin flushed with arousal.
My voice sang with arousal.
My voice shook with arousal.
My voice slurred with arousal.
Arousal curled deep in my
belly.
Arousal pooled low in my
belly.
My body was overwrought
with arousal.
My eyes grew hazy with
arousal.
My eyes went dark with
arousal.
My eyes were bloodshot with
arousal.
My eyes were bright with
arousal.

My eyes were dark with
arousal.
My eyes were full of arousal.
My eyes were hazy with
arousal.
My eyes were heavy with
arousal.
My face glazed over with
arousal.
My throat was thick with
arousal.
My voice was rough with
arousal.
My voice was thick with
arousal.

ASTONISHMENT

Definition: Great surprise.

See AMAZEMENT

Astonishment brightened my gaze.

Astonishment coloured my voice.

Astonishment crept over me.

Astonishment crossed my face.

Astonishment flared inside me.

Astonishment jolted through me.

Astonishment lit my eyes.

Astonishment lit my face.

Astonishment lit my features.

Astonishment made me gasp.

Astonishment parted my lips.

Astonishment rose within me.

Astonishment snaked through me.

Astonishment twisted my gut.

I froze in astonishment.

I gasped in astonishment.

Astonishment came over my face.

Astonishment edged into my voice.

Astonishment flashed on my face.

Astonishment flickered across my face.

Astonishment flickered over my face.

Astonishment flitted across my face.

Astonishment lit up my face.

Astonishment passed across my face.

Astonishment passed over my face.

Astonishment plastered across my face.

Astonishment played across my face.

Astonishment reflected in my eyes.

Astonishment registered on my face.

Astonishment settled on my face.

Astonishment settled over my face.

Astonishment showed in my eyes.

Astonishment sounded in my voice.

My brows arched in astonishment.

My brows climbed in astonishment.

My brows lifted in astonishment.

My brows raised in astonishment.

My brows rose in astonishment.

My ears flickered in astonishment.

My eyebrows arched in
astonishment.
My eyebrows arched with
astonishment.
My eyebrows lifted in
astonishment.
My eyebrows raised in
astonishment.
My eyebrows rose in
astonishment.
My eyebrows rose with
astonishment.
My eyes blinked in
astonishment.
My eyes blinked with
astonishment.
My eyes bloomed with
astonishment.
My eyes brightened with
astonishment.
My eyes filled with
astonishment.
My eyes flared in
astonishment.
My eyes flared with
astonishment.
My eyes flashed from
astonishment.
My eyes flashed with
astonishment.
My eyes flickered with
astonishment.
My eyes fluttered in
astonishment.
My eyes opened in
astonishment.
My eyes popped in
astonishment.

My eyes popped with
astonishment.
My eyes rounded in
astonishment.
My eyes scrunched in
astonishment.
My eyes shut in astonishment.
My eyes stared in
astonishment.
My eyes twinkled with
astonishment.
My eyes widened in
astonishment.
My eyes widened with
astonishment.
My face altered from
astonishment.
My face collapsed in
astonishment.
My face contorted with
astonishment.
My face frozen in
astonishment.
My face relaxed with
astonishment.
My face scrunched in
astonishment.
My face twisted in
astonishment.
My face winced in
astonishment.
My head cocked in
astonishment.
My head jerked in
astonishment.
My head shook in
astonishment.

My head throbbed with astonishment.
My jaw dropped in astonishment.
My jaw gaped in astonishment.
My lips parted in astonishment.
My lips rounded in astonishment.
My mouth dropped in astonishment.
My mouth gaped in astonishment.
My mouth opened in astonishment.
My mouth parted in astonishment.
My skin deepened with astonishment.
My voice filled with astonishment.
My body was motionless with astonishment.
My brows shot up in astonishment.
My eyebrows shot up in astonishment.
My eyebrows went up in astonishment.
My eyes bloomed wide with astonishment.
My eyes flew open in astonishment.
My eyes grew huge with astonishment.
My eyes grew wide with astonishment.
My eyes lit up in astonishment.

My eyes opened wide in astonishment.
My eyes opened wide with astonishment.
My eyes shot up in astonishment.
My eyes were full of astonishment.
My eyes were luminous with astonishment.
My eyes were wide in astonishment.
My eyes were wide with astonishment.
My face lit up in astonishment.
My face screwed up in astonishment.
My face was alive with astonishment.
My face was blank with astonishment.
My face was full of astonishment.
My face was wide with astonishment.
My head was abuzz with astonishment.
My head whipped around in astonishment.
My mouth dropped open in astonishment.
My mouth fell open in astonishment.
My mouth hung open in astonishment.
My mouth was agape in astonishment.

My mouth was wide in
astonishment.
My voice was soft with
astonishment.

ATTRACTION
Definition: The feeling of liking someone, especially sexually, because of the way they look or behave.
See DESIRE

Attraction bubbled through me.
Attraction caressed my mouth.
Attraction clawed at me.
Attraction coursed through me.
Attraction crowded my chest.
Attraction curled through me.
Attraction darkened my irises.
Attraction drifted through me.
Attraction exploded inside me.
Attraction flowed over me.
Attraction flowed through me.
Attraction fluttered inside me.
Attraction glowed inside me.
Attraction gushed through me.
Attraction heated my blood.
Attraction knifed through me.
Attraction laced my voice.
Attraction licked through me.
Attraction made me melt.
Attraction penetrated my heart.
Attraction poured through me.
Attraction pulsed through me.
Attraction pumped through me.
Attraction radiated from me.
Attraction ravaged my face.
Attraction rippled through me.

Attraction rolled through me.
Attraction rose from me.
Attraction rose in me.
Attraction shattered within me.
Attraction slammed into me.
Attraction sluiced through me.
Attraction spiralled through me.
Attraction splintered through me.
Attraction surged through me.
Attraction swelled within me.
Attraction swept through me.
Attraction swirled through me.
Attraction tightened inside me.
Attraction tightened my features.
Attraction wafted through me.
Attraction warmed my insides.
Attraction went through me.
Attraction banked in my eyes.
Attraction combated in my brain.
Attraction danced in my belly.
Attraction flashed in my eyes.
Attraction flickered in my expression.
Attraction flickered in my eyes.

Attraction nipped at my skin.
Attraction ran through my mind.
Attraction throbbed against my belly.
My blood burned with attraction.
My blood heated with attraction.
My body burned with attraction.
My body drugged with attraction.
My body hardened with attraction.
My body heated with attraction.
My body hummed with attraction.
My body jangled with attraction.
My body shivered with attraction.
My body stirred with attraction.
My body thrummed with attraction.
My body twitched with attraction.
My body unfurled with attraction.
My ears shut in attraction.
My eyes blazed with attraction.
My eyes danced with attraction.
My eyes darkened with attraction.
My eyes flared with attraction.
My eyes flickered with attraction.
My eyes gleamed with attraction.
My eyes glittered with attraction.
My eyes glowed with attraction.
My eyes lit with attraction.
My eyes narrowed with attraction.
My eyes shimmered with attraction.
My face flushed with attraction.
My heart burned with attraction.
My heart swelled with attraction.
My pulse raced with attraction.
My skin flushed with attraction.
My voice slurred with attraction.
Attraction curled deep in my belly.
Attraction pooled low in my belly.
I felt a flicker of attraction.
I felt a pull of attraction.
I felt a thrill of attraction.
My body was overwrought with attraction.
My eyes went dark with attraction.
My eyes were dark with attraction.

My eyes were full of attraction.
My eyes were hazy with
attraction.
My eyes were heavy with
attraction.
My face glazed over with
attraction.
My throat was thick with
attraction.
My voice sounded rough with
attraction.
My voice was rough with
attraction.
My voice was thick with
attraction.

AWE

Definition: A feeling of reverential respect mixed with fear or wonder.
See WONDER

Awe brightened my gaze.
Awe coloured my voice.
Awe crept over me.
Awe crossed my face.
Awe flared inside me.
Awe jolted through me.
Awe lit my eyes.
Awe lit my face.
Awe lit my features.
Awe made me gasp.
Awe parted my lips.
Awe rose within me.
Awe snaked through me.
Awe twisted my gut.
I grunted in awe.
Awe came over my face.
Awe edged into my voice.
Awe flashed on my face.
Awe flickered across my face.
Awe flickered over my face.
Awe flitted across my face.
Awe lit up my face.
Awe passed across my face.
Awe passed over my face.
Awe plastered across my face.
Awe played across my face.
Awe reflected in my eyes.
Awe registered on my face.
Awe settled on my face.
Awe settled over my face.
Awe showed in my eyes.
Awe sounded in my voice.
My brows arched in awe.

My brows climbed in awe.
My brows lifted in awe.
My brows raised in awe.
My brows rose in awe.
My ears flickered in awe.
My eyebrows arched in awe.
My eyebrows arched with awe.
My eyebrows lifted in awe.
My eyebrows raised in awe.
My eyebrows rose in awe.
My eyebrows rose with awe.
My eyes blinked in awe.
My eyes blinked with awe.
My eyes bloomed with awe.
My eyes brightened with awe.
My eyes filled with awe.
My eyes flared in awe.
My eyes flared with awe.
My eyes flashed from awe.
My eyes flashed with awe.
My eyes flickered with awe.
My eyes fluttered in awe.
My eyes opened in awe.
My eyes popped in awe.
My eyes popped with awe.
My eyes rounded in awe.
My eyes scrunched in awe.
My eyes shut in awe.
My eyes stared in awe.
My eyes twinkled with awe.
My eyes widened in awe.
My eyes widened with awe.
My face altered from awe.

My face collapsed in awe.
My face contorted with awe.
My face frozen in awe.
My face relaxed with awe.
My face scrunched in awe.
My face twisted in awe.
My face winced in awe.
My head cocked in awe.
My head jerked in awe.
My head shook in awe.
My head throbbed with awe.
My jaw dropped in awe.
My jaw gaped in awe.
My lips parted in awe.
My lips rounded in awe.
My mouth dropped in awe.
My mouth gaped in awe.
My mouth opened in awe.
My mouth parted in awe.
My skin deepened with awe.
My voice filled with awe.
I felt a shiver of awe.
I felt a tinge of awe.
I gave a whistle of awe.
My body was motionless with awe.
My brows shot up in awe.
My eyebrows shot up in awe.
My eyebrows went up in awe.
My eyes bloomed wide with awe.
My eyes flew open in awe.
My eyes grew huge with awe.
My eyes grew wide with awe.
My eyes lit up in awe.
My eyes opened wide in awe.
My eyes opened wide with awe.

My eyes shot up in awe.
My eyes were full of awe.
My eyes were luminous with awe.
My eyes were wide in awe.
My eyes were wide with awe.
My face lit up in awe.
My face screwed up in awe.
My face was alive with awe.
My face was blank with awe.
My face was full of awe.
My face was wide with awe.
My head was abuzz with awe.
My head whipped around in awe.
My mouth dropped open in awe.
My mouth fell open in awe.
My mouth hung open in awe.
My mouth was agape in awe.
My mouth was wide in awe.
My voice was soft with awe.

B

BEWILDERMENT
Definition: A feeling of being perplexed and confused.
See CONFUSION

Bewilderment ate at me.
Bewilderment came over me.
Bewilderment clouded my brain.
Bewilderment clouded my eyes.
Bewilderment clouded my face.
Bewilderment clouded my features.
Bewilderment clouded my mind.
Bewilderment creased my brow.
Bewilderment crossed my face.
Bewilderment crossed my features.
Bewilderment darkened my features.
Bewilderment entered my eyes.
Bewilderment filled my face.
Bewilderment lined my face.
Bewilderment marred my face.
Bewilderment muddled my brain.
Bewilderment pulled at me.

Bewilderment separated my eyebrows.
Bewilderment shimmied through me.
Bewilderment swept over me.
Bewilderment swept through me.
Bewilderment swirled through me.
Bewilderment twisted my face.
I gasped in bewilderment.
I shrugged in bewilderment.
Bewilderment drew my eyebrows together.
Bewilderment etched on my face.
Bewilderment flashed in my eyes.
Bewilderment flickered in my eyes.
Bewilderment passed over my face.
Bewilderment passed over my features.
Bewilderment reigned in my mind.

Bewilderment swirled in my brain.
Bewilderment swirled in my head.
Bewilderment tugged at my mouth.
My brows joined in bewilderment.
My brows tightened in bewilderment.
My eyebrows furrowed in bewilderment.
My eyebrows knitted in bewilderment.
My eyes clouded with bewilderment.
My eyes darkened with bewilderment.
My eyes diluted with bewilderment.
My eyes flickered with bewilderment.
My eyes narrowed in bewilderment.
My eyes shone in bewilderment.
My eyes sparkled with bewilderment.
My eyes stared in bewilderment.
My eyes tilted in bewilderment.
My eyes widened in bewilderment.
My face clouded with bewilderment.
My face flushed with bewilderment.

My face knotted with bewilderment.
My face puckered with bewilderment.
My face twisted in bewilderment.
My face twisted with bewilderment.
My head rang with bewilderment.
My head reeled with bewilderment.
My head spun in bewilderment.
My head spun with bewilderment.
My head turned in bewilderment.
My heart pounded in bewilderment.
My lips parted in bewilderment.
My nose crinkled in bewilderment.
My voice filled with bewilderment.
My eyebrows pulled down in bewilderment.
My eyes opened wide in bewilderment.
My eyes were dark with bewilderment.
My eyes were wide with bewilderment.

BITTERNESS

Definition: Anger and disappointment at being treated unfairly.
See INDIGNATION

Bitterness burned inside me.
Bitterness burned through me.
Bitterness burned within me.
Bitterness churned inside me.
Bitterness churned through me.
Bitterness clenched inside me.
Bitterness clouded my face.
Bitterness coiled inside me.
Bitterness coloured my cheeks.
Bitterness coursed through me.
Bitterness crept into me.
Bitterness entered my voice.
Bitterness filled my throat.
Bitterness laced my voice.
Bitterness lit my eyes.
Bitterness poured over me.
Bitterness stained my cheeks.
Bitterness suffused my cheeks.
Bitterness swelled inside me.
Bitterness tightened my jaw.
Bitterness washed over me.
I smiled with bitterness.
Bitterness burned in my chest.
Bitterness burned in my eyes.
Bitterness came into my voice.
Bitterness chattered in my head.
Bitterness churned in my gut.
Bitterness churned through my belly.
Bitterness coiled in my belly.

Bitterness coursed through my veins.
Bitterness crackled in my eyes.
Bitterness crept into my tone.
Bitterness crept into my voice.
Bitterness curdled inside my belly.
Bitterness edged into my voice.
Bitterness flared in my heart.
Bitterness rose in my throat.
Bitterness shone in my eyes.
Bitterness sprouted in my gut.
Bitterness swelled in my throat.
My body quickened in bitterness.
My body quivered with bitterness.
My chest swelled with bitterness.
My eyebrows climbed in bitterness.
My eyes blazed with bitterness.
My eyes dazzled in bitterness.
My eyes filled with bitterness.
My eyes glittered with bitterness.
My eyes shone with bitterness.
My eyes smouldered with bitterness.
My eyes widened with bitterness.

My face crumpled in bitterness.
My face darkened with bitterness.
My face filled with bitterness.
My face flushed with bitterness.
My face reddened with bitterness.
My face set with bitterness.
My face strained in bitterness.
My face tensed with bitterness.
My face tightened in bitterness.
My face tightened with bitterness.
My face trembled with bitterness.
My face twisted in bitterness.
My face twisted with bitterness.
My face twitched with bitterness.
My head ached in bitterness.
My head sang with bitterness.
My heart filled with bitterness.
My heart seethed with bitterness.
My lips twisted with bitterness.
My stomach boiled with bitterness.
My tone drenched with bitterness.
My tone laden with bitterness.
My tone reeked of bitterness.
My voice crackled with bitterness.

My voice edged with bitterness.
My voice laced with bitterness.
My voice ragged with bitterness.
My voice rattled with bitterness.
My voice sank into bitterness.
My voice shook with bitterness.
My voice tinged with bitterness.
Bitterness burned bright in my eyes.
I felt a kind of bitterness.
I felt a wave of bitterness.
My eyes were wide with bitterness.
My face screwed up in bitterness.
My face turned flush with bitterness.
My face turned red with bitterness.
My face turned rosy with bitterness.
My face was ruddy with bitterness.
My face went dark with bitterness.
My voice trailed off in bitterness.
My voice was alive with bitterness.
My voice was shrill with bitterness.

BLISS

Definition: Perfect happiness.
See HAPPINESS

Bliss brightened my eyes.
Bliss coursed through me.
Bliss crashed through me.
Bliss crawled over me.
Bliss encircled my head.
Bliss exploded inside me.
Bliss exploded within me.
Bliss filled my chest.
Bliss filled my lungs.
Bliss flowed through me.
Bliss hummed through me.
Bliss laced my heart.
Bliss licked through me.
Bliss lit my features.
Bliss melted my bones.
Bliss moved through me.
Bliss pierced my brain.
Bliss poured through me.
Bliss raced through me.
Bliss radiated through me.
Bliss ran through me.
Bliss ripped through me.
Bliss rippled through me.
Bliss roared through me.
Bliss rocked through me.
Bliss rushed through me.
Bliss seared my senses.
Bliss settled over me.
Bliss shot through me.
Bliss shuddered through me.
Bliss sliced through me.
Bliss spiked through me.
Bliss splintered my brain.

Bliss stole through me.
Bliss surged through me.
Bliss swept through me.
Bliss touched my face.
Bliss washed over me.
Bliss washed through me.
Bliss welled inside me.
Bliss went through me.
Bliss whirled through me.
Bliss appeared on my face.
Bliss burned in my stomach.
Bliss flowed from my lips.
Bliss glided through my body.
Bliss infused in my expression.
Bliss raced down my spine.
Bliss radiated from my
expression.
Bliss ran through my voice.
Bliss rivered through my body.
Bliss rocked through my body.
Bliss rumbled from my throat.
Bliss shimmied down my
spine.
Bliss skittered down my body.
Bliss sparked through my
system.
Bliss swept across my face.
Bliss vibrated along my skin.
Bliss washed over my body.
Bliss welled in my eyes.
My body hummed with bliss.
My body jerked in bliss.
My body sighed in bliss.

My body teemed with bliss.
My eyes closed in bliss.
My eyes closed with bliss.
My eyes crinkled with bliss.
My eyes danced with bliss.
My eyes flashed with bliss.
My eyes glazed with bliss.
My eyes gleamed with bliss.
My eyes glowed with bliss.
My eyes rolled with bliss.
My eyes shut with bliss.
My eyes sparkled with bliss.
My eyes widened with bliss.
My face danced with bliss.
My face flushed with bliss.
My face lit with bliss.
My face softened with bliss.
My face wreathed in bliss.
My heart filled with bliss.
My heart fluttered with bliss.
My heart hummed with bliss.
My heart leaped with bliss.
My heart sighed with bliss.
My heart soared with bliss.
My heart thumped with bliss.
My lips twitched with bliss.
My mouth opened in bliss.
My skin mottled with bliss.
My voice softened with bliss.
My eyes slid shut in bliss.
My face grew radiant with
bliss.
My face was aglow with bliss.
My face was rapt with bliss.

BOREDOM

Definition: The state of feeling bored.
See ENNUI

My boredom thickened.
Boredom built inside me.
Boredom came over me.
Boredom clawed at me.
Boredom coloured my
expression.
Boredom coloured my tone.
Boredom coloured my voice.
Boredom crawled over me.
Boredom crossed my face.
Boredom crossed my features.
Boredom flooded my soul.
Boredom lined my voice.
Boredom mounted within me.
I exhaled with boredom.
I frowned with boredom.
I grimaced with boredom.
I groaned with boredom.
I grunted with boredom.
I sighed with boredom.
I snorted with boredom.
Boredom crawled through my
back.
Boredom crept into my eyes.
Boredom crept into my voice.
Boredom etched into my face.
Boredom etched into my
features.
Boredom etched on my face.
Boredom pulled at my mind.
Boredom rolled across my
mind.

Boredom seeped from my
voice.
Boredom showed on my face.
Boredom simmered in my
mind.
I felt edgy with boredom.
I felt numb with boredom.
I was rigid with boredom.
My body ached with boredom.
My eyelids lowered with
boredom.
My eyelids sagged with
boredom.
My eyes brimmed with
boredom.
My eyes bulged with boredom.
My eyes dimmed with
boredom.
My face sagged with boredom.
My gaze flattened with
boredom.
My tone dripped with
boredom.
My tone sagged with boredom.
My voice laced with boredom.
I exhaled a sigh of boredom.
I felt a pang of boredom.
I felt a shiver of boredom.
I felt a wave of boredom.
I heaved a groan of boredom.
I heaved a sigh of boredom.
I released a huff of boredom.
I uttered a grunt of boredom.

My lips pressed thin with
boredom.
My nerves were edgy with
boredom.
My voice was flat with
boredom.
My voice was thick with
boredom.
My voice was thin with
boredom.
A sigh of boredom shimmered
through me.
A wave of boredom came over
me.
A wave of boredom washed
over me.
I let out a sob of boredom.
A look of boredom came over
my face.

C

CHEERFULNESS

Definition: The quality or state of being noticeably happy and optimistic.
See HAPPINESS

Cheerfulness brightened my eyes.
Cheerfulness engorged my heart.
Cheerfulness engulfed my face.
Cheerfulness exploded inside me.
Cheerfulness filled my heart.
Cheerfulness flashed through me.
Cheerfulness flooded through me.
Cheerfulness flowed through me.
Cheerfulness laced my heart.
Cheerfulness leaped through me.
Cheerfulness rushed through me.
Cheerfulness settled my soul.
Cheerfulness stung my eyes.
Cheerfulness surged through me.
Cheerfulness swept through me.

Cheerfulness warmed my insides.
Cheerfulness washed over me.
Cheerfulness washed through me.
Cheerfulness welled inside me.
Cheerfulness went through me.
Cheerfulness whirled through me.
Cheerfulness broke over my face.
Cheerfulness clapped in my chest.
Cheerfulness flickered in my eyes.
Cheerfulness rolled down my face.
Cheerfulness streamed down my cheeks.
Cheerfulness streamed down my face.
Cheerfulness welled in my eyes.
My eyes danced with cheerfulness.

My eyes filled with cheerfulness.
My eyes gleamed with cheerfulness.
My eyes shone with cheerfulness.
My eyes sparkled with cheerfulness.
My face filled with cheerfulness.
My face flooded with cheerfulness.
My face flushed with cheerfulness.
My face glowed with cheerfulness.
My face lit with cheerfulness.
My face wreathed in cheerfulness.
My heart beat with cheerfulness.
My heart burst with cheerfulness.
My heart danced with cheerfulness.
My heart filled with cheerfulness.
My heart flipped with cheerfulness.
My heart fluttered with cheerfulness.
My heart leaped with cheerfulness.
My heart leapt with cheerfulness.
My heart pinged with cheerfulness.

My heart soared with cheerfulness.
My heart swelled with cheerfulness.
My heart thumped with cheerfulness.
My voice brimmed with cheerfulness.
My voice coated with cheerfulness.
My voice inflated with cheerfulness.
My voice rang with cheerfulness.
My eyes were white with cheerfulness.
My face was brilliant with cheerfulness.
My heart was full of cheerfulness.

COMPASSION

Definition: Sympathetic pity and concern for the sufferings or misfortunes of others.
See PITY

Compassion clouded my eyes.
Compassion coloured my words.
Compassion crossed my face.
Compassion darkened my eyes.
Compassion filled my eyes.
Compassion flooded my heart.
Compassion rippled through me.
Compassion rolled through me.
Compassion seeped through me.
Compassion softened my expression.
Compassion stirred in me.
Compassion surged through me.
Compassion touched my eyes.
Compassion touched my voice.
Compassion tugged at me.
Compassion warred inside me.
Compassion welled inside me.
Compassion blazed in my eyes.
Compassion crept into my voice.
Compassion registered in my eyes.
Compassion rolled into my head.

Compassion shone in my eyes.
Compassion shone in my face.
Compassion showed on my face.
Compassion stirred in my gut.
Compassion welled in my chest.
My chest squeezed with compassion.
My chest tightened in compassion.
My eyes brimmed with compassion.
My eyes darkened with compassion.
My eyes filled with compassion.
My eyes flickered with compassion.
My eyes glowed with compassion.
My eyes moistened with compassion.
My eyes softened with compassion.
My eyes warmed with compassion.
My face burned in compassion.
My face filled with compassion.
My face throbbed in compassion.

My face twisted with compassion.
My head throbbed in compassion.
My heart ached with compassion.
My heart clenched with compassion.
My heart filled with compassion.
My heart lurched in compassion.
My heart overflowed with compassion.
My heart sank with compassion.
My heart squeezed in compassion.
My heart swelled with compassion.
My heart twisted with compassion.
My lips twitched in compassion.
My mouth parted in compassion.
My stomach growled in compassion.
My stomach gurgled in compassion.
My stomach knotted with compassion.
My stomach murmured in compassion.
My stomach rumbled in compassion.
My stomach tightened in compassion.

My tone filled with compassion.
My voice dripped with compassion.
My voice filled with compassion.
My voice laced with compassion.
My voice throbbed with compassion.
I felt a deal of compassion.
I felt a flicker of compassion.
I felt a pang of compassion.
I felt a rush of compassion.
I felt a wave of compassion.
I felt an ounce of compassion.
I uttered a cry of compassion.
My eyes were full of compassion.
My eyes were warm with compassion.
My eyes were wide with compassion.
My face was full of compassion.
My face was soft with compassion.
My mouth turned down in compassion.
My mouth went soft with compassion.
My voice pitched low with compassion.
My voice was full of compassion.

CONFUSION

Definition: The state of being bewildered or unclear in one's mind about something.

See BEWILDERMENT

Confusion ate at me.
Confusion came over me.
Confusion clouded my brain.
Confusion clouded my eyes.
Confusion clouded my face.
Confusion clouded my features.
Confusion clouded my mind.
Confusion creased my brow.
Confusion crossed my face.
Confusion crossed my features.
Confusion darkened my features.
Confusion filled my face.
Confusion lined my face.
Confusion marred my face.
Confusion muddled my brain.
Confusion pulled at me.
Confusion separated my eyebrows.
Confusion shimmied through me.
Confusion swept over me.
Confusion swept through me.
Confusion swirled through me.
Confusion twisted my face.
I frowned in confusion.
I muttered in confusion.
I spluttered in confusion.

Confusion drew my eyebrows together.
Confusion etched on my face.
Confusion flashed in my eyes.
Confusion flickered in my eyes.
Confusion passed over my face.
Confusion passed over my features.
Confusion reigned in my mind.
Confusion swirled in my brain.
Confusion swirled in my head.
Confusion tugged at my mouth.
My brows joined in confusion.
My brows tightened in confusion.
My eyebrows furrowed in confusion.
My eyebrows knitted in confusion.
My eyes clouded with confusion.
My eyes darkened with confusion.
My eyes diluted with confusion.
My eyes flickered with confusion.

My eyes narrowed in
confusion.
My eyes sparkled with
confusion.
My eyes stared in confusion.
My eyes tilted in confusion.
My eyes widened in confusion.
My face clouded with
confusion.
My face flushed with
confusion.
My face knotted with
confusion.
My face puckered with
confusion.
My face twisted in confusion.
My head rang with confusion.
My head reeled with
confusion.
My head spun in confusion.
My head spun with confusion.
My head turned in confusion.
My heart pounded in
confusion.
My nose crinkled in confusion.
I felt a moment of confusion.
My eyebrows pulled down in
confusion.
My eyes were dark with
confusion.
My eyes were wide with
confusion.

CONTEMPT

Definition: The feeling that a person or a thing is worthless or beneath consideration.

See SCORN

Contempt curled my lips.
Contempt edged my voice.
Contempt filled my voice.
Contempt tinged my voice.
Contempt touched my voice.
I frowned with contempt.
I snickered with contempt.
I sniffed with contempt.
I snorted with contempt.
I spat in contempt.
I spat with contempt.
Contempt poured from my mouth.
My eyes blazed with contempt.
My eyes filled with contempt.
My eyes flashed with contempt.
My eyes flickered with contempt.
My eyes glowed with contempt.
My eyes narrowed in contempt.
My eyes shone with contempt.
My face flushed with contempt.
My face twisted in contempt.
My face twisted with contempt.
My face wrinkled with contempt.

My face written with contempt.
My heart filled with contempt.
My lips curled in contempt.
My lips curled with contempt.
My lips twisted with contempt.
My mouth twisted in contempt.
My nose flared in contempt.
My tone laced with contempt.
My voice dripped with contempt.
My voice filled with contempt.
My voice jagged with contempt.
My voice laced with contempt.
My voice loaded with contempt.
My voice quavered with contempt.
My voice sharpened with contempt.
My voice touched with contempt.
Contempt lay thick in my voice.
I felt a flash of contempt.
I felt a rush of contempt.
I felt a shudder of contempt.
I felt a surge of contempt.
I felt a twinge of contempt.

I gave a grimace of contempt.
I gave a snort of contempt.
My eyes were full of contempt.
My face was full of contempt.
My voice vibrated with
contempt.
My voice was thick with
contempt.

CONTENTMENT

Definition: A state of happiness and satisfaction.

See HAPPINESS

Contentment brightened my eyes.

Contentment coursed through me.

Contentment crashed through me.

Contentment crawled over me.

Contentment encircled my head.

Contentment exploded inside me.

Contentment exploded within me.

Contentment filled my chest.

Contentment filled my lungs.

Contentment flowed through me.

Contentment hummed through me.

Contentment laced my heart.

Contentment licked through me.

Contentment lit my features.

Contentment melted my bones.

Contentment moved through me.

Contentment pierced my brain.

Contentment poured through me.

Contentment raced through me.

Contentment radiated through me.

Contentment ran through me.

Contentment ripped through me.

Contentment rippled through me.

Contentment roared through me.

Contentment rocked through me.

Contentment rushed through me.

Contentment seared my senses.

Contentment settled over me.

Contentment shot through me.

Contentment shuddered through me.

Contentment sliced through me.

Contentment spiked through me.

Contentment splintered my brain.

Contentment stole through me.

Contentment surged through me.

Contentment swept through me.
Contentment touched my face.
Contentment washed over me.
Contentment washed through me.
Contentment welled inside me.
Contentment went through me.
Contentment whirled through me.
I sighed in contentment.
I sighed with contentment.
I smiled with contentment.
I snorted in contentment.
Contentment appeared on my face.
Contentment burned in my stomach.
Contentment flowed from my lips.
Contentment glided through my body.
Contentment infused in my expression.
Contentment raced down my spine.
Contentment radiated from my expression.
Contentment ran through my voice.
Contentment rivered through my body.
Contentment rocked through my body.

Contentment rumbled from my throat.
Contentment shimmied down my spine.
Contentment skittered down my body.
Contentment sparked through my system.
Contentment swept across my face.
Contentment vibrated along my skin.
Contentment washed over my body.
Contentment welled in my eyes.
My body jerked in contentment.
My body sighed in contentment.
My body teemed with contentment.
My eyes closed in contentment.
My eyes closed with contentment.
My eyes crinkled with contentment.
My eyes danced with contentment.
My eyes flashed with contentment.
My eyes glazed with contentment.
My eyes gleamed with contentment.
My eyes glowed with contentment.

My eyes rolled with
contentment.
My eyes shut with
contentment.
My eyes softened with
contentment.
My eyes sparkled with
contentment.
My eyes widened with
contentment.
My face danced with
contentment.
My face flushed with
contentment.
My face lit with contentment.
My face softened with
contentment.
My face wreathed in
contentment.
My features softened with
contentment.
My heart fluttered with
contentment.
My heart hummed with
contentment.
My heart leaped with
contentment.
My heart sighed with
contentment.
My heart soared with
contentment.
My heart thumped with
contentment.
My lips twitched with
contentment.
My mouth opened in
contentment.

My skin mottled with
contentment.
I felt a glow of contentment.
I felt a kind of contentment.
I felt a wave of contentment.
I felt an upwelling of
contentment.
I gave a smile of contentment.
My eyes slid shut in
contentment.
My face grew radiant with
contentment.
My face was aglow with
contentment.
My face was rapt with
contentment.

D

DELIGHT

Definition: Great pleasure.
See PLEASURE

Delight coursed through me.
Delight crashed through me.
Delight crawled over me.
Delight darkened my eyes.
Delight encircled my head.
Delight exploded within me.
Delight filled my chest.
Delight filled my lungs.
Delight flowed through me.
Delight hummed through me.
Delight licked through me.
Delight melted my bones.
Delight moved through me.
Delight pierced my brain.
Delight poured through me.
Delight raced through me.
Delight radiated through me.
Delight ran through me.
Delight ripped through me.
Delight rippled through me.
Delight roared through me.
Delight rocked through me.
Delight seared my senses.
Delight shot through me.
Delight shuddered through me.
Delight sliced through me.

Delight spiked through me.
Delight splintered my brain.
Delight stole through me.
Delight swept through me.
Delight touched my face.
Delight washed over me.
Delight washed through me.
Delight widened my eyes.
I cackled in delight.
I cackled with delight.
I chuckled with delight.
I gasped in delight.
I gasped with delight.
I grinned with delight.
I groaned with delight.
I shivered with delight.
I sighed with delight.
I smiled in delight.
I smiled with delight.
I whooped with delight.
I yelped with delight.
Delight appeared on my face.
Delight burned in my
stomach.
Delight flowed from my lips.
Delight glided through my
body.

Delight infused in my
expression.
Delight raced down my spine.
Delight ran through my voice.
Delight rang in my voice.
Delight rocked through my
body.
Delight rumbled from my
throat.
Delight shimmied down my
spine.
Delight shone on my face.
Delight skittered down my
body.
Delight sparked through my
system.
Delight swept across my face.
Delight vibrated along my
skin.
Delight washed over my body.
My body jerked in delight.
My body quivered with
delight.
My body sighed in delight.
My body teemed with delight.
My eyebrows danced in
delight.
My eyes beamed with delight.
My eyes closed in delight.
My eyes closed with delight.
My eyes crinkled with delight.
My eyes danced with delight.
My eyes flashed with delight.
My eyes glazed with delight.
My eyes gleamed with delight.
My eyes glittered in delight.
My eyes glowed with delight.
My eyes rolled with delight.

My eyes shimmered with
delight.
My eyes shone with delight.
My eyes shut with delight.
My eyes sparkled with delight.
My eyes twinkled with delight.
My eyes widened in delight.
My eyes widened with delight.
My face danced with delight.
My face flushed with delight.
My face lit with delight.
My head buzzed with delight.
My heart fluttered with
delight.
My heart molten with delight.
My heart sighed with delight.
My lips twitched with delight.
My mouth opened in delight.
My skin mottled with delight.
My voice quavered with
delight.
My voice screeched with
delight.
I exhaled an aaaahhhh of
delight.
I felt a surge of delight.
I gave a bound of delight.
I gave a crow of delight.
I gave a cry of delight.
I gave a laugh of delight.
I gave a shudder of delight.
I gave a sigh of delight.
I gave a squeal of delight.
My eyebrows went up in
delight.
My eyes slid shut in delight.
My eyes were huge with
delight.

My eyes were wide with
delight.
My face grew radiant with
delight.
My face was aglow with
delight.
My face was rapt with delight.

DEPRESSION

Definition: Feelings of severe despondency and dejection.
See MELANCHOLY

Depression came over me.
Depression clouded my expression.
Depression crashed over me.
Depression crept over me.
Depression crossed my face.
Depression crossed my features.
Depression darkened my eyes.
Depression ebbed over me.
Depression entered my voice.
Depression filled my eyes.
Depression filled my voice.
Depression hovered over me.
Depression howled through me.
Depression invaded my eyes.
Depression lined my face.
Depression ravaged my body.
Depression rose off me.
Depression seeped into me.
Depression settled over me.
Depression settled upon me.
Depression sizzled through me.
Depression spiralled through me.
Depression squeezed my chest.
Depression swept through me.
Depression tinged my eyes.
Depression tinged my voice.
Depression tugged at me.
Depression washed over me.

Depression weighed on me.
Depression welled inside me.
Depression came into my eyes.
Depression came into my voice.
Depression crept into my expression.
Depression drifted across my face.
Depression flickered in my eyes.
Depression flickered in my face.
Depression lay in my heart.
Depression lingered in my eyes.
Depression passed over my face.
Depression ran down my spine.
Depression seeped into my muscles.
Depression settled in my heart.
Depression settled on my face.
Depression settled on my shoulders.
Depression showed in my eyes.
Depression welled in my chest.
Depression welled in my eyes.
My eyes drooped with depression.
My eyes filled with depression.

My eyes shadowed in
depression.
My face creased with
depression.
My face crumpled with
depression.
My face darkened with
depression.
My face etched with
depression.
My face filled with depression.
My face sagged with
depression.
My tone laced with depression.
My tone shaded with
depression.
My tone softened with
depression.
My voice broke with
depression.
My voice filled with
depression.
My voice infused with
depression.
My voice laced with
depression.
My voice tinged with
depression.
I felt a weight of depression.
My eyes were full of
depression.
My face was heavy with
depression.
My tone was thick with
depression.
My voice was full of
depression.

My voice was soft with
depression.
A touch of depression came
into my eyes.

DESIRE

Definition: Strong sexual feeling or appetite.

See LUST

Desire bubbled through me.
Desire caressed my mouth.
Desire clawed at me.
Desire coursed through me.
Desire crowded my chest.
Desire curled through me.
Desire darkened my irises.
Desire drifted through me.
Desire exploded inside me.
Desire flowed over me.
Desire flowed through me.
Desire fluttered inside me.
Desire glowed inside me.
Desire gushed through me.
Desire heated my blood.
Desire knifed through me.
Desire laced my voice.
Desire licked through me.
Desire made me melt.
Desire penetrated my heart.
Desire poured through me.
Desire pulsed through me.
Desire pumped through me.
Desire radiated from me.
Desire ravaged my face.
Desire rippled through me.
Desire rose from me.
Desire rose in me.
Desire shattered within me.
Desire slammed into me.
Desire sluiced through me.
Desire spiralled through me.
Desire splintered through me.

Desire surged through me.
Desire swelled within me.
Desire swept through me.
Desire swirled through me.
Desire tightened inside me.
Desire tightened my features.
Desire wafted through me.
Desire warmed my insides.
Desire went through me.
I groaned with desire.
Desire banked in my eyes.
Desire combated in my brain.
Desire danced in my belly.
Desire flashed in my eyes.
Desire flickered in my
expression.
Desire flickered in my eyes.
Desire nipped at my skin.
Desire throbbed against my
belly.
My blood burned with desire.
My blood heated with desire.
My body burned with desire.
My body drugged with desire.
My body hardened with desire.
My body heated with desire.
My body hummed with desire.
My body jangled with desire.
My body shivered with desire.
My body stirred with desire.
My body thrummed with
desire.
My body twitched with desire.

My body unfurled with desire.
My ears shut in desire.
My eyes blazed with desire.
My eyes danced with desire.
My eyes darkened with desire.
My eyes flared with desire.
My eyes flickered with desire.
My eyes gleamed with desire.
My eyes glittered with desire.
My eyes glowed with desire.
My eyes lit with desire.
My eyes narrowed with desire.
My eyes shimmered with desire.
My face flushed with desire.
My heart burned with desire.
My heart swelled with desire.
My pulse raced with desire.
My skin flushed with desire.
My voice slurred with desire.
Desire curled deep in my belly.
Desire pooled low in my belly.
I felt a jolt of desire.
I felt a lack of desire.
I felt a stab of desire.
I felt a surge of desire.
I felt a wave of desire.
My body was overwrought with desire.
My eyes went dark with desire.
My eyes were dark with desire.
My eyes were full of desire.
My eyes were hazy with desire.
My eyes were heavy with desire.
My face glazed over with desire.

My throat was thick with desire.
My voice sounded rough with desire.
My voice was rough with desire.
My voice was thick with desire.

DESPAIR

Definition: The complete loss or absence of hope.
See HOPELESSNESS

Despair battled inside me.
Despair came over me.
Despair clouded my eyes.
Despair cramped my belly.
Despair descended on me.
Despair descended over me.
Despair entered my eyes.
Despair greeted my words.
Despair nagged at me.
Despair poured over me.
Despair rushed through me.
Despair settled over me.
Despair swept over me.
Despair swept through me.
Despair tightened my features.
Despair touched my heart.
Despair weighed on me.
Despair welled inside me.
I bellowed in despair.
I moaned in despair.
I moaned with despair.
I sobbed in despair.
Despair bloomed in my eyes.
Despair came over my face.
Despair crept up my spine.
Despair emanated from my
body.
Despair etched on my face.
Despair flickered across my
face.
Despair glazed in my eyes.
Despair gnawed at my guts.
Despair leaked into my soul.

Despair pressed behind my
eyes.
Despair slid off my face.
Despair surged from my feet.
Despair weighed down my
heart.
Despair welled in my chest.
My body sagged with despair.
My eyes flared with despair.
My eyes widened in despair.
My face broken with despair.
My face crumpled in despair.
My face drawn with despair.
My face filled with despair.
My face lined with despair.
My heart dulled with despair.
My shoulders drooped in
despair.
My shoulders sagged with
despair.
My shoulders sank in despair.
My throat wrinkled with
despair.
My voice cracked with despair.
My voice filled with despair.
My voice ragged with despair.
My voice rose in despair.
My voice sagged with despair.
I felt a pang of despair.
I felt a pit of despair.
I felt a sense of despair.
I felt a surge of despair.
I felt a wave of despair.

I gave a look of despair.
I gave a whimper of despair.
My chest went hollow with
despair.
My eyes were bright with
despair.
My heart felt leaden with
despair.
My heart was full of despair.
My heart welled up with
despair.
My voice was shrill with
despair.

DISAPPOINTMENT

Definition: Sadness or displeasure caused by the non-fulfilment of one's hopes or expectations.
See SADNESS

Disappointment burned within me.

Disappointment coursed through me.

Disappointment crept through me.

Disappointment crossed my face.

Disappointment damped my spirits.

Disappointment darkened my eyes.

Disappointment filled my eyes.

Disappointment filled my face.

Disappointment flared inside me.

Disappointment flitted through me.

Disappointment flooded through me.

Disappointment marred my face.

Disappointment rippled through me.

Disappointment roiled through me.

Disappointment rushed through me.

Disappointment shadowed my smile.

Disappointment tightened my chest.

Disappointment tightened my throat.

Disappointment tinged my voice.

Disappointment trickled through me.

Disappointment washed over me.

Disappointment washed through me.

I frowned with disappointment.

I gasped in disappointment.

I groaned in disappointment.

I groaned with disappointment.

I grunted with disappointment.

I sighed in disappointment.

I sighed with disappointment.

Disappointment ballooned in my chest.

Disappointment etched into my face.

Disappointment etched into my features.

Disappointment etched on my face.

Disappointment flared in my expression.

Disappointment flared in my eyes.

Disappointment flickered in
my eyes.
Disappointment flitted over
my face.
Disappointment glinted in my
eyes.
Disappointment passed across
my face.
Disappointment rang in my
voice.
Disappointment reflected in
my eyes.
Disappointment registered on
my face.
Disappointment simmered in
my tone.
Disappointment slid across my
features.
Disappointment swelled in my
breast.
Disappointment washed over
my face.
Disappointment weighed
down my heart.
My eyes flooded with
disappointment.
My face fell with
disappointment.
My face melted with
disappointment.
My face twisted with
disappointment.
My heart sank in
disappointment.
My mouth curved in
disappointment.
My mouth drooped with
disappointment.

My mouth twisted with
disappointment.
My shoulders slumped with
disappointment.
My voice filled with
disappointment.
My voice laced with
disappointment.
My voice rang with
disappointment.
My voice tinged with
disappointment.
I felt a bit of disappointment.
I felt a drop of
disappointment.
I felt a flare of disappointment.
I felt a lurch of
disappointment.
I felt a mix of disappointment.
I felt a pang of
disappointment.
I felt a prick of
disappointment.
I felt a sense of
disappointment.
I felt a stab of disappointment.
I felt a surge of
disappointment.
I felt a tug of disappointment.
I felt a twinge of
disappointment.
I gave a huff of
disappointment.
I gave a sigh of
disappointment.
My chest felt hollow with
disappointment.

My mouth turned down with
disappointment.
My tone was low with
disappointment.
My voice trailed off in
disappointment.
My voice was flat with
disappointment.
My voice was heavy with
disappointment.
My voice was sharp with
disappointment.

DISDAIN
Definition: The feeling that someone or something is unworthy of
one's consideration or respect.
See CONTEMPT

Disdain curled my lips.
Disdain edged my voice.
Disdain filled my voice.
Disdain tinged my voice.
Disdain touched my voice.
I sniffed in disdain.
I sniffed with disdain.
I snorted with disdain.
Disdain poured from my
mouth.
My eyes blazed with disdain.
My eyes filled with disdain.
My eyes flashed with disdain.
My eyes flickered with disdain.
My eyes glowed with disdain.
My eyes narrowed in disdain.
My eyes shone with disdain.
My face flushed with disdain.
My face twisted in disdain.
My face twisted with disdain.
My face wrinkled with disdain.
My face written with disdain.
My heart filled with disdain.
My lips curled in disdain.
My lips curled with disdain.
My lips twisted with disdain.
My mouth twisted in disdain.
My nose flared in disdain.
My tone laced with disdain.
My voice dripped with disdain.
My voice filled with disdain.
My voice jagged with disdain.

My voice laced with disdain.
My voice loaded with disdain.
My voice quavered with
disdain.
My voice sharpened with
disdain.
My voice touched with
disdain.
My voice vibrated with
disdain.
Disdain lay thick in my voice.
My eyes were full of disdain.
My face was full of disdain.
My voice was thick with
disdain.

DISGUST

Definition: A feeling of revulsion or strong disapproval aroused by something unpleasant or offensive.
See REVULSION

Disgust altered my face.
Disgust ate at me.
Disgust came over me.
Disgust choked my throat.
Disgust coloured my voice.
Disgust crossed my face.
Disgust filled my face.
Disgust flooded over me.
Disgust pervaded my tone.
Disgust puckered my lips.
Disgust ripped through me.
Disgust rippled through me.
Disgust rolled through me.
Disgust tinged my voice.
Disgust trickled over me.
I frowned in disgust.
I frowned with disgust.
I grimaced in disgust.
I grimaced with disgust.
I grunted in disgust.
I grunted with disgust.
I muttered in disgust.
I scowled in disgust.
I shuddered with disgust.
I sighed in disgust.
I sneered with disgust.
I sniffed in disgust.
I snorted in disgust.
I snorted with disgust.
I sobbed with disgust.
I spat in disgust.
I swallowed in disgust.

Disgust came across my face.
Disgust dripped in my tone.
Disgust flooded into my heart.
Disgust fought in my throat.
Disgust fought in my voice.
Disgust glowed in my eyes.
Disgust made my stomach churn.
Disgust rose in my stomach.
Disgust seeped from my pores.
Disgust wiggled down my frame.
My eyes widened in disgust.
My face clouded with disgust.
My face contorted in disgust.
My face creased with disgust.
My face filled with disgust.
My face grimaced in disgust.
My face twisted in disgust.
My face twisted with disgust.
My face wrinkled in disgust.
My face wrinkled with disgust.
My gut clenched with disgust.
My gut tightened with disgust.
My heart burned with disgust.
My lips curled in disgust.
My lips curled with disgust.
My lips snarled in disgust.
My lips twisted in disgust.
My mouth twisted in disgust.
My mouth twisted with disgust.

My nose crinkled in disgust.
My nose wrinkled in disgust.
My nose wrinkled with disgust.
My skin tingled with disgust.
My stomach heaved with disgust.
My tone filled with disgust.
My voice laced with disgust.
My voice thickened with disgust.
My voice tightened with disgust.
I exhaled a breath of disgust.
I felt a rush of disgust.
I felt a surge of disgust.
I felt a wave of disgust.
I gave a grimace of disgust.
I gave a groan of disgust.
I gave a grunt of disgust.
I gave a huff of disgust.
I gave a shudder of disgust.
I gave a snort of disgust.
I gave a wave of disgust.
I muttered a sound of disgust.
I muttered a word of disgust.
My face creased up in disgust.
My face screwed up with disgust.
My face was stiff with disgust.
My mouth cocked open in disgust.
My mouth squashed up in disgust.
My tone was harsh with disgust.
My voice trailed off in disgust.

My voice was thick with disgust.
My face was a mask of disgust.

DISILLUSIONMENT

Definition: A feeling of disappointment resulting from the discovery that something is not as good as one believed it to be.
See DISAPPOINTMENT

Disillusionment burned within me.
Disillusionment coursed through me.
Disillusionment crept through me.
Disillusionment crossed my face.
Disillusionment damped my spirits.
Disillusionment darkened my eyes.
Disillusionment filled my eyes.
Disillusionment filled my face.
Disillusionment flared inside me.
Disillusionment flitted through me.
Disillusionment flooded over me.
Disillusionment flooded through me.
Disillusionment marred my face.
Disillusionment rippled through me.
Disillusionment roiled through me.
Disillusionment rushed through me.
Disillusionment shadowed my smile.

Disillusionment tightened my chest.
Disillusionment tightened my throat.
Disillusionment tinged my voice.
Disillusionment trickled through me.
Disillusionment washed over me.
Disillusionment washed through me.
Disillusionment ballooned in my chest.
Disillusionment crept into my eyes.
Disillusionment etched into my face.
Disillusionment etched into my features.
Disillusionment etched on my face.
Disillusionment flared in my expression.
Disillusionment flared in my eyes.
Disillusionment flickered in my eyes.
Disillusionment flitted over my face.
Disillusionment glinted in my eyes.

Disillusionment passed across my face.
Disillusionment rang in my voice.
Disillusionment reflected in my eyes.
Disillusionment registered on my face.
Disillusionment simmered in my tone.
Disillusionment slid across my features.
Disillusionment swelled in my breast.
Disillusionment washed over my face.
Disillusionment weighed down my heart.
My eyes flooded with disillusionment.
My face fell with disillusionment.
My face melted with disillusionment.
My face twisted with disillusionment.
My head drooped in disillusionment.
My heart sank in disillusionment.
My mouth curved in disillusionment.
My mouth drooped with disillusionment.
My mouth twisted with disillusionment.
My shoulders slumped with disillusionment.

My voice filled with disillusionment.
My voice laced with disillusionment.
My voice rang with disillusionment.
My voice tinged with disillusionment.
My words tinged with disillusionment.
My chest felt hollow with disillusionment.
My eyes were dark with disillusionment.
My eyes were huge with disillusionment.
My mouth turned down with disillusionment.
My tone was low with disillusionment.
My voice trailed off in disillusionment.
My voice was flat with disillusionment.
My voice was heavy with disillusionment.
My voice was sharp with disillusionment.

DISLIKE

Definition: A feeling of distaste or hostility.

See HATE

Dislike blurred my vision.
Dislike coursed through me.
Dislike simmered inside me.
Dislike twisted my features.
Dislike bubbled in my gut.
Dislike combusted behind my ribs.
Dislike crawled over my skin.
Dislike etched in my face.
Dislike etched on my face.
Dislike passed over my face.
Dislike rose in my gut.
Dislike rose in my throat.
Dislike smouldered in my eyes.
My body quivered with dislike.
My eyes brimmed with dislike.
My eyes bulged with dislike.
My eyes burned with dislike.
My eyes filled with dislike.
My eyes flared with dislike.
My eyes flashed with dislike.
My eyes flickered with dislike.
My eyes glared with dislike.
My eyes glazed in dislike.
My eyes gleamed with dislike.
My eyes glittered with dislike.
My eyes glowed with dislike.
My eyes locked in dislike.
My eyes narrowed as dislike.
My eyes narrowed in dislike.
My eyes narrowed with dislike.
My eyes seethed with dislike.
My face brimmed with dislike.

My face contorted with dislike.
My face darkened in dislike.
My face flushed with dislike.
My face loaded with dislike.
My face masked in dislike.
My face twisted in dislike.
My face twisted with dislike.
My heart filled with dislike.
My heart seethed with dislike.
My mouth twisted in dislike.
My mouth twisted with dislike.
My skin tingled with dislike.
My throat constricted with dislike.
My voice filled with dislike.
My voice saturated with dislike.
Dislike burned deep in my soul.
I felt a stab of dislike.
I felt a wave of dislike.
My body was taut with dislike.
My eyes were alive with dislike.
My eyes were cold with dislike.
My eyes were dead with dislike.
My eyes were full of dislike.
My eyes were wide with dislike.
My face was stiff with dislike.
My face was venomous with dislike.

My heart was full of dislike.

DISMAY

Definition: Concern and distress caused by something unexpected.
See ALARM

Dismay clawed through me.
Dismay creased my face.
Dismay crossed my face.
Dismay crossed my features.
Dismay filled my eyes.
Dismay painted my face.
Dismay plucked at me.
Dismay pulsed through me.
Dismay rang through me.
Dismay ripped through me.
Dismay rose in me.
Dismay shot through me.
Dismay spurred my pulse.
Dismay streaked through me.
Dismay washed over me.
Dismay wedged into me.
Dismay widened my eyes.
Dismay buzzed in my head.
Dismay came over my face.
Dismay flashed in my eyes.
Dismay flickered in my eyes.
Dismay jingled on my wrist.
Dismay passed across my face.
Dismay probed into my brain.
Dismay raced into my eyes.
Dismay raced through my
chest.
Dismay registered in my eyes.
Dismay ripped through my
gut.
Dismay shot through my eyes.
Dismay sounded in my brain.

Dismay strummed through my
nerves.
Dismay tingled inside my
brain.
My body buzzed with dismay.
My body stiffened with
dismay.
My body tingled with dismay.
My brows lifted in dismay.
My ears extended in dismay.
My eyes blazed with dismay.
My eyes blinked in dismay.
My eyes rounded in dismay.
My eyes widened in dismay.
My eyes widened with dismay.
My face contorted with
dismay.
My face crumpled with
dismay.
My face fell in dismay.
My face filled with dismay.
My face flushed with dismay.
My face frozen in dismay.
My face paled in dismay.
My head jerked with dismay.
My head turned in dismay.
My heart leapt with dismay.
My heart thumped with
dismay.
My mouth opened in dismay.
My mouth quivered with
dismay.

My stomach crawled with
dismay.
My voice cracked with dismay.
My voice rose in dismay.
My voice rose with dismay.
I felt a flutter of dismay.
I felt a lurch of dismay.
I felt a pang of dismay.
I felt a sense of dismay.
I felt a shiver of dismay.
I felt a slide of dismay.
I felt a stab of dismay.
I felt a swoop of dismay.
I gave a cry of dismay.
I gave a squeal of dismay.
My body was taut with dismay.
My eyes opened wide in
dismay.
My eyes went wide with
dismay.
My eyes were bright with
dismay.
My eyes were frantic with
dismay.
My eyes were full of dismay.
My eyes were huge with
dismay.
My eyes were unblinking with
dismay.
My eyes were wide in dismay.
My eyes were wide with
dismay.
My head jerked up in dismay.
My mouth flapped open in
dismay.
My spine was rigid in dismay.
My voice cried out with
dismay.

My voice rose up in dismay.
My voice shouted out in
dismay.
My voice was full of dismay.
My voice was weak with
dismay.

DISPLEASURE

Definition: A feeling of annoyance or disapproval.

See ANNOYANCE

Displeasure clouded my face.
Displeasure crawled through me.
Displeasure crossed my face.
Displeasure crossed my forehead.
Displeasure entered my expression.
Displeasure entered my voice.
Displeasure filled my face.
Displeasure grated my voice.
Displeasure laced my voice.
Displeasure moved through me.
Displeasure rose in me.
Displeasure sifted through me.
Displeasure washed over me.
Displeasure burned in my gut.
Displeasure crept into my expression.
Displeasure crept into my voice.
Displeasure descended over my features.
Displeasure faded from my expression.
Displeasure flared on my face.
Displeasure flashed across my face.
Displeasure flashed in my eyes.
Displeasure flickered across my face.

Displeasure flickered in my eyes.
Displeasure flickered over my face.
Displeasure passed through my eyes.
Displeasure rang in my words.
Displeasure ripped through my body.
Displeasure scratched at my temper.
Displeasure settled over my face.
Displeasure washed across my face.
My brows lowered in displeasure.
My eyebrows furrowed in displeasure.
My eyes flashed with displeasure.
My eyes flickered with displeasure.
My eyes gleamed with displeasure.
My eyes glowed with displeasure.
My eyes narrowed in displeasure.
My eyes snapped with displeasure.
My eyes went from displeasure.

My face crawled with
displeasure.
My face tightened with
displeasure.
My face twisted in displeasure.
My face went from displeasure.
My head jerked in displeasure.
My head throbbed with
displeasure.
My lips crimped with
displeasure.
My lips thinned with
displeasure.
My lips tightened in
displeasure.
My mouth tightened in
displeasure.
My mouth tightened with
displeasure.
My tone rose with displeasure.
My voice laced with
displeasure.
My voice ragged with
displeasure.
My voice rasped with
displeasure.
My voice rose with displeasure.
My voice strained with
displeasure.
My voice tinged with
displeasure.
I gave a shudder of displeasure.
My eyes were sharp with
displeasure.
My face grew pinched with
displeasure.
My face was a line of
displeasure.

My face was a pile of
displeasure.

DISTRESS
Definition: Extreme anxiety, sorrow, or pain.
See ANXIETY

Distress ate into me.
Distress churned inside me.
Distress clawed at me.
Distress coursed through me.
Distress crossed my face.
Distress filled my voice.
Distress flooded over me.
Distress knotted my gut.
Distress knotted my insides.
Distress knotted my shoulders.
Distress knotted my stomach.
Distress lined my face.
Distress pinched my lips.
Distress pumped my heart.
Distress ran through me.
Distress rushed through me.
Distress scraped my spine.
Distress slipped from me.
Distress squeezed my belly.
Distress swept over me.
Distress swept through me.
Distress swirled through me.
Distress tightened my breath.
Distress tightened my features.
Distress tightened my shoulders.
Distress touched my heart.
Distress tugged at me.
Distress washed over me.
Distress washed through me.
Distress weighed on me.
Distress went through me.
Distress wormed through me.

I moaned in distress.
Distress came into my eyes.
Distress churned in my gut.
Distress coursed through my veins.
Distress crawled up my back.
Distress crept into my voice.
Distress crept up my spine.
Distress emanated from my body.
Distress etched across my face.
Distress flickered in my eyes.
Distress glazed in my eyes.
Distress nagged at my mind.
Distress plucked at my chest.
Distress pressed against my chest.
Distress pulsed through my body.
Distress pumped through my veins.
Distress roared in my head.
Distress roiled in my gut.
Distress rose in my throat.
Distress slithered up my spine.
Distress spilled through my guts.
Distress sprinted across my eyes.
Distress swept through my body.
Distress trembled in my stomach.

Distress whispered in my gut.
My body hummed with distress.
My eyebrows furrowed in distress.
My eyes clouded with distress.
My eyes flared with distress.
My eyes widened in distress.
My face creased in distress.
My face creased with distress.
My face crumpled in distress.
My face flooded with distress.
My face flushed with distress.
My face lined with distress.
My face pinched with distress.
My face twisted with distress.
My face wisped with distress.
My head throbbed with distress.
My jaw worked with distress.
My mouth puckered with distress.
My nose quivered with distress.
My shoulders knotted with distress.
My stomach clenched in distress.
My stomach cramped with distress.
My stomach knotted with distress.
My voice broken with distress.
My voice cracked with distress.
My voice marbled with distress.
My voice rose in distress.

My voice strained with distress.
My voice tinged with distress.
Distress caused my throat to tighten.
I felt a flutter of distress.
I felt a rush of distress.
My eyes were bright with distress.
My face was full of distress.
My mouth was dry with distress.
My spine went cold with distress.
My voice was shrill with distress.
My voice was taut with distress.
My voice was thin with distress.

DOUBT

Definition: A feeling of uncertainty or lack of conviction.

See SCEPTICISM

Doubt came over me.
Doubt chewed at me.
Doubt clouded my expression.
Doubt clouded my features.
Doubt covered my expression.
Doubt crashed over me.
Doubt crept over me.
Doubt crossed my face.
Doubt crossed my features.
Doubt darkened my eyes.
Doubt darkened my face.
Doubt descended on me.
Doubt descended over me.
Doubt ebbed over me.
Doubt entered my voice.
Doubt filled my eyes.
Doubt filled my voice.
Doubt hovered over me.
Doubt howled through me.
Doubt invaded my eyes.
Doubt lined my face.
Doubt obscured my vision.
Doubt ravaged my body.
Doubt rose off me.
Doubt seeped into me.
Doubt settled on me.
Doubt settled over me.
Doubt sizzled through me.
Doubt spiralled through me.
Doubt squeezed my chest.
Doubt swept over me.
Doubt swept through me.
Doubt tinged my eyes.

Doubt tinged my voice.
Doubt tugged at me.
Doubt washed over me.
Doubt weighed on me.
Doubt welled inside me.
I darkened with doubt.
My face registered doubt.
Doubt came into my eyes.
Doubt came into my voice.
Doubt crept into my expression.
Doubt drifted across my face.
Doubt flickered in my eyes.
Doubt flickered in my face.
Doubt flickered in my mind.
Doubt flickered through my mind.
Doubt lay in my heart.
Doubt lingered in my eyes.
Doubt passed over my face.
Doubt ran down my spine.
Doubt seeped into my muscles.
Doubt settled in my heart.
Doubt settled on my face.
Doubt settled on my shoulders.
Doubt shone in my face.
Doubt showed in my eyes.
Doubt welled in my chest.
Doubt welled in my eyes.
I was paralyzed with doubt.
My eyes drooped with doubt.
My eyes filled with doubt.

My eyes shadowed in doubt.
My face clenched with doubt.
My face creased with doubt.
My face crumpled with doubt.
My face darkened with doubt.
My face descended with doubt.
My face drawn in doubt.
My face etched with doubt.
My face filled with doubt.
My face sagged with doubt.
My face sunk in doubt.
My mind beset with doubt.
My tone laced with doubt.
My tone shaded with doubt.
My tone softened with doubt.
My voice filled with doubt.
My voice infused with doubt.
My voice laced with doubt.
My voice laden with doubt.
My voice tinged with doubt.
My eyes were full of doubt.
My face was heavy with doubt.
My tone was thick with doubt.
My voice was full of doubt.
My voice was heavy with
doubt.
My voice was soft with doubt.
A touch of doubt came into
my eyes.

DREAD

Definition: Great fear or apprehension.
See FEAR

Dread blocked my throat.
Dread came over me.
Dread clenched my chest.
Dread coursed through me.
Dread crashed over me.
Dread crept over me.
Dread entered my mind.
Dread fell on me.
Dread filled my chest.
Dread filled my guts.
Dread filled my heart.
Dread grew inside me.
Dread gripped my bowels.
Dread gripped my stomach.
Dread hung over me.
Dread knotted my stomach.
Dread mushroomed inside me.
Dread rose in me.
Dread settled into me.
Dread settled over me.
Dread slammed into me.
Dread swelled within me.
Dread swept over me.
Dread swept through me.
Dread tightened my stomach.
Dread twisted my stomach.
Dread washed over me.
Dread went through me.
Dread balled in my belly.
Dread balled in my stomach.
Dread coiled in my stomach.
Dread crept over my body.
Dread gnawed at my stomach.

Dread hummed in my gut.
Dread landed in my stomach.
Dread ran up my spine.
Dread roared through my body.
Dread rose in my gut.
Dread sank into my veins.
Dread seeped through my veins.
Dread settled in my stomach.
Dread squirmed inside my gut.
Dread stirred in my heart.
Dread stomped down my spine.
Dread swirled inside my chest.
Dread tightened around my throat.
Dread uncoiled in my gut.
Dread washed through my bloodstream.
Dread went down my back.
My body tingled with dread.
My eyes filled with dread.
My face painted in dread.
My heart filled with dread.
My heart fluttered with dread.
My heart gripped with dread.
My heart swelled with dread.
My skin crawled with dread.
My stomach knotted with dread.
My stomach tightened with dread.

My stomach turned in dread.
My voice distorted with dread.
My voice shook with dread.
My voice trembled with dread.
I felt a chill of dread.
I felt a flutter of dread.
I felt a moment of dread.
I felt a pang of dread.
I felt a sense of dread.
I felt a shiver of dread.
I felt a shudder of dread.
I felt a thump of dread.
I felt a tingle of dread.
I felt a tremor of dread.
I felt a trickle of dread.
I felt an upsurge of dread.
My blood went cold with
dread.
My body was heavy with
dread.
My eyes were full of dread.
My face was bloodless with
dread.
My heart was heavy with
dread.
My voice was heavy with
dread.
My voice was hoarse with
dread.
My voice was taut with dread.

E

EAGERNESS
Definition: Enthusiasm to do or to have something.
See ENTHUSIASM

Eagerness boiled inside me.
Eagerness bubbled through me.
Eagerness caressed my mouth.
Eagerness clawed at me.
Eagerness clouded my mind.
Eagerness coursed through me.
Eagerness crowded my chest.
Eagerness curled through me.
Eagerness darkened my eyes.
Eagerness darkened my irises.
Eagerness dilated my eyes.
Eagerness drifted through me.
Eagerness entered my voice.
Eagerness exploded inside me.
Eagerness exploded within me.
Eagerness filled my head.
Eagerness flowed over me.
Eagerness flowed through me.
Eagerness fluttered inside me.
Eagerness glowed inside me.
Eagerness gushed through me.
Eagerness heated my blood.
Eagerness knifed through me.
Eagerness laced my voice.
Eagerness licked through me.
Eagerness lit my eyes.

Eagerness made me melt.
Eagerness penetrated my heart.
Eagerness poured through me.
Eagerness pulsed through me.
Eagerness pumped through me.
Eagerness radiated from me.
Eagerness ravaged my face.
Eagerness reddened my cheeks.
Eagerness rippled through me.
Eagerness rose from me.
Eagerness rose in me.
Eagerness shattered within me.
Eagerness slammed into me.
Eagerness sluiced through me.
Eagerness spiralled through me.
Eagerness splintered through me.
Eagerness surged through me.
Eagerness swelled within me.
Eagerness swept through me.
Eagerness swirled through me.
Eagerness thickened my voice.
Eagerness tightened inside me.
Eagerness tightened my features.

Eagerness wafted through me.
Eagerness warmed my insides.
Eagerness washed through me.
Eagerness went through me.
Eagerness banked in my eyes.
Eagerness combated in my
brain.
Eagerness danced in my belly.
Eagerness exploded in my
chest.
Eagerness flamed in my
expression.
Eagerness flared in my eyes.
Eagerness flashed in my eyes.
Eagerness flashed into my eyes.
Eagerness flickered in my
expression.
Eagerness flickered in my eyes.
Eagerness glittered in my eyes.
Eagerness nipped at my skin.
Eagerness settled over my face.
Eagerness swept across my
face.
Eagerness throbbed against my
belly.
My blood burned with
eagerness.
My blood heated with
eagerness.
My body burned with
eagerness.
My body drugged with
eagerness.
My body hardened with
eagerness.
My body heated with
eagerness.

My body hummed with
eagerness.
My body jangled with
eagerness.
My body shivered with
eagerness.
My body stirred with
eagerness.
My body thrummed with
eagerness.
My body twitched with
eagerness.
My body unfurled with
eagerness.
My body vibrated with
eagerness.
My ears shut in eagerness.
My eyes blazed with eagerness.
My eyes danced with
eagerness.
My eyes darkened with
eagerness.
My eyes dilated with eagerness.
My eyes filled with eagerness.
My eyes flared with eagerness.
My eyes flickered with
eagerness.
My eyes glazed with eagerness.
My eyes gleamed with
eagerness.
My eyes glittered with
eagerness.
My eyes glowed with
eagerness.
My eyes hooded with
eagerness.
My eyes lit with eagerness.

My eyes narrowed with eagerness.
My eyes shimmered with eagerness.
My eyes shone with eagerness.
My eyes sparkled with eagerness.
My face filled with eagerness.
My face flushed with eagerness.
My face mottled with eagerness.
My face shone with eagerness.
My head bobbed with eagerness.
My heart burned with eagerness.
My heart swelled with eagerness.
My pulse raced with eagerness.
My skin blushed with eagerness.
My skin flushed with eagerness.
My voice bubbled with eagerness.
My voice sang with eagerness.
My voice shook with eagerness.
My voice slurred with eagerness.
Eagerness curled deep in my belly.
Eagerness pooled low in my belly.
My body was overwrought with eagerness.

My eyes grew hazy with eagerness.
My eyes went dark with eagerness.
My eyes were bloodshot with eagerness.
My eyes were bright with eagerness.
My eyes were dark with eagerness.
My eyes were full of eagerness.
My eyes were hazy with eagerness.
My eyes were heavy with eagerness.
My face glazed over with eagerness.
My throat was thick with eagerness.
My voice was rough with eagerness.
My voice was thick with eagerness.

ECSTASY

Definition: An overwhelming feeling of great happiness or joyful excitement.

See HAPPINESS

Ecstasy brightened my eyes.
Ecstasy coursed through me.
Ecstasy crashed over me.
Ecstasy crashed through me.
Ecstasy crawled over me.
Ecstasy encircled my head.
Ecstasy exploded inside me.
Ecstasy exploded within me.
Ecstasy filled my chest.
Ecstasy filled my features.
Ecstasy filled my lungs.
Ecstasy flowed through me.
Ecstasy heated my blood.
Ecstasy hummed through me.
Ecstasy laced my heart.
Ecstasy licked through me.
Ecstasy lit my eyes.
Ecstasy lit my features.
Ecstasy melted my bones.
Ecstasy moved through me.
Ecstasy passed through me.
Ecstasy pierced my brain.
Ecstasy poured through me.
Ecstasy raced through me.
Ecstasy radiated through me.
Ecstasy ran through me.
Ecstasy ripped through me.
Ecstasy rippled through me.
Ecstasy roared through me.
Ecstasy rocked through me.
Ecstasy rushed through me.
Ecstasy seared my senses.

Ecstasy settled over me.
Ecstasy shot through me.
Ecstasy shuddered through me.
Ecstasy sliced through me.
Ecstasy spiked through me.
Ecstasy splintered my brain.
Ecstasy stole through me.
Ecstasy surged through me.
Ecstasy swept through me.
Ecstasy touched my face.
Ecstasy washed over me.
Ecstasy washed through me.
Ecstasy welled inside me.
Ecstasy went through me.
Ecstasy whirled through me.
I groaned in ecstasy.
I moaned in ecstasy.
I sighed with ecstasy.
Ecstasy appeared on my face.
Ecstasy burned in my stomach.
Ecstasy flowed from my lips.
Ecstasy glided through my body.
Ecstasy glowed upon my face.
Ecstasy infused in my expression.
Ecstasy raced down my spine.
Ecstasy radiated from my expression.
Ecstasy ran through my voice.
Ecstasy rippled through my body.

Ecstasy rivered through my
body.
Ecstasy rocked through my
body.
Ecstasy rumbled from my
throat.
Ecstasy shimmied down my
spine.
Ecstasy skittered down my
body.
Ecstasy sparked through my
system.
Ecstasy swept across my face.
Ecstasy vibrated along my skin.
Ecstasy washed over my body.
Ecstasy welled in my eyes.
My body agitated with ecstasy.
My body jerked in ecstasy.
My body sighed in ecstasy.
My body teemed with ecstasy.
My eyes closed in ecstasy.
My eyes closed with ecstasy.
My eyes crinkled with ecstasy.
My eyes danced with ecstasy.
My eyes flashed with ecstasy.
My eyes glazed with ecstasy.
My eyes gleamed with ecstasy.
My eyes glowed with ecstasy.
My eyes narrowed in ecstasy.
My eyes rolled with ecstasy.
My eyes shut with ecstasy.
My eyes sparkled with ecstasy.
My eyes widened with ecstasy.
My face danced with ecstasy.
My face flushed with ecstasy.
My face lit with ecstasy.
My face softened with ecstasy.
My face wreathed in ecstasy.

My face written with ecstasy.
My heart fluttered with
ecstasy.
My heart hummed with
ecstasy.
My heart leaped with ecstasy.
My heart sighed with ecstasy.
My heart soared with ecstasy.
My heart thumped with
ecstasy.
My lips twitched with ecstasy.
My mouth opened in ecstasy.
My skin mottled with ecstasy.
My voice moaned in ecstasy.
I felt a kind of ecstasy.
My eyes clamped shut in
ecstasy.
My eyes slid shut in ecstasy.
My face grew radiant with
ecstasy.
My face was aglow with
ecstasy.
My face was rapt with ecstasy.

ELATION

Definition: Great happiness and exhilaration.

See HAPPINESS

Elation brightened my eyes.
Elation coursed through me.
Elation crashed through me.
Elation crawled over me.
Elation encircled my head.
Elation exploded inside me.
Elation exploded within me.
Elation filled my chest.
Elation filled my lungs.
Elation filled my veins.
Elation flowed through me.
Elation hummed through me.
Elation laced my heart.
Elation licked through me.
Elation lit my features.
Elation melted my bones.
Elation moved through me.
Elation pierced my brain.
Elation poured through me.
Elation raced through me.
Elation radiated through me.
Elation ran through me.
Elation ripped through me.
Elation rippled through me.
Elation roared through me.
Elation rocked through me.
Elation rushed through me.
Elation seared my senses.
Elation settled over me.
Elation shot through me.
Elation shuddered through me.
Elation sliced through me.

Elation spiked through me.
Elation splintered my brain.
Elation stole through me.
Elation suffused my features.
Elation surged through me.
Elation swept through me.
Elation touched my face.
Elation washed over me.
Elation washed through me.
Elation welled inside me.
Elation went through me.
Elation whirled through me.
I grinned with elation.
I sighed with elation.
Elation appeared on my face.
Elation burned in my stomach.
Elation flowed from my lips.
Elation glided through my body.
Elation infused in my expression.
Elation raced down my spine.
Elation radiated from my expression.
Elation ran through my voice.
Elation rivered through my body.
Elation rocked through my body.
Elation rumbled from my throat.
Elation shimmied down my spine.

Elation skittered down my
body.
Elation sparked through my
system.
Elation swept across my face.
Elation vibrated along my skin.
Elation washed over my body.
Elation welled in my eyes.
My body jerked in elation.
My body sighed in elation.
My body teemed with elation.
My eyes closed in elation.
My eyes closed with elation.
My eyes crinkled with elation.
My eyes danced with elation.
My eyes flashed with elation.
My eyes glazed with elation.
My eyes gleamed with elation.
My eyes glowed with elation.
My eyes rolled with elation.
My eyes shut with elation.
My eyes sparkled with elation.
My eyes widened with elation.
My face danced with elation.
My face flushed with elation.
My face lit with elation.
My face softened with elation.
My face wreathed in elation.
My heart fluttered with
elation.
My heart hummed with
elation.
My heart leaped with elation.
My heart sighed with elation.
My heart soared with elation.
My heart thumped with
elation.
My lips twitched with elation.

My mouth opened in elation.
My skin mottled with elation.
I felt a burst of elation.
I felt a combination of elation.
I felt a flutter of elation.
I felt a sense of elation.
I felt a stab of elation.
I felt a surge of elation.
I felt a wave of elation.
My eyes slid shut in elation.
My face grew radiant with
elation.
My face was aglow with
elation.
My face was rapt with elation.

EMBARRASSMENT

Definition: A feeling of self-consciousness, shame, or awkwardness.
See SHAME

Embarrassment burned my cheeks.
Embarrassment clouded my face.
Embarrassment coloured my face.
Embarrassment fell over me.
Embarrassment flicked at me.
Embarrassment flitted past me.
Embarrassment flooded my cheeks.
Embarrassment flooded through me.
Embarrassment heated my cheeks.
Embarrassment heated my face.
Embarrassment made me flush.
Embarrassment poured through me.
Embarrassment reddened my cheeks.
Embarrassment stole through me.
Embarrassment swept over me.
Embarrassment swept through me.
Embarrassment tinged my voice.
Embarrassment warmed my face.

I blushed in embarrassment.
I blushed with embarrassment.
I flushed with embarrassment.
I muttered with embarrassment.
I shrugged with embarrassment.
I shuddered in embarrassment.
Embarrassment burned in my cheeks.
Embarrassment flickered on my face.
Embarrassment fluttered across my belly.
Embarrassment gnawed at my thoughts.
Embarrassment lodged in my throat.
Embarrassment rose in my cheeks.
Embarrassment rushed down my spine.
Embarrassment skated up my spine.
I grew hot with embarrassment.
I grew warm with embarrassment.
My cheeks burned with embarrassment.
My cheeks flushed with embarrassment.

My ears quivered with embarrassment.
My ears shifted in embarrassment.
My ears stiffened in embarrassment.
My ears stiffened with embarrassment.
My ears twitched with embarrassment.
My ears vibrated in embarrassment.
My ears wriggled with embarrassment.
My expression softened with embarrassment.
My eyes closed in embarrassment.
My eyes narrowed in embarrassment.
My eyes warred with embarrassment.
My face burned with embarrassment.
My face coloured with embarrassment.
My face flamed with embarrassment.
My face flushed from embarrassment.
My face flushed with embarrassment.
My face fluttered from embarrassment.
My face heated with embarrassment.
My throat tightened with embarrassment.

My tone edged with embarrassment.
My tone softened with embarrassment.
My voice coated with embarrassment.
I felt a blush of embarrassment.
I felt a flash of embarrassment.
I felt a flicker of embarrassment.
I felt a flush of embarrassment.
I felt a mixture of embarrassment.
I felt a moment of embarrassment.
I felt a stab of embarrassment.
I felt a twinge of embarrassment.
I gave a squeak of embarrassment.
I gave a whine of embarrassment.
My body felt hot with embarrassment.
My body went hot with embarrassment.
My cheeks flushed red with embarrassment.
My cheeks grew warm with embarrassment.
My cheeks were warm with embarrassment.
My face felt hot with embarrassment.
My neck flushed red with embarrassment.

My neck grew hot with
embarrassment.
My throat seized up with
embarrassment.
My voice was gruff with
embarrassment.
My voice was stiff with
embarrassment.
My voice was tight with
embarrassment.

ENERVATION

Definition: A feeling of being drained of energy or vitality.

My enervation thickened.
Enervation built inside me.
Enervation came over me.
Enervation clawed at me.
Enervation coloured my expression.
Enervation coloured my tone.
Enervation coloured my voice.
Enervation crawled over me.
Enervation crossed my face.
Enervation crossed my features.
Enervation flooded my soul.
Enervation lined my voice.
Enervation mounted within me.
I exhaled with enervation.
I frowned with enervation.
I grimaced with enervation.
I groaned with enervation.
I grunted with enervation.
I sighed with enervation.
I snorted with enervation.
Enervation crawled through my back.
Enervation crept into my eyes.
Enervation crept into my voice.
Enervation etched into my face.
Enervation etched into my features.
Enervation etched on my face.
Enervation pulled at my mind.

Enervation rolled across my mind.
Enervation seeped from my voice.
Enervation showed on my face.
Enervation simmered in my mind.
I felt edgy with enervation.
I felt numb with enervation.
I was rigid with enervation.
My body ached with enervation.
My eyelids lowered with enervation.
My eyelids sagged with enervation.
My eyes brimmed with enervation.
My eyes bulged with enervation.
My eyes dimmed with enervation.
My face sagged with enervation.
My gaze flattened with enervation.
My tone dripped with enervation.
My tone sagged with enervation.
My voice laced with enervation.
I exhaled a sigh of enervation.
I felt a pang of enervation.

I felt a shiver of enervation.
I felt a wave of enervation.
I heaved a groan of enervation.
I heaved a sigh of enervation.
I released a huff of enervation.
I uttered a grunt of enervation.
My lips pressed thin with
enervation.
My nerves were edgy with
enervation.
My voice was flat with
enervation.
My voice was thick with
enervation.
My voice was thin with
enervation.
A sigh of enervation
shimmered through me.
A wave of enervation came
over me.
A wave of enervation washed
over me.
I let out a sob of enervation.
A look of enervation came
over my face.

ENNUI

Definition: A feeling of listlessness and dissatisfaction arising from a lack of occupation or excitement.

See BOREDOM

My ennui thickened.
Ennui built inside me.
Ennui came over me.
Ennui clawed at me.
Ennui coloured my expression.
Ennui coloured my tone.
Ennui coloured my voice.
Ennui crawled over me.
Ennui crossed my face.
Ennui crossed my features.
Ennui flooded my soul.
Ennui lined my voice.
Ennui mounted within me.
I exhaled with ennui.
I frowned with ennui.
I grimaced with ennui.
I groaned with ennui.
I grunted with ennui.
I sighed with ennui.
I snorted with ennui.
Ennui crawled through my back.
Ennui crept into my eyes.
Ennui crept into my voice.
Ennui etched into my face.
Ennui etched into my features.
Ennui etched on my face.
Ennui pulled at my mind.
Ennui rolled across my mind.
Ennui seeped from my voice.
Ennui showed on my face.
Ennui simmered in my mind.

I felt edgy with ennui.
I felt numb with ennui.
I was rigid with ennui.
My body ached with ennui.
My eyelids lowered with ennui.
My eyelids sagged with ennui.
My eyes brimmed with ennui.
My eyes bulged with ennui.
My eyes dimmed with ennui.
My face sagged with ennui.
My gaze flattened with ennui.
My tone dripped with ennui.
My tone sagged with ennui.
My voice laced with ennui.
I exhaled a sigh of ennui.
I felt a pang of ennui.
I felt a shiver of ennui.
I felt a wave of ennui.
I heaved a groan of ennui.
I heaved a sigh of ennui.
I released a huff of ennui.
I uttered a grunt of ennui.
My lips pressed thin with ennui.
My nerves were edgy with ennui.
My voice was flat with ennui.
My voice was thick with ennui.
My voice was thin with ennui.
A sigh of ennui shimmered through me.

A wave of ennui came over me.
A wave of ennui washed over
me.
I let out a sob of ennui.
A look of ennui came over my
face.

ENTHUSIASM

Definition: Intense and eager enjoyment, interest, or approval.
See PASSION

Enthusiasm boiled inside me.
Enthusiasm bubbled through me.
Enthusiasm caressed my mouth.
Enthusiasm clawed at me.
Enthusiasm clouded my mind.
Enthusiasm coursed through me.
Enthusiasm crowded my chest.
Enthusiasm curled through me.
Enthusiasm darkened my eyes.
Enthusiasm darkened my irises.
Enthusiasm dilated my eyes.
Enthusiasm drifted through me.
Enthusiasm entered my voice.
Enthusiasm exploded inside me.
Enthusiasm exploded within me.
Enthusiasm filled my head.
Enthusiasm flowed over me.
Enthusiasm flowed through me.
Enthusiasm fluttered inside me.
Enthusiasm glowed inside me.
Enthusiasm gushed through me.
Enthusiasm heated my blood.

Enthusiasm knifed through me.
Enthusiasm laced my voice.
Enthusiasm licked through me.
Enthusiasm lit my eyes.
Enthusiasm made me melt.
Enthusiasm penetrated my heart.
Enthusiasm poured through me.
Enthusiasm pulsed through me.
Enthusiasm pumped through me.
Enthusiasm radiated from me.
Enthusiasm ravaged my face.
Enthusiasm reddened my cheeks.
Enthusiasm rippled through me.
Enthusiasm rose from me.
Enthusiasm rose in me.
Enthusiasm shattered within me.
Enthusiasm slammed into me.
Enthusiasm sluiced through me.
Enthusiasm spiralled through me.
Enthusiasm splintered through me.

Enthusiasm surged through me.
Enthusiasm swelled within me.
Enthusiasm swept through me.
Enthusiasm swirled through me.
Enthusiasm thickened my voice.
Enthusiasm tightened inside me.
Enthusiasm tightened my features.
Enthusiasm wafted through me.
Enthusiasm warmed my insides.
Enthusiasm washed through me.
Enthusiasm went through me.
Enthusiasm banked in my eyes.
Enthusiasm combated in my brain.
Enthusiasm danced in my belly.
Enthusiasm exploded in my chest.
Enthusiasm flamed in my expression.
Enthusiasm flared in my eyes.
Enthusiasm flashed in my eyes.
Enthusiasm flashed into my eyes.
Enthusiasm flickered in my expression.
Enthusiasm flickered in my eyes.
Enthusiasm glittered in my eyes.

Enthusiasm nipped at my skin.
Enthusiasm throbbed against my belly.
My blood burned with enthusiasm.
My blood heated with enthusiasm.
My body burned with enthusiasm.
My body drugged with enthusiasm.
My body hardened with enthusiasm.
My body heated with enthusiasm.
My body hummed with enthusiasm.
My body jangled with enthusiasm.
My body shivered with enthusiasm.
My body stirred with enthusiasm.
My body thrummed with enthusiasm.
My body twitched with enthusiasm.
My body unfurled with enthusiasm.
My body vibrated with enthusiasm.
My ears shut in enthusiasm.
My eyes blazed with enthusiasm.
My eyes danced with enthusiasm.
My eyes darkened with enthusiasm.

My eyes dilated with enthusiasm.
My eyes filled with enthusiasm.
My eyes flared with enthusiasm.
My eyes flickered with enthusiasm.
My eyes glazed with enthusiasm.
My eyes gleamed with enthusiasm.
My eyes glittered with enthusiasm.
My eyes glowed with enthusiasm.
My eyes hooded with enthusiasm.
My eyes lit with enthusiasm.
My eyes narrowed with enthusiasm.
My eyes shimmered with enthusiasm.
My eyes shone with enthusiasm.
My eyes sparkled with enthusiasm.
My face filled with enthusiasm.
My face flushed with enthusiasm.
My face mottled with enthusiasm.
My heart burned with enthusiasm.
My heart swelled with enthusiasm.

My pulse raced with enthusiasm.
My skin blushed with enthusiasm.
My skin flushed with enthusiasm.
My voice bubbled with enthusiasm.
My voice sang with enthusiasm.
My voice shook with enthusiasm.
My voice slurred with enthusiasm.
Enthusiasm curled deep in my belly.
Enthusiasm pooled low in my belly.
I felt a measure of enthusiasm.
My body was overwrought with enthusiasm.
My eyes grew hazy with enthusiasm.
My eyes went dark with enthusiasm.
My eyes were bloodshot with enthusiasm.
My eyes were bright with enthusiasm.
My eyes were dark with enthusiasm.
My eyes were full of enthusiasm.
My eyes were hazy with enthusiasm.
My eyes were heavy with enthusiasm.

My face glazed over with
enthusiasm.
My throat was thick with
enthusiasm.
My voice was rough with
enthusiasm.
My voice was thick with
enthusiasm.

ENVY

Definition: A feeling of discontented or resentful longing aroused by someone else's possessions, qualities, or luck.

See JEALOUSY

Envy ate at me.
Envy bloomed inside me.
Envy bubbled through me.
Envy caressed my mouth.
Envy clawed at me.
Envy coursed through me.
Envy crawled over me.
Envy crowded my chest.
Envy curdled inside me.
Envy curled through me.
Envy darkened my irises.
Envy drifted through me.
Envy exploded inside me.
Envy flowed over me.
Envy flowed through me.
Envy fluttered inside me.
Envy glowed inside me.
Envy gushed through me.
Envy heated my blood.
Envy knifed through me.
Envy laced my voice.
Envy licked through me.
Envy made me melt.
Envy mushroomed inside me.
Envy penetrated my heart.
Envy poured through me.
Envy pulsed through me.
Envy pumped through me.
Envy radiated from me.
Envy ravaged my face.
Envy rippled through me.
Envy rose from me.

Envy rose in me.
Envy scratched at me.
Envy shattered within me.
Envy slammed into me.
Envy sluiced through me.
Envy snaked inside me.
Envy snaked through me.
Envy speared through me.
Envy spiralled through me.
Envy splintered through me.
Envy stirred in me.
Envy suffused my body.
Envy surged through me.
Envy swelled within me.
Envy swept through me.
Envy swirled through me.
Envy tightened inside me.
Envy tightened my features.
Envy traipsed through me.
Envy wafted through me.
Envy warmed my insides.
Envy washed through me.
Envy went through me.
Envy banked in my eyes.
Envy burned in my gut.
Envy combated in my brain.
Envy danced in my belly.
Envy flared in my heart.
Envy flashed in my eyes.
Envy flickered in my expression.
Envy flickered in my eyes.

Envy nipped at my skin.
Envy sparked through my
mind.
Envy throbbed against my
belly.
My blood burned with envy.
My blood heated with envy.
My body burned with envy.
My body drugged with envy.
My body hardened with envy.
My body heated with envy.
My body hummed with envy.
My body jangled with envy.
My body shivered with envy.
My body stirred with envy.
My body thrummed with
envy.
My body twitched with envy.
My body unfurled with envy.
My ears shut in envy.
My eyes blazed with envy.
My eyes danced with envy.
My eyes darkened with envy.
My eyes flared with envy.
My eyes flickered with envy.
My eyes gleamed with envy.
My eyes glittered with envy.
My eyes glowed with envy.
My eyes lit with envy.
My eyes narrowed with envy.
My eyes shimmered with envy.
My face crazed with envy.
My face flushed with envy.
My heart burned with envy.
My heart swelled with envy.
My pulse raced with envy.
My skin flushed with envy.
My voice rang with envy.

My voice slurred with envy.
Envy curled deep in my belly.
Envy pooled low in my belly.
I felt a bit of envy.
I felt a flash of envy.
I felt a flicker of envy.
I felt a pang of envy.
I felt a prickle of envy.
I felt a sense of envy.
I felt a stab of envy.
I felt a surge of envy.
I felt a swish of envy.
I felt a thrust of envy.
I felt a tinge of envy.
I felt a twinge of envy.
I felt a twist of envy.
My body was overwrought
with envy.
My eyes went dark with envy.
My eyes were dark with envy.
My eyes were full of envy.
My eyes were hazy with envy.
My eyes were heavy with envy.
My face glazed over with envy.
My throat was thick with envy.
My voice sounded rough with
envy.
My voice was rough with envy.
My voice was thick with envy.

EUPHORIA

Definition: A feeling or state of intense excitement and happiness.
See HAPPINESS

Euphoria brightened my eyes.
Euphoria coursed through me.
Euphoria crashed through me.
Euphoria crawled over me.
Euphoria encircled my head.
Euphoria exploded inside me.
Euphoria exploded within me.
Euphoria filled my chest.
Euphoria filled my lungs.
Euphoria flowed through me.
Euphoria hummed through
me.
Euphoria laced my heart.
Euphoria licked through me.
Euphoria lit my features.
Euphoria melted my bones.
Euphoria moved through me.
Euphoria pierced my brain.
Euphoria poured through me.
Euphoria raced through me.
Euphoria radiated through me.
Euphoria ran through me.
Euphoria ripped through me.
Euphoria rippled through me.
Euphoria roared through me.
Euphoria rocked through me.
Euphoria rushed through me.
Euphoria seared my senses.
Euphoria settled over me.
Euphoria shot through me.
Euphoria shuddered through
me.
Euphoria sliced through me.

Euphoria spiked through me.
Euphoria splintered my brain.
Euphoria stole through me.
Euphoria surged through me.
Euphoria swept through me.
Euphoria touched my face.
Euphoria washed over me.
Euphoria washed through me.
Euphoria welled inside me.
Euphoria went through me.
Euphoria whirled through me.
Euphoria appeared on my face.
Euphoria burned in my
stomach.
Euphoria flowed from my lips.
Euphoria flushed through my
body.
Euphoria glided through my
body.
Euphoria infused in my
expression.
Euphoria raced down my
spine.
Euphoria radiated from my
expression.
Euphoria ran through my
voice.
Euphoria rattled through my
veins.
Euphoria rippled through my
body.
Euphoria rivered through my
body.

Euphoria rocked through my body.
Euphoria rumbled from my throat.
Euphoria shimmied down my spine.
Euphoria skittered down my body.
Euphoria sparked through my system.
Euphoria swept across my face.
Euphoria vibrated along my skin.
Euphoria washed over my body.
Euphoria welled in my eyes.
My body jerked in euphoria.
My body sighed in euphoria.
My body teemed with euphoria.
My eyes closed in euphoria.
My eyes closed with euphoria.
My eyes crinkled with euphoria.
My eyes danced with euphoria.
My eyes flashed with euphoria.
My eyes glazed with euphoria.
My eyes gleamed with euphoria.
My eyes glowed with euphoria.
My eyes rolled with euphoria.
My eyes shut with euphoria.
My eyes sparkled with euphoria.
My eyes widened with euphoria.
My face danced with euphoria.
My face flushed with euphoria.
My face lit with euphoria.
My face softened in euphoria.
My face wreathed in euphoria.
My heart fluttered with euphoria.
My heart hummed with euphoria.
My heart leaped with euphoria.
My heart sighed with euphoria.
My heart soared with euphoria.
My heart thumped with euphoria.
My lips twitched with euphoria.
My mouth opened in euphoria.
My skin mottled with euphoria.
My eyes slid shut in euphoria.
My face grew radiant with euphoria.
My face was aglow with euphoria.
My face was rapt with euphoria.

EXASPERATION

Definition: A feeling of intense irritation or annoyance.
See IRRITATION

Exasperation clouded my face.
Exasperation crawled through me.
Exasperation crossed my face.
Exasperation crossed my forehead.
Exasperation entered my expression.
Exasperation entered my voice.
Exasperation filled my face.
Exasperation grated my voice.
Exasperation laced my voice.
Exasperation moved through me.
Exasperation rose in me.
Exasperation sifted through me.
Exasperation touched my voice.
Exasperation washed over me.
I exhaled in exasperation.
I grimaced with exasperation.
I groaned in exasperation.
I sighed in exasperation.
Exasperation burned in my gut.
Exasperation crept into my expression.
Exasperation crept into my voice.
Exasperation descended over my features.
Exasperation flared on my face.

Exasperation flashed across my face.
Exasperation flashed in my eyes.
Exasperation flickered across my face.
Exasperation flickered in my eyes.
Exasperation flickered over my face.
Exasperation passed through my eyes.
Exasperation rang in my words.
Exasperation ripped through my body.
Exasperation scratched at my temper.
Exasperation settled over my face.
Exasperation washed across my face.
My brows lowered in exasperation.
My eyebrows furrowed in exasperation.
My eyes flashed with exasperation.
My eyes flickered with exasperation.
My eyes gleamed with exasperation.

My eyes glowed with
exasperation.
My eyes narrowed in
exasperation.
My eyes snapped with
exasperation.
My eyes went from
exasperation.
My face clouded with
exasperation.
My face crawled with
exasperation.
My face flushed with
exasperation.
My face tightened with
exasperation.
My face twisted in
exasperation.
My face went from
exasperation.
My head jerked in
exasperation.
My head throbbed with
exasperation.
My lips crimped with
exasperation.
My lips tightened in
exasperation.
My mouth tightened in
exasperation.
My mouth tightened with
exasperation.
My tone reeked of
exasperation.
My tone rose with
exasperation.
My voice ragged with
exasperation.

My voice rasped with
exasperation.
My voice rose in exasperation.
My voice rose with
exasperation.
My voice strained with
exasperation.
My voice tinged with
exasperation.
I exhaled a blast of
exasperation.
I gave a sigh of exasperation.
I gave a snort of exasperation.
My eyes were sharp with
exasperation.
My face grew pinched with
exasperation.
My voice was full of
exasperation.

EXCITEMENT

Definition: A feeling of great enthusiasm and eagerness.

See EXHILARATION

Excitement brightened my face.

Excitement coiled in me.

Excitement coursed through me.

Excitement crossed my face.

Excitement entered my voice.

Excitement flowed through me.

Excitement grew inside me.

Excitement heated my blood.

Excitement jabbed my brain.

Excitement mounted inside me.

Excitement moved through me.

Excitement painted my features.

Excitement pulsed through me.

Excitement quickened my breath.

Excitement raced through me.

Excitement ran through me.

Excitement rippled through me.

Excitement rose in me.

Excitement rose inside me.

Excitement rose within me.

Excitement rushed through me.

Excitement skittered through me.

Excitement stirred in me.

Excitement swept over me.

Excitement swept through me.

Excitement tickled my stomach.

Excitement touched my voice.

Excitement washed over me.

Excitement went through me.

I beamed with excitement.

I bubbled with excitement.

I shivered with excitement.

I whooped with excitement.

Excitement blazed in my eyes.

Excitement bubbled in my voice.

Excitement budded in my chest.

Excitement burgeoned in my loins.

Excitement closed on my chest.

Excitement coursed through my veins.

Excitement crept down my back.

Excitement crept into my voice.

Excitement fizzed in my chest.

Excitement flashed into my bones.

Excitement gleamed in my eyes.

Excitement played across my face.
Excitement poked at my belly.
Excitement ran up my spine.
Excitement rippled through my veins.
Excitement rose in my chest.
Excitement rose in my voice.
Excitement stirred along my nerve.
Excitement welled in my breast.
My blood heated with excitement.
My body quivered with excitement.
My chest bubbled with excitement.
My chest pounded with excitement.
My ears flapped in excitement.
My ears fluttered with excitement.
My ears quivered with excitement.
My eyes blazed with excitement.
My eyes burned with excitement.
My eyes danced with excitement.
My eyes flashed in excitement.
My eyes flashed with excitement.
My eyes gleamed with excitement.
My eyes glinted with excitement.

My eyes glistened with excitement.
My eyes glittered with excitement.
My eyes shone in excitement.
My eyes shone with excitement.
My eyes sparkled with excitement.
My eyes twinkled with excitement.
My eyes widened in excitement.
My eyes widened with excitement.
My face filled with excitement.
My face flickered with excitement.
My face flushed with excitement.
My face glowed with excitement.
My face polished with excitement.
My face shone with excitement.
My face swelled with excitement.
My face tingled with excitement.
My head bobbed in excitement.
My head twitched with excitement.
My heart beat with excitement.
My heart filled with excitement.

My heart fluttered with excitement.
My heart pounded with excitement.
My heart quickened in excitement.
My heart quickened with excitement.
My heart raced with excitement.
My heart thumped with excitement.
My lips quivered with excitement.
My mouth twitched with excitement.
My nose twitched in excitement.
My pulse kicked with excitement.
My pulse pounded with excitement.
My pulse raced with excitement.
My skin glowed with excitement.
My stomach churned with excitement.
My stomach squirmed with excitement.
My voice cracked with excitement.
My voice filled with excitement.
My voice rang with excitement.
My voice rose in excitement.
My voice rose with excitement.

My voice shook with excitement.
My voice squeaked with excitement.
My voice tinged with excitement.
My voice trembled with excitement.
Excitement caused my voice to rise.
I felt a beat of excitement.
I felt a bolt of excitement.
I felt a bubble of excitement.
I felt a burn of excitement.
I felt a burst of excitement.
I felt a buzz of excitement.
I felt a chill of excitement.
I felt a current of excitement.
I felt a flicker of excitement.
I felt a flush of excitement.
I felt a flutter of excitement.
I felt a frisson of excitement.
I felt a jolt of excitement.
I felt a kind of excitement.
I felt a lift of excitement.
I felt a mix of excitement.
I felt a moment of excitement.
I felt a prickle of excitement.
I felt a pulse of excitement.
I felt a quiver of excitement.
I felt a rush of excitement.
I felt a sense of excitement.
I felt a shiver of excitement.
I felt a spark of excitement.
I felt a spurt of excitement.
I felt a stab of excitement.
I felt a stir of excitement.
I felt a surge of excitement.

I felt a thrill of excitement.
I felt a tickle of excitement.
I felt a tinge of excitement.
I felt a tingle of excitement.
I felt a tremor of excitement.
I felt a tug of excitement.
I felt a twinge of excitement.
I felt a wave of excitement.
I felt that tingle of excitement.
I gave a bark of excitement.
I gave a shiver of excitement.
My eyes burned bright with
excitement.
My eyes grew big with
excitement.
My eyes lit up in excitement.
My eyes lit up with
excitement.
My eyes were alight with
excitement.
My eyes were alive with
excitement.
My eyes were big with
excitement.
My eyes were bright with
excitement.
My eyes were brilliant with
excitement.
My eyes were fierce with
excitement.
My eyes were frantic with
excitement.
My eyes were full of
excitement.
My eyes were wide with
excitement.
My face flushed grey with
excitement.

My face lit up with excitement.
My face was bright with
excitement.
My neck felt prickly with
excitement.
My skin was clammy with
excitement.
My skin was electric with
excitement.
My stomach screwed up with
excitement.
My voice was full of
excitement.
My voice was hoarse with
excitement.

EXHILARATION

Definition: A feeling of excitement, happiness, or elation.

See EXCITEMENT

Exhilaration brightened my face.

Exhilaration came over me.

Exhilaration coiled in me.

Exhilaration coursed through me.

Exhilaration crossed my face.

Exhilaration entered my voice.

Exhilaration filled my chest.

Exhilaration filled my stomach.

Exhilaration flooded through me.

Exhilaration flowed through me.

Exhilaration grew inside me.

Exhilaration heated my blood.

Exhilaration jabbed my brain.

Exhilaration mounted inside me.

Exhilaration moved through me.

Exhilaration painted my features.

Exhilaration pulsed through me.

Exhilaration quickened my breath.

Exhilaration raced through me.

Exhilaration ran through me.

Exhilaration rippled through me.

Exhilaration rose in me.

Exhilaration rose inside me.

Exhilaration rose within me.

Exhilaration rushed through me.

Exhilaration settled over me.

Exhilaration skittered through me.

Exhilaration stirred in me.

Exhilaration surged through me.

Exhilaration swept over me.

Exhilaration swept through me.

Exhilaration tickled my stomach.

Exhilaration touched my voice.

Exhilaration washed over me.

Exhilaration went through me.

Exhilaration blazed in my eyes.

Exhilaration bubbled in my voice.

Exhilaration budded in my chest.

Exhilaration burgeoned in my loins.

Exhilaration closed on my chest.

Exhilaration coursed through my veins.

Exhilaration crept down my back.

Exhilaration crept into my voice.

Exhilaration fizzed in my chest.

Exhilaration flashed into my bones.

Exhilaration gleamed in my eyes.

Exhilaration played across my face.

Exhilaration poked at my belly.

Exhilaration ran up my spine.

Exhilaration rippled through my veins.

Exhilaration rose in my chest.

Exhilaration rose in my voice.

Exhilaration stirred along my nerve.

Exhilaration welled in my breast.

My blood heated with exhilaration.

My body quivered with exhilaration.

My chest bubbled with exhilaration.

My chest pounded with exhilaration.

My ears flapped in exhilaration.

My ears fluttered with exhilaration.

My ears quivered with exhilaration.

My eyes blazed with exhilaration.

My eyes burned with exhilaration.

My eyes danced with exhilaration.

My eyes flashed in exhilaration.

My eyes flashed with exhilaration.

My eyes gleamed with exhilaration.

My eyes glinted with exhilaration.

My eyes glistened with exhilaration.

My eyes glittered with exhilaration.

My eyes shone in exhilaration.

My eyes shone with exhilaration.

My eyes sparkled with exhilaration.

My eyes twinkled with exhilaration.

My eyes widened in exhilaration.

My eyes widened with exhilaration.

My face filled with exhilaration.

My face flickered with exhilaration.

My face flushed with exhilaration.

My face glowed with exhilaration.

My face polished with exhilaration.

My face shone with exhilaration.

My face swelled with exhilaration.
My face tingled with exhilaration.
My head bobbed in exhilaration.
My head twitched with exhilaration.
My heart beat with exhilaration.
My heart filled with exhilaration.
My heart fluttered with exhilaration.
My heart pounded with exhilaration.
My heart quickened in exhilaration.
My heart quickened with exhilaration.
My heart raced with exhilaration.
My heart thumped with exhilaration.
My lips quivered with exhilaration.
My mouth twitched with exhilaration.
My nose twitched in exhilaration.
My pulse kicked with exhilaration.
My pulse pounded with exhilaration.
My pulse raced with exhilaration.
My skin glowed with exhilaration.

My stomach churned with exhilaration.
My stomach squirmed with exhilaration.
My voice cracked with exhilaration.
My voice filled with exhilaration.
My voice rang with exhilaration.
My voice rose in exhilaration.
My voice rose with exhilaration.
My voice shook with exhilaration.
My voice squeaked with exhilaration.
My voice tinged with exhilaration.
My voice trembled with exhilaration.
Exhilaration caused my voice to rise.
I felt a rush of exhilaration.
I felt a sense of exhilaration.
I felt a surge of exhilaration.
I felt a wave of exhilaration.
My eyes burned bright with exhilaration.
My eyes grew big with exhilaration.
My eyes lit up in exhilaration.
My eyes lit up with exhilaration.
My eyes were alight with exhilaration.
My eyes were alive with exhilaration.

My eyes were big with
exhilaration.
My eyes were bright with
exhilaration.
My eyes were brilliant with
exhilaration.
My eyes were fierce with
exhilaration.
My eyes were frantic with
exhilaration.
My eyes were full of
exhilaration.
My eyes were wide with
exhilaration.
My face flushed grey with
exhilaration.
My face lit up with
exhilaration.
My face was bright with
exhilaration.
My neck felt prickly with
exhilaration.
My skin was clammy with
exhilaration.
My skin was electric with
exhilaration.
My stomach screwed up with
exhilaration.
My voice was full of
exhilaration.
My voice was hoarse with
exhilaration.

F

FEAR

Definition: An unpleasant emotion caused by the threat of danger,
pain, or harm.
See TERROR

Fear arced through me.
Fear ate at me.
Fear ate into me.
Fear bled into me.
Fear blurred my vision.
Fear boiled inside me.
Fear bubbled in me.
Fear burned my nostrils.
Fear chilled my spine.
Fear clawed at me.
Fear clenched my stomach.
Fear clogged my thoughts.
Fear clogged my throat.
Fear clouded my brain.
Fear clouded my expression.
Fear clouded my eyes.
Fear clutched my heart.
Fear coated my mouth.
Fear consumed my face.
Fear coursed through me.
Fear cramped my chest.
Fear crashed into me.
Fear crashed through me.
Fear crawled through me.
Fear crept over me.
Fear crossed my face.

Fear crowded my chest.
Fear crowded my throat.
Fear cut through me.
Fear darkened my eyes.
Fear darkened my face.
Fear darted through me.
Fear dried my mouth.
Fear exploded inside me.
Fear fell over me.
Fear filled my eyes.
Fear filled my face.
Fear filled my mind.
Fear flared in me.
Fear flooded into me.
Fear flooded my mind.
Fear flooded my veins.
Fear flowed into me.
Fear grabbed at me.
Fear grew within me.
Fear gripped my gut.
Fear gripped my heart.
Fear gripped my soul.
Fear gripped my stomach.
Fear gripped my throat.
Fear iced my veins.
Fear jack-knifed through me.

Fear jolted through me.
Fear knifed through me.
Fear knotted my insides.
Fear laced my voice.
Fear lanced through me.
Fear leaped through me.
Fear licked at me.
Fear lined my face.
Fear lit inside me.
Fear lit my eyes.
Fear lit my nerves.
Fear made me sweat.
Fear moved through me.
Fear mushroomed inside me.
Fear nagged at me.
Fear painted my face.
Fear plucked at me.
Fear poured through me.
Fear pricked my spine.
Fear prodded my mind.
Fear pulsed through me.
Fear pumped through me.
Fear raced through me.
Fear racked my body.
Fear radiated from me.
Fear raged inside me.
Fear raked through me.
Fear ran over me.
Fear ran through me.
Fear rifled through me.
Fear ripped through me.
Fear rippled through me.
Fear rode through me.
Fear roiled inside me.
Fear roiled through me.
Fear rolled through me.
Fear rose in me.
Fear rose inside me.

Fear rushed through me.
Fear seized my chest.
Fear seized my stomach.
Fear shivered through me.
Fear shot through me.
Fear shuddered through me.
Fear skimmed my nerves.
Fear slammed into me.
Fear slithered through me.
Fear snaked through me.
Fear soured my stomach.
Fear spiralled inside me.
Fear spiralled through me.
Fear squeezed my chest.
Fear squeezed my heart.
Fear squeezed my lungs.
Fear stabbed through me.
Fear stilled my fingers.
Fear streaked my face.
Fear streaked through me.
Fear struck through me.
Fear surged through me.
Fear swelled inside me.
Fear swept over me.
Fear swept through me.
Fear swirled through me.
Fear thundered through me.
Fear tied my stomach.
Fear tightened around me.
Fear tightened my chest.
Fear tightened my lungs.
Fear tightened my nerves.
Fear tightened my skin.
Fear tinged my words.
Fear travelled through me.
Fear trickled over me.
Fear turned my stomach.
Fear washed my face.

Fear washed over me.
Fear washed through me.
Fear went through me.
Fear whipped through me.
Fear widened my eyes.
Fear wormed through me.
I filled with fear.
I fluttered with fear.
I froze with fear.
I gasped in fear.
I muttered in fear.
I shivered from fear.
I shivered in fear.
I shuddered with fear.
I yelped with fear.
Fear blew through my heart.
Fear bloomed in my face.
Fear blossomed in my belly.
Fear burned in my throat.
Fear burrowed into my spine.
Fear caught in my throat.
Fear churned in my gut.
Fear clamped around my neck.
Fear clawed at my chest.
Fear clawed at my heart.
Fear clawed at my insides.
Fear clawed at my throat.
Fear clawed up my spine.
Fear closed around my heart.
Fear closed up my throat.
Fear coursed through my body.
Fear crawled along my collar.
Fear crawled on my skin.
Fear crawled through my
limbs.
Fear crawled up my spine.
Fear crept down my spine.
Fear crept into my expression.

Fear crept through my body.
Fear crept up my spine.
Fear etched in my eyes.
Fear etched into my
expression.
Fear etched into my eyes.
Fear etched on my face.
Fear etched on my features.
Fear fell across my eyes.
Fear flashed in my eyes.
Fear flickered in my eyes.
Fear fluttered through my
breast.
Fear grew in my eyes.
Fear grew in my gut.
Fear jammed in my throat.
Fear knotted in my belly.
Fear lifted from my heart.
Fear lingered in my voice.
Fear lumped in my throat.
Fear made my chest tight.
Fear made my knees weak.
Fear made my throat sore.
Fear oozed from my pores.
Fear played across my face.
Fear played over my face.
Fear poured through my body.
Fear pressed against my heart.
Fear pried open my heart.
Fear ran down my spine.
Fear ran through my bowels.
Fear ran through my veins.
Fear ran up my spine.
Fear reflected in my eyes.
Fear reflected in my face.
Fear registered in my eyes.
Fear ripped through my
stomach.

Fear rippled across my skin.
Fear rolled down my cheeks.
Fear rolled through my
stomach.
Fear rose in my gut.
Fear rose in my throat.
Fear seeped into my mind.
Fear settled in my stomach.
Fear shone from my eyes.
Fear shone in my eyes.
Fear shot down my spine.
Fear shot up my spine.
Fear showed in my eyes.
Fear showed on my face.
Fear slammed into my brain.
Fear sliced through my
midsection.
Fear slid down my spine.
Fear slithered along my skin.
Fear slithered through my
belly.
Fear slithered up my spine.
Fear smouldered in my
stomach.
Fear snaked along my spine.
Fear snatched at my heart.
Fear streamed down my face.
Fear surged through my gut.
Fear swirled in my stomach.
Fear tightened between my
shoulders.
Fear tightened in my stomach.
Fear traipsed up my spine.
Fear trembled down my spine.
Fear tugged at my legs.
Fear wafted up my spine.
Fear washed through my
mouth.

My body convulsed in fear.
My body pulsed with fear.
My body quivered with fear.
My body shook with fear.
My body shuddered with fear.
My body trembled in fear.
My body trembled with fear.
My body vibrated with fear.
My chest clenched with fear.
My chest seized with fear.
My eyes blazed with fear.
My eyes brimmed with fear.
My eyes bulged in fear.
My eyes bulged with fear.
My eyes clouded with fear.
My eyes darkened with fear.
My eyes darted in fear.
My eyes dilated with fear.
My eyes filled with fear.
My eyes flashed with fear.
My eyes flickered with fear.
My eyes glazed with fear.
My eyes glittered with fear.
My eyes inked with fear.
My eyes marbled with fear.
My eyes popped with fear.
My eyes protruded with fear.
My eyes rolled in fear.
My eyes shone with fear.
My eyes simmered with fear.
My eyes touched with fear.
My eyes widened in fear.
My eyes widened with fear.
My face contorted with fear.
My face distorted with fear.
My face drawn in fear.
My face etched with fear.
My face filled with fear.

My face frozen in fear.
My face frozen with fear.
My face pinched with fear.
My face tightened with fear.
My face twisted in fear.
My face twisted with fear.
My face twitched with fear.
My heart banged with fear.
My heart clutched in fear.
My heart drummed with fear.
My heart filled with fear.
My heart frozen with fear.
My heart hammered with fear.
My heart pounded in fear.
My heart pounded with fear.
My heart protested in fear.
My heart sank with fear.
My heart seized with fear.
My heart squeezed with fear.
My heart thudded with fear.
My heartbeat stuttered in fear.
My lips compressed in fear.
My mouth contorted with
fear.
My mouth writhed with fear.
My nerves jangled with fear.
My skin chilled with fear.
My skin pricked with fear.
My skin prickled with fear.
My throat clamped with fear.
My throat clogged with fear.
My throat constricted in fear.
My throat constricted with
fear.
My throat dried in fear.
My throat parched from fear.
My throat tightened with fear.
My tone laced with fear.

My voice chattered with fear.
My voice choked with fear.
My voice cracked from fear.
My voice cracked with fear.
My voice edged with fear.
My voice hushed with fear.
My voice laced with fear.
My voice muted with fear.
My voice quavered with fear.
My voice quivered with fear.
My voice ragged with fear.
My voice rose in fear.
My voice shook with fear.
My voice tinged with fear.
My voice trembled with fear.
My voice vibrated with fear.
My voice whined with fear.
I felt a burst of fear.
I felt a chill of fear.
I felt a flash of fear.
I felt a flutter of fear.
I felt a goad of fear.
I felt a jab of fear.
I felt a jolt of fear.
I felt a knife of fear.
I felt a knot of fear.
I felt a lancet of fear.
I felt a mixture of fear.
I felt a moment of fear.
I felt a note of fear.
I felt a pang of fear.
I felt a prickle of fear.
I felt a pulse of fear.
I felt a quiver of fear.
I felt a ridge of fear.
I felt a ripple of fear.
I felt a rush of fear.
I felt a sense of fear.

I felt a shaft of fear.
I felt a shiver of fear.
I felt a shudder of fear.
I felt a slick of fear.
I felt a spark of fear.
I felt a spasm of fear.
I felt a spike of fear.
I felt a spurt of fear.
I felt a stab of fear.
I felt a surge of fear.
I felt a swell of fear.
I felt a thrill of fear.
I felt a tingle of fear.
I felt a tremor of fear.
I felt a twinge of fear.
I felt a whisper of fear.
I felt a whorl of fear.
I felt an ache of fear.
I felt an icicle of fear.
I gave a tremor of fear.
I sniffed a sliver of fear.
I swallowed a lump of fear.
My body was electric with fear.
My eyes grew huge with fear.
My eyes grew wide with fear.
My eyes opened wide in fear.
My eyes opened wide with fear.
My eyes snapped wide with fear.
My eyes squeezed shut with fear.
My eyes were big with fear.
My eyes were black with fear.
My eyes were blind with fear.
My eyes were bright with fear.
My eyes were crazy with fear.
My eyes were dark with fear.

My eyes were full of fear.
My eyes were glassy with fear.
My eyes were grey with fear.
My eyes were huge with fear.
My eyes were large with fear.
My eyes were wide with fear.
My eyes were wild with fear.
My face was ashen with fear.
My face was crazy with fear.
My face was frantic with fear.
My heart became cold with fear.
My heart was full of fear.
My mouth fell open in fear.
My mouth grew dry with fear.
My mouth hung open in fear.
My mouth was dry with fear.
My shoulders were tense with fear.
My stomach turned sick with fear.
My throat was raw with fear.
My throat was thick with fear.
My voice pitched high with fear.
My voice was shrill with fear.

FONDNESS

Definition: Affection or liking for someone or something.
See AFFECTION

Fondness came over me.
Fondness crossed my face.
Fondness fell over me.
Fondness filled my eyes.
Fondness filled my mind.
Fondness flowed around me.
Fondness pierced my heart.
Fondness saturated my voice.
Fondness surged through me.
Fondness swept through me.
Fondness warred inside me.
Fondness washed over me.
Fondness washed through me.
Fondness welled inside me.
Fondness blazed in my eyes.
Fondness burned in my eyes.
Fondness crept into my voice.
Fondness gleamed in my eyes.
Fondness radiated from my face.
Fondness shimmered in my expression.
Fondness shone in my eyes.
Fondness shone through my tears.
Fondness stirred in my breast.
My chest squeezed with fondness.
My chest swelled with fondness.
My eyes brimmed with fondness.
My eyes darkened with fondness.
My eyes filled with fondness.
My eyes glowed with fondness.
My eyes moistened with fondness.
My eyes shimmered with fondness.
My eyes shone with fondness.
My eyes softened with fondness.
My face filled with fondness.
My face suffused with fondness.
My heart ached with fondness.
My heart engorged with fondness.
My heart filled with fondness.
My heart fluttered with fondness.
My heart looked for fondness.
My heart overflowed with fondness.
My heart soared with fondness.
My heart squeezed with fondness.
My heart swelled with fondness.
My heart swollen with fondness.
My heart warmed with fondness.

My throat tightened as
fondness.
My tone filled with fondness.
My voice deepened with
fondness.
My voice throbbed with
fondness.
My eyes lit up with fondness.
My eyes were full of fondness.
My eyes were misty with
fondness.
My eyes were warm with
fondness.
My face was soft with
fondness.
My heart was full of fondness.
My heart was heavy with
fondness.
My voice was full of fondness.

FRIGHT

Definition: A sudden intense feeling of fear.
See FEAR

Fright arced through me.
Fright ate at me.
Fright ate into me.
Fright bled into me.
Fright blurred my vision.
Fright boiled inside me.
Fright bubbled in me.
Fright burned my nostrils.
Fright chilled my spine.
Fright clawed at me.
Fright clenched my stomach.
Fright clogged my thoughts.
Fright clogged my throat.
Fright clouded my brain.
Fright clouded my expression.
Fright clouded my eyes.
Fright clutched my heart.
Fright coated my mouth.
Fright consumed my face.
Fright coursed through me.
Fright cramped my chest.
Fright crashed into me.
Fright crashed through me.
Fright crawled through me.
Fright crept over me.
Fright crossed my face.
Fright crowded my chest.
Fright crowded my throat.
Fright cut through me.
Fright darkened my eyes.
Fright darkened my face.
Fright darted through me.
Fright dried my mouth.

Fright exploded inside me.
Fright fell over me.
Fright filled my eyes.
Fright filled my face.
Fright filled my mind.
Fright flared in me.
Fright flooded into me.
Fright flooded my mind.
Fright flooded my veins.
Fright flowed into me.
Fright grabbed at me.
Fright grew within me.
Fright gripped my gut.
Fright gripped my heart.
Fright gripped my soul.
Fright gripped my stomach.
Fright gripped my throat.
Fright iced my veins.
Fright jack-knifed through me.
Fright jolted through me.
Fright knifed through me.
Fright knotted my insides.
Fright laced my voice.
Fright lanced through me.
Fright leaped through me.
Fright licked at me.
Fright lined my face.
Fright lit inside me.
Fright lit my eyes.
Fright lit my nerves.
Fright made me sweat.
Fright moved through me.
Fright mushroomed inside me.

Fright nagged at me.
Fright painted my face.
Fright plucked at me.
Fright poured through me.
Fright pricked my spine.
Fright prodded my mind.
Fright pulsed through me.
Fright pumped through me.
Fright raced through me.
Fright racked my body.
Fright radiated from me.
Fright raged inside me.
Fright raked through me.
Fright ran over me.
Fright ran through me.
Fright rifled through me.
Fright ripped through me.
Fright rippled through me.
Fright rode through me.
Fright roiled inside me.
Fright roiled through me.
Fright rolled through me.
Fright rose in me.
Fright rose inside me.
Fright rushed through me.
Fright seized my chest.
Fright seized my stomach.
Fright shivered through me.
Fright shot through me.
Fright shuddered through me.
Fright skimmed my nerves.
Fright slammed into me.
Fright slithered through me.
Fright snaked through me.
Fright soured my stomach.
Fright spiralled inside me.
Fright spiralled through me.
Fright squeezed my chest.

Fright squeezed my heart.
Fright squeezed my lungs.
Fright stabbed through me.
Fright stilled my fingers.
Fright streaked my face.
Fright streaked through me.
Fright struck through me.
Fright surged through me.
Fright swelled inside me.
Fright swept over me.
Fright swept through me.
Fright swirled through me.
Fright thundered through me.
Fright tied my stomach.
Fright tightened around me.
Fright tightened my chest.
Fright tightened my lungs.
Fright tightened my nerves.
Fright tightened my skin.
Fright tinged my words.
Fright travelled through me.
Fright trickled over me.
Fright turned my stomach.
Fright washed my face.
Fright washed over me.
Fright washed through me.
Fright went through me.
Fright whipped through me.
Fright widened my eyes.
Fright wormed through me.
I froze in fright.
I gasped in fright.
Fright blew through my heart.
Fright bloomed in my face.
Fright blossomed in my belly.
Fright burned in my throat.
Fright burrowed into my
spine.

Fright caught in my throat.
Fright churned in my gut.
Fright clamped around my neck.
Fright clawed at my chest.
Fright clawed at my heart.
Fright clawed at my insides.
Fright clawed at my throat.
Fright clawed up my spine.
Fright closed around my heart.
Fright closed up my throat.
Fright coursed through my body.
Fright crawled along my collar.
Fright crawled on my skin.
Fright crawled through my limbs.
Fright crawled up my spine.
Fright crept down my spine.
Fright crept into my expression.
Fright crept through my body.
Fright crept up my spine.
Fright etched in my eyes.
Fright etched into my expression.
Fright etched into my eyes.
Fright etched on my face.
Fright etched on my features.
Fright fell across my eyes.
Fright flashed in my eyes.
Fright flickered in my eyes.
Fright fluttered through my breast.
Fright grew in my eyes.
Fright grew in my gut.
Fright jammed in my throat.
Fright knotted in my belly.

Fright lifted from my heart.
Fright lingered in my voice.
Fright lumped in my throat.
Fright made my chest tight.
Fright made my knees weak.
Fright made my throat sore.
Fright oozed from my pores.
Fright played across my face.
Fright played over my face.
Fright poured through my body.
Fright pressed against my heart.
Fright pried open my heart.
Fright ran down my spine.
Fright ran through my bowels.
Fright ran through my veins.
Fright ran up my spine.
Fright reflected in my eyes.
Fright reflected in my face.
Fright registered in my eyes.
Fright ripped through my stomach.
Fright rippled across my skin.
Fright rolled down my cheeks.
Fright rolled through my stomach.
Fright rose in my gut.
Fright rose in my throat.
Fright seeped into my mind.
Fright settled in my stomach.
Fright shone from my eyes.
Fright shone in my eyes.
Fright shot down my spine.
Fright shot up my spine.
Fright showed in my eyes.
Fright showed on my face.
Fright slammed into my brain.

Fright sliced through my
midsection.
Fright slid down my spine.
Fright slithered along my skin.
Fright slithered through my
belly.
Fright slithered up my spine.
Fright smouldered in my
stomach.
Fright snaked along my spine.
Fright snatched at my heart.
Fright streamed down my face.
Fright surged through my gut.
Fright swirled in my stomach.
Fright tightened between my
shoulders.
Fright tightened in my
stomach.
Fright traipsed up my spine.
Fright trembled down my
spine.
Fright tugged at my legs.
Fright wafted up my spine.
Fright washed through my
mouth.
My body convulsed in fright.
My body pulsed with fright.
My body quivered with fright.
My body shook with fright.
My body shuddered with
fright.
My body trembled in fright.
My body trembled with fright.
My body vibrated with fright.
My chest clenched with fright.
My chest seized with fright.
My eyes blazed with fright.
My eyes brimmed with fright.

My eyes bulged in fright.
My eyes bulged with fright.
My eyes clouded with fright.
My eyes darkened with fright.
My eyes darted in fright.
My eyes dilated with fright.
My eyes filled with fright.
My eyes flashed with fright.
My eyes flickered with fright.
My eyes glazed with fright.
My eyes glittered with fright.
My eyes inked with fright.
My eyes marbled with fright.
My eyes popped with fright.
My eyes protruded with fright.
My eyes rolled in fright.
My eyes shone with fright.
My eyes simmered with fright.
My eyes touched with fright.
My eyes widened in fright.
My eyes widened with fright.
My face contorted with fright.
My face distorted with fright.
My face drawn in fright.
My face etched in fright.
My face etched with fright.
My face filled with fright.
My face frozen in fright.
My face frozen with fright.
My face pinched with fright.
My face tightened with fright.
My face twisted in fright.
My face twisted with fright.
My face twitched with fright.
My head pounded with fright.
My heart banged with fright.
My heart clutched in fright.

My heart drummed with
fright.
My heart filled with fright.
My heart frozen with fright.
My heart hammered with
fright.
My heart laboured with fright.
My heart pounded in fright.
My heart pounded with fright.
My heart protested in fright.
My heart sank with fright.
My heart seized with fright.
My heart squeezed with fright.
My heart thudded with fright.
My heartbeat stuttered in
fright.
My lips compressed in fright.
My mouth contorted with
fright.
My mouth writhed with fright.
My nerves jangled with fright.
My skin chilled with fright.
My skin pricked with fright.
My skin prickled with fright.
My throat clamped with
fright.
My throat clogged with fright.
My throat constricted in
fright.
My throat constricted with
fright.
My throat dried in fright.
My throat parched from fright.
My throat tightened with
fright.
My tone laced with fright.
My voice chattered with fright.
My voice choked with fright.

My voice cracked from fright.
My voice cracked with fright.
My voice edged with fright.
My voice hushed with fright.
My voice laced with fright.
My voice muted with fright.
My voice quavered with fright.
My voice quivered with fright.
My voice ragged with fright.
My voice rose in fright.
My voice shook with fright.
My voice tinged with fright.
My voice trembled with fright.
My voice vibrated with fright.
My voice whined with fright.
I felt a moment of fright.
I felt a stir of fright.
I gave a gasp of fright.
I gave a squeak of fright.
My body was electric with
fright.
My eyes grew huge with fright.
My eyes grew wide with fright.
My eyes opened wide in fright.
My eyes opened wide with
fright.
My eyes snapped wide with
fright.
My eyes squeezed shut with
fright.
My eyes went huge with fright.
My eyes went wide with fright.
My eyes were big with fright.
My eyes were black with fright.
My eyes were blind with fright.
My eyes were bright with
fright.
My eyes were crazy with fright.

My eyes were dark with fright.
My eyes were full of fright.
My eyes were glassy with
fright.
My eyes were grey with fright.
My eyes were huge with fright.
My eyes were large with fright.
My eyes were wide in fright.
My eyes were wide with fright.
My eyes were wild with fright.
My face was ashen with fright.
My face was crazy with fright.
My face was frantic with
fright.
My face was full of fright.
My heart became cold with
fright.
My heart was full of fright.
My mouth fell open in fright.
My mouth grew dry with
fright.
My mouth hung open in
fright.
My mouth was dry with fright.
My shoulders were tense with
fright.
My stomach turned sick with
fright.
My throat was raw with fright.
My throat was thick with
fright.
My voice pitched high with
fright.
My voice was shrill with fright.

FRUSTRATION

Definition: The feeling of being upset or annoyed as a result of being unable to change or achieve something.

See EXASPERATION

Frustration built inside me.
Frustration burned my eyes.
Frustration clawed at me.
Frustration coiled inside me.
Frustration coloured my tone.
Frustration crawled through me.
Frustration crossed my face.
Frustration crossed my features.
Frustration flooded through me.
Frustration flushed my face.
Frustration fuelled my anger.
Frustration knifed through me.
Frustration knotted my belly.
Frustration knotted my gut.
Frustration knotted my shoulders.
Frustration lined my face.
Frustration mounted within me.
Frustration painted my face.
Frustration rolled through me.
Frustration scalded my eyelids.
Frustration sharpened my voice.
Frustration shrunk my lungs.
Frustration surged over me.
Frustration thickened my voice.

Frustration tore through me.
Frustration twisted my expression.
Frustration welled inside me.
I exhaled in frustration.
I exhaled with frustration.
I frowned in frustration.
I grimaced in frustration.
I groaned with frustration.
I grunted in frustration.
I sighed in frustration.
I sighed with frustration.
I snorted in frustration.
Frustration came over my face.
Frustration clamped around my throat.
Frustration crept into my voice.
Frustration etched into my face.
Frustration etched on my face.
Frustration flowed in my breasts.
Frustration glinted in my eyes.
Frustration pulled at my features.
Frustration pulled my eyebrows together.
Frustration seeped into my voice.
Frustration shimmered in my voice.

Frustration showed on my
face.
Frustration simmered in my
veins.
Frustration welled in my gut.
My body trembled with
frustration.
My eyes blazed with
frustration.
My eyes bulged in frustration.
My eyes narrowed in
frustration.
My eyes narrowed with
frustration.
My eyes rimmed with
frustration.
My face flattened in
frustration.
My face painted with
frustration.
My head growled in
frustration.
My jaw clenched in
frustration.
My jaw worked in frustration.
My shoulders sagged in
frustration.
My voice brimmed with
frustration.
My voice cracked with
frustration.
My voice filled with
frustration.
My voice lowered in
frustration.
My voice pitched with
frustration.
My voice rose in frustration.

I exhaled a gust of frustration.
I exhaled a sigh of frustration.
I felt a flash of frustration.
I felt a pang of frustration.
I felt a rush of frustration.
I felt a stab of frustration.
I felt a wave of frustration.
I gave a cry of frustration.
I gave a groan of frustration.
I gave a grunt of frustration.
I gave a sigh of frustration.
I gave a sob of frustration.
I muttered a sound of
frustration.
I sighed a huff of frustration.
My body was taut with
frustration.
My face was rigid with
frustration.
My voice was edgy with
frustration.
My voice was gravelly with
frustration.
My voice was rough with
frustration.
My voice was sharp with
frustration.
My voice was thick with
frustration.

FURY

Definition: Wild or violent anger.

See ANGER

Fury blackened my heart.
Fury boiled inside me.
Fury boiled through me.
Fury clogged my throat.
Fury contorted my face.
Fury darkened my eyes.
Fury darkened my face.
Fury erupted in me.
Fury flattened my lips.
Fury grew inside me.
Fury iced my veins.
Fury leapt inside me.
Fury lined my face.
Fury painted my face.
Fury poured through me.
Fury pumped through me.
Fury radiated from me.
Fury raged through me.
Fury railed through me.
Fury ran through me.
Fury rolled through me.
Fury rose in me.
Fury rose inside me.
Fury seethed inside me.
Fury simmered inside me.
Fury snaked through me.
Fury spurned my adrenaline.
Fury surged through me.
Fury swept through me.
Fury twisted my insides.
I burned with fury.
I muttered in fury.
I simmered with fury.

I sobbed in fury.
Fury bled through my veins.
Fury burned in my brain.
Fury crept into my tone.
Fury etched on my face.
Fury exploded on my face.
Fury flashed across my face.
Fury ignited in my veins.
Fury raced through my blood.
Fury raged on my face.
Fury seethed in my eyes.
Fury seethed through my veins.
Fury settled into my bones.
Fury shone in my eyes.
Fury sizzled through my blood.
Fury slammed into my chest.
Fury washed over my face.
Fury washed through my veins.
My body raged with fury.
My body shook with fury.
My body throbbed with fury.
My body trembled with fury.
My eyes blazed with fury.
My eyes bugged in fury.
My eyes bulged in fury.
My eyes bulged with fury.
My eyes burned with fury.
My eyes darkened with fury.
My eyes fired with fury.
My eyes flashed in fury.
My eyes flashed with fury.
My eyes glared with fury.

My eyes glowed with fury.
My eyes narrowed in fury.
My eyes shone with fury.
My eyes sparked with fury.
My eyes widened in fury.
My face blotched with fury.
My face contorted in fury.
My face contorted with fury.
My face darkened with fury.
My face flushed with fury.
My face paled with fury.
My face twisted with fury.
My mouth trembled with fury.
My spine bristled with fury.
My stomach twisted in fury.
My tone edged with fury.
My voice crackled with fury.
My voice filled with fury.
My voice rose in fury.
My voice trembled with fury.
My voice vibrated with fury.
I felt a bolt of fury.
I felt a flash of fury.
I felt a sense of fury.
I felt a thrust of fury.
I gave a cry of fury.
I gave a growl of fury.
My blood ran hot with fury.
My eyes were bright with fury.
My eyes were full of fury.
My eyes were narrow in fury.
My eyes were narrow with
fury.
My eyes were red with fury.
My eyes were wide with fury.
My eyes were wild with fury.
My face went pale with fury.
My lips were white with fury.

G

GAIETY

Definition: The state or quality of being light-hearted or cheerful.
See CHEERFULNESS

Gaiety brightened my eyes.
Gaiety engorged my heart.
Gaiety engulfed my face.
Gaiety exploded inside me.
Gaiety filled my heart.
Gaiety flashed through me.
Gaiety flooded through me.
Gaiety flowed through me.
Gaiety laced my heart.
Gaiety leaped through me.
Gaiety rushed through me.
Gaiety settled my soul.
Gaiety stung my eyes.
Gaiety surged through me.
Gaiety swept through me.
Gaiety warmed my insides.
Gaiety washed over me.
Gaiety washed through me.
Gaiety welled inside me.
Gaiety went through me.
Gaiety whirled through me.
Gaiety broke over my face.
Gaiety clapped in my chest.
Gaiety flickered in my eyes.
Gaiety rolled down my face.
Gaiety streamed down my
cheeks.

Gaiety streamed down my face.
Gaiety welled in my eyes.
My eyes danced with gaiety.
My eyes filled with gaiety.
My eyes gleamed with gaiety.
My eyes shone with gaiety.
My eyes sparkled with gaiety.
My face filled with gaiety.
My face flooded with gaiety.
My face flushed with gaiety.
My face glowed with gaiety.
My face lit with gaiety.
My face wreathed in gaiety.
My heart beat with gaiety.
My heart burst with gaiety.
My heart danced with gaiety.
My heart filled with gaiety.
My heart flipped with gaiety.
My heart fluttered with gaiety.
My heart leaped with gaiety.
My heart leapt with gaiety.
My heart pinged with gaiety.
My heart soared with gaiety.
My heart swelled with gaiety.
My heart thumped with gaiety.
My voice brimmed with gaiety.
My voice coated with gaiety.

My voice inflated with gaiety.
My voice rang with gaiety.
My eyes were white with
gaiety.
My face was brilliant with
gaiety.
My heart was full of gaiety.

GLADNESS

Definition: A feeling of joy and exhilaration.

See JOY

Gladness coursed through me.
Gladness darkened my eyes.
Gladness engorged my heart.
Gladness engulfed my face.
Gladness filled my heart.
Gladness flashed through me.
Gladness flooded through me.
Gladness leapt through me.
Gladness raced through me.
Gladness rippled through me.
Gladness settled my soul.
Gladness stung my eyes.
Gladness surged through me.
Gladness swept through me.
Gladness warmed my insides.
Gladness washed through me.
Gladness welled inside me.
Gladness widened my eyes.
Gladness broke over my face.
Gladness clapped in my chest.
Gladness flickered in my eyes.
Gladness rang in my voice.
Gladness rolled down my face.
Gladness shone on my face.
Gladness streamed down my cheeks.
Gladness streamed down my face.
My body quivered with gladness.
My eyebrows danced in gladness.
My eyes beamed with gladness.
My eyes danced with gladness.
My eyes filled with gladness.
My eyes gleamed with gladness.
My eyes glittered in gladness.
My eyes shimmered with gladness.
My eyes shone with gladness.
My eyes sparkled with gladness.
My eyes twinkled with gladness.
My eyes widened in gladness.
My eyes widened with gladness.
My face filled with gladness.
My face flooded with gladness.
My face glowed with gladness.
My face lit with gladness.
My head buzzed with gladness.
My heart beat with gladness.
My heart burst with gladness.
My heart danced with gladness.
My heart filled with gladness.
My heart flipped with gladness.
My heart fluttered with gladness.
My heart leapt with gladness.
My heart molten with gladness.
My heart pinged with gladness.

My heart warmed with
gladness.
My voice brimmed with
gladness.
My voice quavered with
gladness.
My voice screeched with
gladness.
My eyebrows went up in
gladness.
My eyes were huge with
gladness.
My eyes were white with
gladness.
My eyes were wide with
gladness.
My face was brilliant with
gladness.
My heart was full of gladness.
My nerves cried out in
gladness.

GLEE

Definition: Great delight, especially from one's own good fortune or another's misfortune.

See DELIGHT

Glee coursed through me.
Glee crashed through me.
Glee crawled over me.
Glee darkened my eyes.
Glee encircled my head.
Glee exploded within me.
Glee filled my chest.
Glee filled my lungs.
Glee flooded through me.
Glee flowed through me.
Glee hummed through me.
Glee licked through me.
Glee melted my bones.
Glee moved through me.
Glee pierced my brain.
Glee poured through me.
Glee raced through me.
Glee radiated through me.
Glee ran through me.
Glee ripped through me.
Glee rippled through me.
Glee roared through me.
Glee rocked through me.
Glee seared my senses.
Glee shot through me.
Glee shuddered through me.
Glee sliced through me.
Glee spiked through me.
Glee splintered my brain.
Glee stole through me.
Glee swept through me.
Glee touched my face.

Glee washed over me.
Glee washed through me.
Glee widened my eyes.
I chuckled in glee.
Glee appeared on my face.
Glee burned in my stomach.
Glee flowed from my lips.
Glee glided through my body.
Glee infused in my expression.
Glee raced down my spine.
Glee ran through my voice.
Glee rang in my voice.
Glee rocked through my body.
Glee rumbled from my throat.
Glee shimmied down my spine.
Glee shone on my face.
Glee showed on my face.
Glee skittered down my body.
Glee sparked through my system.
Glee swept across my face.
Glee vibrated along my skin.
Glee washed over my body.
My body jerked in glee.
My body quivered with glee.
My body sighed in glee.
My body teemed with glee.
My eyebrows danced in glee.
My eyes beamed with glee.
My eyes closed in glee.
My eyes closed with glee.

My eyes crinkled with glee.
My eyes danced with glee.
My eyes flashed with glee.
My eyes glazed with glee.
My eyes gleamed with glee.
My eyes glittered in glee.
My eyes glowed with glee.
My eyes rolled with glee.
My eyes shimmered with glee.
My eyes shone with glee.
My eyes shut with glee.
My eyes sparkled with glee.
My eyes twinkled with glee.
My eyes widened in glee.
My eyes widened with glee.
My face danced with glee.
My face filled with glee.
My face flushed with glee.
My face lit with glee.
My head buzzed with glee.
My head tossed in glee.
My heart fluttered with glee.
My heart leaped with glee.
My heart molten with glee.
My heart sighed with glee.
My lips twitched with glee.
My mouth opened in glee.
My mouth perked with glee.
My skin mottled with glee.
My voice quavered with glee.
My voice screeched with glee.
I felt a flutter of glee.
I felt a hint of glee.
My eyebrows went up in glee.
My eyes slid shut in glee.
My eyes were full of glee.
My eyes were huge with glee.
My eyes were wide with glee.

My face grew radiant with glee.
My face lit up with glee.
My face was aglow with glee.
My face was rapt with glee.

GLOOM

Definition: A state of depression or despondency.

See DEPRESSION

Gloom came over me.
Gloom clouded my expression.
Gloom crashed over me.
Gloom crept over me.
Gloom crossed my face.
Gloom crossed my features.
Gloom darkened my eyes.
Gloom descended on me.
Gloom descended over me.
Gloom ebbed over me.
Gloom entered my voice.
Gloom filled my eyes.
Gloom filled my voice.
Gloom howled through me.
Gloom invaded my eyes.
Gloom lined my face.
Gloom obscured my vision.
Gloom rose off me.
Gloom seeped into me.
Gloom settled on me.
Gloom settled over me.
Gloom settled upon me.
Gloom sizzled through me.
Gloom spiralled through me.
Gloom squeezed my chest.
Gloom swept over me.
Gloom swept through me.
Gloom tinged my eyes.
Gloom tinged my voice.
Gloom tugged at me.
Gloom washed over me.
Gloom weighed on me.
Gloom welled inside me.

Gloom came into my eyes.
Gloom came into my voice.
Gloom crept into my expression.
Gloom drifted across my face.
Gloom flickered in my eyes.
Gloom flickered in my face.
Gloom lay in my heart.
Gloom lingered in my eyes.
Gloom passed over my face.
Gloom seeped into my muscles.
Gloom settled on my face.
Gloom showed in my eyes.
Gloom welled in my chest.
Gloom welled in my eyes.
My eyes drooped with gloom.
My eyes filled with gloom.
My eyes shadowed in gloom.
My face creased with gloom.
My face crumpled with gloom.
My face darkened with gloom.
My face descended with gloom.
My face drawn in gloom.
My face etched with gloom.
My face filled with gloom.
My face sagged with gloom.
My face sunk in gloom.
My tone laced with gloom.
My tone shaded with gloom.
My tone softened with gloom.
My voice broke with gloom.

My voice filled with gloom.
My voice infused with gloom.
My voice laced with gloom.
My voice tinged with gloom.
I felt a sense of gloom.
My eyes were full of gloom.
My face was heavy with gloom.
My tone was thick with gloom.
My voice was full of gloom.
My voice was soft with gloom.
A touch of gloom came into
my eyes.

GRIEF

Definition: Intense sorrow, especially caused by someone's death.
See SORROW

Grief brushed my face.
Grief clawed inside me.
Grief clenched my chest.
Grief crossed my brow.
Grief darkened my eyes.
Grief filled my face.
Grief flashed through me.
Grief infiltrated my smile.
Grief laced my voice.
Grief lined my eyes.
Grief passed through me.
Grief shadowed my eyes.
Grief sliced into me.
Grief strafed my heart.
Grief swelled inside me.
Grief tore into me.
Grief twisted my face.
Grief welled inside me.
I bellowed with grief.
Grief coursed through my body.
Grief etched in my face.
Grief radiated from my eyes.
Grief rose from my skin.
Grief surfaced through my skin.
Grief tore at my heart.
My body convulsed with grief.
My eyes dulled with grief.
My eyes filled with grief.
My eyes haunted with grief.
My eyes shaded with grief.
My eyes swam with grief.

My face collapsed with grief.
My face contorted with grief.
My face drawn with grief.
My face frozen in grief.
My face lined with grief.
My face shrouded in grief.
My face smudged with grief.
My face twisted with grief.
My face wrinkled with grief.
My head bent in grief.
My head bowed in grief.
My head lifted in grief.
My heart clenched with grief.
My heart filled with grief.
My heart submerged in grief.
My shoulders hunched with grief.
My throat tightened with grief.
My voice cracked with grief.
My voice ragged with grief.
My voice stricken with grief.
I felt a flash of grief.
I felt a pang of grief.
I felt a spasm of grief.
I felt a surge of grief.
I felt a swell of grief.
I felt a tide of grief.
My eyes moistened over with grief.
My eyes were black with grief.
My eyes were red with grief.
My eyes were vacant with grief.

My eyes were wide with grief.
My face folded up in grief.
My voice was full of grief.
My voice was heavy with grief.
My voice was hoarse with grief.

GUILT

Definition: A feeling of having committed wrong or failed in an obligation.

Guilt ate at me.
Guilt clawed at me.
Guilt clogged my throat.
Guilt crept through me.
Guilt darkened my eyes.
Guilt filled my heart.
Guilt flooded my face.
Guilt gnawed at me.
Guilt grew inside me.
Guilt haunted my eyes.
Guilt held my tongue.
Guilt lined my face.
Guilt made me wince.
Guilt nagged at me.
Guilt niggled at me.
Guilt nipped at me.
Guilt nudged my conscience.
Guilt pierced my eyes.
Guilt plagued my features.
Guilt poured off me.
Guilt preyed on me.
Guilt ran through me.
Guilt riddled my face.
Guilt ripped through me.
Guilt rose inside me.
Guilt scratched at me.
Guilt seized my soul.
Guilt settled over me.
Guilt slammed against me.
Guilt slammed into me.
Guilt sliced through me.
Guilt snapped at me.
Guilt split my heart.

Guilt squeezed my heart.
Guilt stabbed my chest.
Guilt stained my cheeks.
Guilt streaked through me.
Guilt surged through me.
Guilt swept over me.
Guilt tugged at me.
Guilt twisted my insides.
Guilt washed over me.
Guilt weighed on me.
Guilt welled inside me.
Guilt went through me.
I flushed with guilt.
Guilt ate at my gut.
Guilt boomed in my head.
Guilt coursed through my body.
Guilt crept down my throat.
Guilt crept up my spine.
Guilt flashed into my eyes.
Guilt flickered inside my chest.
Guilt flinched in my stomach.
Guilt flitted down my spine.
Guilt gnawed on my conscience.
Guilt lodged in my throat.
Guilt made my cheeks flush.
Guilt made my chest ache.
Guilt made my head swim.
Guilt made my stomach knot.
Guilt pressed against my chest.
Guilt pressed against my ribs.
Guilt pulsed through my body.

Guilt rose into my throat.
Guilt sat in my stomach.
Guilt slid down my spine.
Guilt soured in my stomach.
Guilt stabbed at my stomach.
Guilt stabbed into my chest.
Guilt tightened in my chest.
Guilt tingled along my nerves.
Guilt weighed on my
shoulders.
Guilt welled in my chest.
My body racked with guilt.
My chest tightened with guilt.
My eyes shrouded with guilt.
My face flushed with guilt.
My gut knotted with guilt.
I felt a dash of guilt.
I felt a draught of guilt.
I felt a flash of guilt.
I felt a flicker of guilt.
I felt a flood of guilt.
I felt a flush of guilt.
I felt a jab of guilt.
I felt a kind of guilt.
I felt a lot of guilt.
I felt a mixture of guilt.
I felt a moment of guilt.
I felt a pang of guilt.
I felt a rush of guilt.
I felt a sense of guilt.
I felt a shard of guilt.
I felt a spasm of guilt.
I felt a stab of guilt.
I felt a sting of guilt.
I felt a surge of guilt.
I felt a tickle of guilt.
I felt a tinge of guilt.
I felt a touch of guilt.

I felt a tug of guilt.
I felt a twinge of guilt.
I felt a twist of guilt.
I felt a wave of guilt.
I felt an ache of guilt.
I felt an ounce of guilt.
I felt an upwelling of guilt.
My stomach was sick with
guilt.

H

HAPPINESS

Definition: The state of being happy.
See CONTENTMENT

Happiness brightened my eyes.
Happiness coursed through me.
Happiness crashed through me.
Happiness crawled over me.
Happiness encircled my head.
Happiness exploded inside me.
Happiness exploded within me.
Happiness filled my chest.
Happiness filled my lungs.
Happiness flowed through me.
Happiness hummed through me.
Happiness laced my heart.
Happiness licked through me.
Happiness lit my features.
Happiness melted my bones.
Happiness moved through me.
Happiness pierced my brain.
Happiness poured through me.
Happiness raced through me.
Happiness radiated through me.
Happiness ran through me.

Happiness ripped through me.
Happiness rippled through me.
Happiness roared through me.
Happiness rocked through me.
Happiness rushed through me.
Happiness seared my senses.
Happiness settled over me.
Happiness shot through me.
Happiness shuddered through me.
Happiness sliced through me.
Happiness spiked through me.
Happiness splintered my brain.
Happiness stole through me.
Happiness surged through me.
Happiness swept through me.
Happiness touched my face.
Happiness washed over me.
Happiness washed through me.
Happiness welled inside me.
Happiness went through me.
Happiness whirled through me.

Happiness appeared on my face.
Happiness burned in my stomach.
Happiness flowed from my lips.
Happiness glided through my body.
Happiness infused in my expression.
Happiness raced down my spine.
Happiness radiated from my expression.
Happiness ran through my voice.
Happiness rivered through my body.
Happiness rocked through my body.
Happiness rumbled from my throat.
Happiness shimmied down my spine.
Happiness skittered down my body.
Happiness sparked through my system.
Happiness swept across my face.
Happiness vibrated along my skin.
Happiness washed over my body.
Happiness welled in my eyes.
My body jerked in happiness.
My body sighed in happiness.

My body teemed with happiness.
My eyes closed in happiness.
My eyes closed with happiness.
My eyes crinkled with happiness.
My eyes danced with happiness.
My eyes flashed with happiness.
My eyes glazed with happiness.
My eyes gleamed with happiness.
My eyes glowed with happiness.
My eyes rolled with happiness.
My eyes shut with happiness.
My eyes sparkled with happiness.
My eyes widened with happiness.
My face danced with happiness.
My face flushed with happiness.
My face lit with happiness.
My face softened with happiness.
My face wreathed in happiness.
My heart fluttered with happiness.
My heart hummed with happiness.
My heart leaped with happiness.
My heart sighed with happiness.

My heart soared with
happiness.
My heart thumped with
happiness.
My lips twitched with
happiness.
My mouth opened in
happiness.
My skin mottled with
happiness.
I felt a burst of happiness.
I felt a dart of happiness.
I felt a jolt of happiness.
I felt a sense of happiness.
I felt a sunburst of happiness.
I felt a surge of happiness.
I felt a wave of happiness.
I gave a kick of happiness.
My eyes slid shut in happiness.
My face grew radiant with
happiness.
My face was aglow with
happiness.
My face was rapt with
happiness.

HATE

Definition: Intense dislike.
See LOATHING

Hate blurred my vision.
Hate coursed through me.
Hate simmered inside me.
Hate twisted my features.
Hate bubbled in my gut.
Hate combusted behind my
ribs.
Hate crawled over my skin.
Hate etched in my face.
Hate etched on my face.
Hate passed over my face.
Hate rose in my gut.
Hate rose in my throat.
Hate smouldered in my eyes.
My body quivered with hate.
My eyes brimmed with hate.
My eyes bulged with hate.
My eyes burned with hate.
My eyes filled with hate.
My eyes flared with hate.
My eyes flashed with hate.
My eyes flickered with hate.
My eyes glared with hate.
My eyes glazed in hate.
My eyes gleamed with hate.
My eyes glittered with hate.
My eyes glowed with hate.
My eyes locked in hate.
My eyes narrowed in hate.
My eyes narrowed with hate.
My eyes seethed with hate.
My face brimmed with hate.
My face contorted with hate.

My face darkened in hate.
My face flushed with hate.
My face loaded with hate.
My face masked in hate.
My face twisted in hate.
My face twisted with hate.
My heart filled with hate.
My heart seethed with hate.
My mouth twisted in hate.
My mouth twisted with hate.
My skin tingled with hate.
My throat constricted with
hate.
My voice filled with hate.
My voice saturated with hate.
Hate burned deep in my soul.
I felt a flash of hate.
My body was taut with hate.
My eyes were alive with hate.
My eyes were cold with hate.
My eyes were dead with hate.
My eyes were full of hate.
My eyes were wide with hate.
My face was stiff with hate.
My face was venomous with
hate.
My heart was full of hate.

HATRED

Definition: Intense dislike.
See LOATHING

Hatred blurred my vision.
Hatred coursed through me.
Hatred simmered inside me.
Hatred twisted my features.
Hatred bubbled in my gut.
Hatred combusted behind my ribs.
Hatred crawled over my skin.
Hatred etched in my face.
Hatred etched on my face.
Hatred passed over my face.
Hatred rose in my gut.
Hatred rose in my throat.
Hatred smouldered in my eyes.
My body quivered with hatred.
My eyes brimmed with hatred.
My eyes bulged with hatred.
My eyes burned with hatred.
My eyes filled with hatred.
My eyes flared with hatred.
My eyes flashed with hatred.
My eyes flickered with hatred.
My eyes glared with hatred.
My eyes glazed in hatred.
My eyes gleamed with hatred.
My eyes glittered with hatred.
My eyes glowed with hatred.
My eyes locked in hatred.
My eyes narrowed as hatred.
My eyes narrowed in hatred.
My eyes narrowed with hatred.
My eyes seethed with hatred.
My face brimmed with hatred.

My face contorted with hatred.
My face darkened in hatred.
My face flushed with hatred.
My face loaded with hatred.
My face masked in hatred.
My face twisted in hatred.
My face twisted with hatred.
My heart filled with hatred.
My heart seethed with hatred.
My mouth twisted in hatred.
My mouth twisted with hatred.
My skin tingled with hatred.
My throat constricted with hatred.
My voice filled with hatred.
My voice saturated with hatred.
Hatred burned deep in my soul.
I felt a bolt of hatred.
I felt a mix of hatred.
I felt a wave of hatred.
I felt an amount of hatred.
My body was taut with hatred.
My eyes were alive with hatred.
My eyes were cold with hatred.
My eyes were dead with hatred.
My eyes were full of hatred.
My eyes were wide with hatred.
My face was stiff with hatred.

My face was venomous with
hatred.
My heart was full of hatred.

HOMESICKNESS

Definition: A feeling of longing for one's home during a period of absence from it.

See LONGING

Homesickness bubbled through me.
Homesickness caressed my mouth.
Homesickness clawed at me.
Homesickness coursed through me.
Homesickness crowded my chest.
Homesickness curled through me.
Homesickness darkened my irises.
Homesickness drifted through me.
Homesickness exploded inside me.
Homesickness flowed over me.
Homesickness flowed through me.
Homesickness fluttered inside me.
Homesickness glowed inside me.
Homesickness gushed through me.
Homesickness heated my blood.
Homesickness knifed through me.
Homesickness laced my voice.

Homesickness licked through me.
Homesickness made me melt.
Homesickness penetrated my heart.
Homesickness poured through me.
Homesickness pulsed through me.
Homesickness pumped through me.
Homesickness radiated from me.
Homesickness radiated through me.
Homesickness ravaged my face.
Homesickness rippled through me.
Homesickness rolled over me.
Homesickness rose from me.
Homesickness rose in me.
Homesickness shattered within me.
Homesickness slammed into me.
Homesickness sluiced through me.
Homesickness spiralled through me.
Homesickness splintered through me.

Homesickness sprouted inside me.
Homesickness surged through me.
Homesickness surged within me.
Homesickness swelled within me.
Homesickness swept over me.
Homesickness swept through me.
Homesickness swirled through me.
Homesickness tightened inside me.
Homesickness tightened my features.
Homesickness tightened my throat.
Homesickness tugged at me.
Homesickness wafted through me.
Homesickness warmed my insides.
Homesickness washed over me.
Homesickness went through me.
Homesickness banked in my eyes.
Homesickness combated in my brain.
Homesickness danced in my belly.
Homesickness flashed in my eyes.
Homesickness flickered in my expression.

Homesickness flickered in my eyes.
Homesickness nipped at my skin.
Homesickness swept through my body.
Homesickness throbbed against my belly.
My blood burned with homesickness.
My blood heated with homesickness.
My body burned with homesickness.
My body drugged with homesickness.
My body hardened with homesickness.
My body heated with homesickness.
My body hummed with homesickness.
My body jangled with homesickness.
My body shivered with homesickness.
My body stirred with homesickness.
My body throbbed with homesickness.
My body thrummed with homesickness.
My body twitched with homesickness.
My body unfurled with homesickness.
My chest clenched with homesickness.

My ears shut in homesickness.
My eyes blazed with
homesickness.
My eyes danced with
homesickness.
My eyes darkened with
homesickness.
My eyes flared with
homesickness.
My eyes flickered with
homesickness.
My eyes gleamed with
homesickness.
My eyes glittered with
homesickness.
My eyes glowed with
homesickness.
My eyes lit with homesickness.
My eyes narrowed with
homesickness.
My eyes shimmered with
homesickness.
My face filled with
homesickness.
My face flushed with
homesickness.
My heart burned with
homesickness.
My heart filled with
homesickness.
My heart fluttered with
homesickness.
My heart swelled with
homesickness.
My pulse raced with
homesickness.
My skin flushed with
homesickness.

My voice slurred with
homesickness.
Homesickness curled deep in
my belly.
Homesickness pooled low in
my belly.
I felt a pang of homesickness.
I felt a twinge of homesickness.
My body was overwrought
with homesickness.
My eyes went dark with
homesickness.
My eyes were dark with
homesickness.
My eyes were full of
homesickness.
My eyes were hazy with
homesickness.
My eyes were heavy with
homesickness.
My eyes were unclouded with
homesickness.
My face glazed over with
homesickness.
My throat was thick with
homesickness.
My voice sounded rough with
homesickness.
My voice was rough with
homesickness.
My voice was thick with
homesickness.

HOPE

Definition: A feeling of expectation and desire for a particular thing to happen.

See DESIRE

Hope bloomed within me.
Hope brightened my eyes.
Hope brightened my face.
Hope bubbled inside me.
Hope filled my chest.
Hope filled my eyes.
Hope flared in me.
Hope flared inside me.
Hope flickered in me.
Hope flooded my soul.
Hope grew inside me.
Hope kindled inside me.
Hope laced my voice.
Hope passed through me.
Hope ran through me.
Hope ripped through me.
Hope rose in me.
Hope rushed through me.
Hope stirred inside me.
Hope surged through me.
Hope swelled inside me.
Hope washed over me.
Hope welled inside me.
Hope went through me.
Hope bloomed in my chest.
Hope blossomed in my heart.
Hope blossomed in my mind.
Hope budded in my chest.
Hope budded in my heart.
Hope came into my eyes.
Hope dawned on my face.
Hope exploded in my chest.

Hope flared in my gaze.
Hope flashed over my face.
Hope flashed through my mind.
Hope flicked across my face.
Hope flickered across my face.
Hope glimmered in my eyes.
Hope glowed in my eyes.
Hope quickened in my breast.
Hope sprang in my face.
Hope stirred in my heart.
Hope surged in my breast.
Hope swelled in my bosom.
Hope swelled in my chest.
Hope wormed through my chest.
My chest filled with hope.
My eyes brightened with hope.
My eyes glimmered with hope.
My eyes shone with hope.
My eyes widened with hope.
My face bloomed with hope.
My face went from hope.
My heart jumped with hope.
My heart pounded with hope.
My heart swelled with hope.
My nerves vibrated with hope.
I felt a burst of hope.
I felt a flare of hope.
I felt a flash of hope.
I felt a flicker of hope.
I felt a flush of hope.

I felt a glimmer of hope.
I felt a leap of hope.
I felt a mix of hope.
I felt a mixture of hope.
I felt a moment of hope.
I felt a ping of hope.
I felt a ray of hope.
I felt a renewal of hope.
I felt a rush of hope.
I felt a sense of hope.
I felt a sort of hope.
I felt a spark of hope.
I felt a spring of hope.
I felt a spurt of hope.
I felt a stab of hope.
I felt a stir of hope.
I felt a surge of hope.
I felt a thrill of hope.
I felt a tickle of hope.
I felt a tinge of hope.
I felt a touch of hope.
I felt a twinge of hope.
I felt a whisper of hope.
I gave a leap of hope.
My eyes burned incandescent
with hope.
My eyes lit up with hope.
My eyes were full of hope.
My eyes were shiny with hope.
My eyes were wide with hope.
My face lit up with hope.
My face was alive with hope.
My face was bright with hope.

HOPELESSNESS

Definition: A feeling or state of despair.

See DESPAIR

Hopelessness battled inside me.

Hopelessness came over me.

Hopelessness clouded my eyes.

Hopelessness cramped my belly.

Hopelessness descended on me.

Hopelessness descended over me.

Hopelessness entered my eyes.

Hopelessness greeted my words.

Hopelessness nagged at me.

Hopelessness poured over me.

Hopelessness rushed through me.

Hopelessness settled over me.

Hopelessness swept over me.

Hopelessness swept through me.

Hopelessness tightened my features.

Hopelessness touched my heart.

Hopelessness weighed on me.

Hopelessness welled inside me.

Hopelessness bloomed in my eyes.

Hopelessness came over my face.

Hopelessness crept up my spine.

Hopelessness emanated from my body.

Hopelessness etched on my face.

Hopelessness flickered across my face.

Hopelessness glazed in my eyes.

Hopelessness gnawed at my guts.

Hopelessness leaked into my soul.

Hopelessness pressed behind my eyes.

Hopelessness slid off my face.

Hopelessness surged from my feet.

Hopelessness weighed down my heart.

Hopelessness welled in my chest.

My body sagged with hopelessness.

My eyes flared with hopelessness.

My eyes widened in hopelessness.

My face broken with hopelessness.

My face crumpled in hopelessness.

My face drawn with hopelessness.

My face filled with
hopelessness.
My face lined with
hopelessness.
My heart dulled with
hopelessness.
My shoulders drooped in
hopelessness.
My shoulders sagged with
hopelessness.
My shoulders sank in
hopelessness.
My throat wrinkled with
hopelessness.
My voice cracked with
hopelessness.
My voice filled with
hopelessness.
My voice ragged with
hopelessness.
My voice rose in hopelessness.
My voice sagged with
hopelessness.
I felt a wave of hopelessness.
My chest went hollow with
hopelessness.
My eyes were bright with
hopelessness.
My heart felt leaden with
hopelessness.
My heart was full of
hopelessness.
My heart welled up with
hopelessness.
My voice was shrill with
hopelessness.

HORROR

Definition: An intense feeling of fear, shock, or disgust.

See TERROR

Horror altered my tone.
Horror blinded my eyes.
Horror crossed my face.
Horror crossed my features.
Horror filled my eyes.
Horror filled my features.
Horror flooded through me.
Horror raced through me.
Horror rolled through me.
Horror spilled through me.
Horror streaked my face.
Horror struck my face.
Horror surged through me.
Horror swept through me.
Horror washed over me.
Horror washed through me.
Horror widened my eyes.
I froze in horror.
I froze with horror.
I gasped in horror.
I gasped with horror.
I groaned in horror.
I shuddered in horror.
I shuddered with horror.
Horror bloomed in my chest.
Horror broke through my lips.
Horror burned in my eyes.
Horror came into my eyes.
Horror crawled across my face.
Horror crept across my face.
Horror crept into my voice.
Horror crept up my spine.
Horror dawned in my eyes.

Horror dawned on my face.
Horror etched on my face.
Horror etched onto my face.
Horror flashed in my eyes.
Horror flashed through my mind.
Horror flitted over my face.
Horror landed on my shoulder.
Horror registered on my face.
Horror ripped into my heart.
Horror seeped across my features.
Horror showed on my face.
Horror sprang into my eyes.
Horror stamped on my face.
Horror stole across my face.
Horror stole over my brain.
Horror washed over my face.
My body shook with horror.
My eyes bulged in horror.
My eyes dulled with horror.
My eyes opened in horror.
My eyes started with horror.
My eyes widened in horror.
My eyes widened with horror.
My face crumpled with horror.
My face flushed with horror.
My face froze in horror.
My face strained with horror.
My face twisted in horror.
My gut twisted with horror.
My mouth opened in horror.

My mouth twisted with
horror.
My throat contracted with
horror.
My voice cried in horror.
My voice rose in horror.
My voice tinged with horror.
I felt a burst of horror.
I felt a pang of horror.
I felt a prickle of horror.
I felt a thrill of horror.
I felt a tremor of horror.
I felt a wave of horror.
I gave a shout of horror.
I gave a squeak of horror.
My eyes opened wide in
horror.
My eyes seemed full of horror.
My eyes went wide in horror.
My eyes went wide with
horror.
My eyes were huge with
horror.
My eyes were wide in horror.
My eyes were wide with
horror.
My face became transfixed
with horror.
My face opened up in horror.
My face turned waxy with
horror.
My mouth fell open in horror.
My throat was dry with
horror.
My voice grew hushed with
horror.

HOSTILITY

Definition: Hostile behaviour.

Hostility burned inside me.
Hostility burned through me.
Hostility burned within me.
Hostility churned inside me.
Hostility churned through me.
Hostility clenched inside me.
Hostility clouded my face.
Hostility coiled inside me.
Hostility coloured my cheeks.
Hostility coursed through me.
Hostility crept into me.
Hostility entered my voice.
Hostility filled my throat.
Hostility laced my humour.
Hostility laced my voice.
Hostility lit my eyes.
Hostility poured over me.
Hostility radiated from me.
Hostility stained my cheeks.
Hostility suffused my cheeks.
Hostility swelled inside me.
Hostility tightened my jaw.
Hostility washed over me.
Hostility burned in my chest.
Hostility burned in my eyes.
Hostility came into my voice.
Hostility chattered in my
head.
Hostility churned in my gut.
Hostility churned through my
belly.
Hostility coiled in my belly.
Hostility coursed through my
veins.

Hostility crackled in my eyes.
Hostility crept into my tone.
Hostility crept into my voice.
Hostility curdled inside my
belly.
Hostility edged into my voice.
Hostility flared in my heart.
Hostility grew in my eyes.
Hostility rose in my throat.
Hostility shone in my eyes.
Hostility sprouted in my gut.
Hostility swelled in my throat.
My body quickened in
hostility.
My body quivered with
hostility.
My chest swelled with
hostility.
My eyebrows climbed in
hostility.
My eyes blazed with hostility.
My eyes dazzled in hostility.
My eyes filled with hostility.
My eyes flashed with hostility.
My eyes glinted with hostility.
My eyes glittered with
hostility.
My eyes shone with hostility.
My eyes smouldered with
hostility.
My eyes widened with
hostility.
My face crumpled in hostility.

My face darkened with hostility.
My face filled with hostility.
My face flushed with hostility.
My face reddened with hostility.
My face set with hostility.
My face strained in hostility.
My face tensed with hostility.
My face tightened in hostility.
My face tightened with hostility.
My face trembled with hostility.
My face twisted in hostility.
My face twisted with hostility.
My face twitched with hostility.
My head ached in hostility.
My head sang with hostility.
My heart filled with hostility.
My heart seethed with hostility.
My lips twisted with hostility.
My stomach boiled with hostility.
My tone drenched with hostility.
My tone laden with hostility.
My tone reeked of hostility.
My voice crackled with hostility.
My voice edged with hostility.
My voice laced with hostility.
My voice ragged with hostility.
My voice rattled with hostility.
My voice sank with hostility.
My voice shook with hostility.

My voice tinged with hostility.
Hostility burned bright in my eyes.
My eyes were wide with hostility.
My face screwed up in hostility.
My face turned flush with hostility.
My face turned red with hostility.
My face turned rosy with hostility.
My face was ruddy with hostility.
My face went dark with hostility.
My voice trailed off in hostility.
My voice was alive with hostility.
My voice was shrill with hostility.

HUMILIATION

Definition: The action of humiliating someone or the state of being humiliated.

See EMBARRASSMENT

Humiliation ate at me.
Humiliation brightened my face.
Humiliation burned through me.
Humiliation clawed at me.
Humiliation coiled in me.
Humiliation coursed through me.
Humiliation crossed my face.
Humiliation entered my voice.
Humiliation flooded my cheeks.
Humiliation flowed through me.
Humiliation grew inside me.
Humiliation heated my blood.
Humiliation heated my cheeks.
Humiliation heated my face.
Humiliation jabbed my brain.
Humiliation mounted inside me.
Humiliation moved through me.
Humiliation painted my features.
Humiliation pulsed through me.
Humiliation quickened my breath.

Humiliation raced through me.
Humiliation ran through me.
Humiliation rippled through me.
Humiliation rose in me.
Humiliation rose inside me.
Humiliation rose within me.
Humiliation rushed through me.
Humiliation scorched my face.
Humiliation seared my cheeks.
Humiliation seeped through me.
Humiliation skittered through me.
Humiliation slashed my cheeks.
Humiliation stirred in me.
Humiliation stung my face.
Humiliation swept over me.
Humiliation swept through me.
Humiliation tickled my stomach.
Humiliation touched my voice.
Humiliation warmed my face.
Humiliation washed over me.
Humiliation went through me.
Humiliation blazed in my eyes.

Humiliation bubbled in my
voice.
Humiliation budded in my
chest.
Humiliation burgeoned in my
loins.
Humiliation closed on my
chest.
Humiliation coursed through
my veins.
Humiliation crept down my
back.
Humiliation crept into my
voice.
Humiliation fizzed in my
chest.
Humiliation flashed into my
bones.
Humiliation gleamed in my
eyes.
Humiliation played across my
face.
Humiliation poked at my
belly.
Humiliation ran up my spine.
Humiliation rippled through
my veins.
Humiliation rose in my chest.
Humiliation rose in my voice.
Humiliation stirred along my
nerve.
Humiliation streamed from
my eyes.
Humiliation welled in my
breast.
My blood heated with
humiliation.

My body quivered with
humiliation.
My chest bubbled with
humiliation.
My chest pounded with
humiliation.
My ears flapped in
humiliation.
My ears fluttered with
humiliation.
My ears quivered with
humiliation.
My eyes blazed with
humiliation.
My eyes burned with
humiliation.
My eyes danced with
humiliation.
My eyes flashed in
humiliation.
My eyes flashed with
humiliation.
My eyes flickered with
humiliation.
My eyes gleamed with
humiliation.
My eyes glinted with
humiliation.
My eyes glistened with
humiliation.
My eyes glittered with
humiliation.
My eyes shone in humiliation.
My eyes shone with
humiliation.
My eyes sparkled with
humiliation.

My eyes twinkled with humiliation.
My eyes widened in humiliation.
My eyes widened with humiliation.
My face burned with humiliation.
My face filled with humiliation.
My face flickered with humiliation.
My face flushed with humiliation.
My face glowed with humiliation.
My face polished with humiliation.
My face shone with humiliation.
My face swelled with humiliation.
My face tingled with humiliation.
My head bobbed in humiliation.
My head twitched with humiliation.
My heart beat with humiliation.
My heart filled with humiliation.
My heart fluttered with humiliation.
My heart pounded with humiliation.
My heart quickened in humiliation.

My heart quickened with humiliation.
My heart raced with humiliation.
My heart thumped with humiliation.
My lips quivered with humiliation.
My mouth twitched with humiliation.
My nose twitched in humiliation.
My pulse kicked with humiliation.
My pulse pounded with humiliation.
My pulse raced with humiliation.
My shoulders drooped in humiliation.
My skin glowed with humiliation.
My stomach churned with humiliation.
My stomach squirmed with humiliation.
My voice choked with humiliation.
My voice cracked with humiliation.
My voice filled with humiliation.
My voice rang with humiliation.
My voice rose in humiliation.
My voice rose with humiliation.

My voice shook with humiliation.
My voice squeaked with humiliation.
My voice tinged with humiliation.
My voice trembled with humiliation.
Humiliation caused my voice to rise.
My eyes burned bright with humiliation.
My eyes grew big with humiliation.
My eyes lit up in humiliation.
My eyes lit up with humiliation.
My eyes were alight with humiliation.
My eyes were alive with humiliation.
My eyes were big with humiliation.
My eyes were bright with humiliation.
My eyes were brilliant with humiliation.
My eyes were fierce with humiliation.
My eyes were frantic with humiliation.
My eyes were full of humiliation.
My eyes were wide with humiliation.
My face flushed grey with humiliation.

My face grew hot with humiliation.
My face lit up with humiliation.
My face was bright with humiliation.
My neck felt prickly with humiliation.
My skin was clammy with humiliation.
My skin was electric with humiliation.
My stomach screwed up with humiliation.
My voice was full of humiliation.
My voice was hoarse with humiliation.

HURT

Definition: Emotional pain or distress.

See DISTRESS

Hurt ate into me.
Hurt churned inside me.
Hurt clawed at me.
Hurt closed my throat.
Hurt coursed through me.
Hurt crossed my face.
Hurt filled my voice.
Hurt flooded over me.
Hurt knotted my gut.
Hurt knotted my insides.
Hurt knotted my shoulders.
Hurt knotted my stomach.
Hurt lined my face.
Hurt lingered inside me.
Hurt pinched my lips.
Hurt pumped my heart.
Hurt ran through me.
Hurt ripped through me.
Hurt rushed through me.
Hurt scraped my spine.
Hurt slipped from me.
Hurt squeezed my belly.
Hurt swept over me.
Hurt swept through me.
Hurt swirled through me.
Hurt tightened my breath.
Hurt tightened my features.
Hurt tightened my shoulders.
Hurt touched my heart.
Hurt tugged at me.
Hurt washed over me.
Hurt washed through me.
Hurt weighed on me.

Hurt went through me.
Hurt wormed through me.
Hurt came into my eyes.
Hurt churned in my gut.
Hurt coursed through my veins.
Hurt crawled up my back.
Hurt crept into my voice.
Hurt crept up my spine.
Hurt emanated from my body.
Hurt etched across my face.
Hurt flickered in my eyes.
Hurt glazed in my eyes.
Hurt nagged at my mind.
Hurt plucked at my chest.
Hurt pressed against my chest.
Hurt pulsed through my body.
Hurt pumped through my veins.
Hurt roared in my head.
Hurt roiled in my gut.
Hurt rose in my throat.
Hurt shimmered in my eyes.
Hurt slithered up my spine.
Hurt spilled through my guts.
Hurt sprinted across my eyes.
Hurt swept through my body.
Hurt trembled in my stomach.
Hurt whispered in my gut.
My body hummed with hurt.
My eyebrows furrowed in hurt.
My eyes clouded with hurt.
My eyes flared with hurt.

My eyes flickered with hurt.
My eyes widened in hurt.
My face creased in hurt.
My face creased with hurt.
My face crumpled in hurt.
My face etched in hurt.
My face flooded with hurt.
My face flushed with hurt.
My face lined with hurt.
My face pinched with hurt.
My face twisted with hurt.
My face wisped with hurt.
My head throbbed with hurt.
My jaw worked with hurt.
My mouth puckered with
hurt.
My nose quivered with hurt.
My shoulders knotted with
hurt.
My stomach clenched in hurt.
My stomach cramped with
hurt.
My stomach knotted with
hurt.
My voice broken with hurt.
My voice cracked with hurt.
My voice marbled with hurt.
My voice rose in hurt.
My voice strained with hurt.
My voice tinged with hurt.
Hurt caused my throat to
tighten.
My eyes opened wide with
hurt.
My eyes were bright with hurt.
My face was full of hurt.
My mouth was dry with hurt.
My spine went cold with hurt.

My voice was shrill with hurt.
My voice was taut with hurt.
My voice was thin with hurt.

HYSTERIA

Definition: Exaggerated or uncontrollable emotion or excitement.
See EXCITEMENT

Hysteria brightened my face.
Hysteria coiled in me.
Hysteria coursed through me.
Hysteria crossed my face.
Hysteria entered my voice.
Hysteria flowed through me.
Hysteria grew inside me.
Hysteria heated my blood.
Hysteria jabbed my brain.
Hysteria mounted inside me.
Hysteria moved through me.
Hysteria painted my features.
Hysteria pulsed through me.
Hysteria quickened my breath.
Hysteria raced through me.
Hysteria ran through me.
Hysteria rippled through me.
Hysteria rose in me.
Hysteria rose inside me.
Hysteria rose within me.
Hysteria rushed through me.
Hysteria skittered through me.
Hysteria stirred in me.
Hysteria swept over me.
Hysteria swept through me.
Hysteria tickled my stomach.
Hysteria touched my voice.
Hysteria washed over me.
Hysteria went through me.
Hysteria blazed in my eyes.
Hysteria bubbled in my chest.
Hysteria bubbled in my throat.
Hysteria bubbled in my voice.

Hysteria budded in my chest.
Hysteria burgeoned in my loins.
Hysteria closed on my chest.
Hysteria coursed through my veins.
Hysteria crept down my back.
Hysteria crept into my voice.
Hysteria fizzed in my chest.
Hysteria flashed into my bones.
Hysteria gleamed in my eyes.
Hysteria played across my face.
Hysteria poked at my belly.
Hysteria quivered through my voice.
Hysteria ran up my spine.
Hysteria rippled through my veins.
Hysteria rose in my chest.
Hysteria rose in my voice.
Hysteria stirred along my nerve.
Hysteria twitched in my chest.
Hysteria welled in my breast.
My blood heated with hysteria.
My body quivered with hysteria.
My chest bubbled with hysteria.
My chest pounded with hysteria.
My ears flapped in hysteria.

My ears fluttered with hysteria.
My ears quivered with hysteria.
My eyes blazed with hysteria.
My eyes burned with hysteria.
My eyes danced with hysteria.
My eyes flashed in hysteria.
My eyes flashed with hysteria.
My eyes gleamed with hysteria.
My eyes glinted with hysteria.
My eyes glistened with hysteria.
My eyes glittered with hysteria.
My eyes shone in hysteria.
My eyes shone with hysteria.
My eyes sparkled with hysteria.
My eyes twinkled with hysteria.
My eyes widened in hysteria.
My eyes widened with hysteria.
My face filled with hysteria.
My face flickered with hysteria.
My face flushed with hysteria.
My face glowed with hysteria.
My face polished with hysteria.
My face shone with hysteria.
My face swelled with hysteria.
My face tingled with hysteria.
My head bobbed in hysteria.
My head twitched with hysteria.
My heart beat with hysteria.
My heart filled with hysteria.
My heart fluttered with hysteria.
My heart pounded with hysteria.

My heart quickened in hysteria.
My heart quickened with hysteria.
My heart raced with hysteria.
My heart thumped with hysteria.
My lips quivered with hysteria.
My mouth twitched with hysteria.
My nose twitched in hysteria.
My pulse kicked with hysteria.
My pulse pounded with hysteria.
My pulse raced with hysteria.
My skin glowed with hysteria.
My stomach churned with hysteria.
My stomach squirmed with hysteria.
My voice cracked with hysteria.
My voice filled with hysteria.
My voice rang with hysteria.
My voice rose in hysteria.
My voice rose with hysteria.
My voice shook with hysteria.
My voice squeaked with hysteria.
My voice tinged with hysteria.
My voice trembled with hysteria.
Hysteria caused my voice to rise.
My eyes burned bright with hysteria.
My eyes grew big with hysteria.
My eyes lit up in hysteria.

My eyes lit up with hysteria.
My eyes were alight with
hysteria.
My eyes were alive with
hysteria.
My eyes were big with hysteria.
My eyes were bright with
hysteria.
My eyes were brilliant with
hysteria.
My eyes were fierce with
hysteria.
My eyes were frantic with
hysteria.
My eyes were full of hysteria.
My eyes were wide with
hysteria.
My face flushed grey with
hysteria.
My face lit up with hysteria.
My face was bright with
hysteria.
My neck felt prickly with
hysteria.
My skin was clammy with
hysteria.
My skin was electric with
hysteria.
My stomach screwed up with
hysteria.
My voice was full of hysteria.
My voice was hoarse with
hysteria.

I

INDIGNATION

Definition: Anger or annoyance provoked by what is perceived as unfair treatment.
See RESENTMENT

I gasped with indignation.
Indignation burned inside me.
Indignation burned through me.
Indignation burned within me.
Indignation churned inside me.
Indignation churned through me.
Indignation clenched inside me.
Indignation clouded my face.
Indignation coiled inside me.
Indignation coloured my cheeks.
Indignation coursed through me.
Indignation crept into me.
Indignation entered my voice.
Indignation lit my eyes.
Indignation stained my cheeks.
Indignation suffused my cheeks.
Indignation swelled inside me.
Indignation tightened my jaw.
Indignation washed over me.

Indignation burned in my chest.
Indignation burned in my eyes.
Indignation came into my voice.
Indignation chattered in my head.
Indignation churned in my gut.
Indignation churned through my belly.
Indignation coiled in my belly.
Indignation coursed through my veins.
Indignation crackled in my eyes.
Indignation crept into my tone.
Indignation crept into my voice.
Indignation curdled inside my belly.
Indignation flared in my heart.
Indignation sprouted in my gut.

Indignation swelled in my throat.
My body quivered with indignation.
My chest swelled with indignation.
My eyes blazed with indignation.
My eyes glittered with indignation.
My eyes shone with indignation.
My eyes smouldered with indignation.
My eyes widened with indignation.
My face crumpled in indignation.
My face darkened with indignation.
My face flushed with indignation.
My face reddened with indignation.
My face set with indignation.
My face strained in indignation.
My face tensed with indignation.
My face tightened in indignation.
My face tightened with indignation.
My face trembled with indignation.
My face twisted in indignation.
My face twisted with indignation.
My face twitched with indignation.
My head sang with indignation.
My lips twisted with indignation.
My stomach boiled with indignation.
My voice crackled with indignation.
My voice edged with indignation.
My voice ragged with indignation.
My voice rattled with indignation.
My voice shook with indignation.
Indignation burned bright in my eyes.
My eyes were wide with indignation.
My face screwed up in indignation.
My face turned flush with indignation.
My face turned red with indignation.
My face turned rosy with indignation.
My face was ruddy with indignation.
My face went dark with indignation.
My voice was alive with indignation.

My voice was shrill with indignation.

IRRITATION

Definition: The state of feeling annoyed, impatient, or slightly angry.
See ANNOYANCE

I bellowed in irritation.
I flushed with irritation.
I frowned with irritation.
I grunted in irritation.
I sighed with irritation.
Irritation clouded my face.
Irritation crawled through me.
Irritation crossed my face.
Irritation crossed my forehead.
Irritation entered my
expression.
Irritation entered my voice.
Irritation filled my face.
Irritation grated my voice.
Irritation laced my voice.
Irritation moved through me.
Irritation rose in me.
Irritation sifted through me.
Irritation washed over me.
Irritation burned in my gut.
Irritation crept into my
expression.
Irritation crept into my voice.
Irritation descended over my
features.
Irritation flared on my face.
Irritation flashed across my
face.
Irritation flashed in my eyes.
Irritation flickered across my
face.
Irritation flickered in my eyes.

Irritation flickered over my
face.
Irritation passed through my
eyes.
Irritation rang in my words.
Irritation ripped through my
body.
Irritation scratched at my
temper.
Irritation settled over my face.
Irritation washed across my
face.
My brows lowered in
irritation.
My eyebrows furrowed in
irritation.
My eyes flashed with irritation.
My eyes flickered with
irritation.
My eyes gleamed with
irritation.
My eyes glowed with irritation.
My eyes narrowed in irritation.
My eyes snapped with
irritation.
My eyes went from irritation.
My face crawled with
irritation.
My face tightened with
irritation.
My face twisted in irritation.
My face went from irritation.
My head jerked in irritation.

My head throbbed with
irritation.
My lips crimped with
irritation.
My lips tightened in irritation.
My mouth tightened in
irritation.
My mouth tightened with
irritation.
My tone rose with irritation.
My voice ragged with
irritation.
My voice rasped with
irritation.
My voice rose with irritation.
My voice strained with
irritation.
My voice tinged with
irritation.
I felt a bubble of irritation.
I felt a flash of irritation.
I felt a flicker of irritation.
I felt a flush of irritation.
I felt a gust of irritation.
I felt a knot of irritation.
I felt a moment of irritation.
I felt a prickle of irritation.
I felt a rush of irritation.
I felt a spasm of irritation.
I felt a spike of irritation.
I felt a stab of irritation.
I felt a surge of irritation.
I felt a twinge of irritation.
I felt a wave of irritation.
I gave a shrug of irritation.
My eyes were sharp with
irritation.

My face grew pinched with
irritation.

J

JEALOUSY
Definition: The state or feeling of being jealous.
See ENVY

Jealousy ate at me.
Jealousy bloomed inside me.
Jealousy bubbled through me.
Jealousy caressed my mouth.
Jealousy clawed at me.
Jealousy coursed through me.
Jealousy crawled over me.
Jealousy crowded my chest.
Jealousy curdled inside me.
Jealousy curled through me.
Jealousy darkened my irises.
Jealousy drifted through me.
Jealousy exploded inside me.
Jealousy flowed over me.
Jealousy flowed through me.
Jealousy fluttered inside me.
Jealousy glowed inside me.
Jealousy gushed through me.
Jealousy heated my blood.
Jealousy knifed through me.
Jealousy laced my voice.
Jealousy licked through me.
Jealousy made me melt.
Jealousy mushroomed inside me.
Jealousy penetrated my heart.
Jealousy poured through me.

Jealousy pulsed through me.
Jealousy pumped through me.
Jealousy radiated from me.
Jealousy ravaged my face.
Jealousy rippled through me.
Jealousy rose from me.
Jealousy rose in me.
Jealousy scratched at me.
Jealousy shattered within me.
Jealousy slammed into me.
Jealousy sluiced through me.
Jealousy snaked inside me.
Jealousy snaked through me.
Jealousy speared through me.
Jealousy spiralled through me.
Jealousy splintered through me.
Jealousy stirred in me.
Jealousy suffused my body.
Jealousy surged through me.
Jealousy swelled within me.
Jealousy swept through me.
Jealousy swirled through me.
Jealousy tightened inside me.
Jealousy tightened my features.
Jealousy traipsed through me.
Jealousy wafted through me.

Jealousy warmed my insides.
Jealousy washed through me.
Jealousy went through me.
Jealousy banked in my eyes.
Jealousy burned in my gut.
Jealousy combated in my brain.
Jealousy danced in my belly.
Jealousy flared in my heart.
Jealousy flashed in my eyes.
Jealousy flickered in my expression.
Jealousy flickered in my eyes.
Jealousy nipped at my skin.
Jealousy sparked through my mind.
Jealousy throbbed against my belly.
My blood burned with jealousy.
My blood heated with jealousy.
My body burned with jealousy.
My body drugged with jealousy.
My body hardened with jealousy.
My body heated with jealousy.
My body hummed with jealousy.
My body jangled with jealousy.
My body shivered with jealousy.
My body stirred with jealousy.
My body thrummed with jealousy.
My body twitched with jealousy.

My body unfurled with jealousy.
My ears shut in jealousy.
My eyes blazed with jealousy.
My eyes danced with jealousy.
My eyes darkened with jealousy.
My eyes flared with jealousy.
My eyes flickered with jealousy.
My eyes gleamed with jealousy.
My eyes glittered with jealousy.
My eyes glowed with jealousy.
My eyes lit with jealousy.
My eyes narrowed with jealousy.
My eyes shimmered with jealousy.
My face crazed with jealousy.
My face flushed with jealousy.
My heart burned with jealousy.
My heart swelled with jealousy.
My pulse raced with jealousy.
My skin flushed with jealousy.
My voice rang with jealousy.
My voice slurred with jealousy.
I felt a bit of jealousy.
I felt a bolt of jealousy.
I felt a flash of jealousy.
I felt a moment of jealousy.
I felt a pang of jealousy.
I felt a rush of jealousy.
I felt a spark of jealousy.
I felt a spurt of jealousy.
I felt a stab of jealousy.
I felt a surge of jealousy.
I felt a tinge of jealousy.
I felt a twinge of jealousy.

I felt a twist of jealousy.
Jealousy curled deep in my
belly.
Jealousy pooled low in my
belly.
My body was overwrought
with jealousy.
My eyes went dark with
jealousy.
My eyes were dark with
jealousy.
My eyes were full of jealousy.
My eyes were hazy with
jealousy.
My eyes were heavy with
jealousy.
My face glazed over with
jealousy.
My throat was thick with
jealousy.
My voice sounded rough with
jealousy.
My voice was rough with
jealousy.
My voice was thick with
jealousy.

JOY

Definition: A feeling of great pleasure and happiness.
See DELIGHT

I whooped with joy.
I yelped with joy.
Joy coursed through me.
Joy darkened my eyes.
Joy engorged my heart.
Joy engulfed my face.
Joy filled my heart.
Joy flashed through me.
Joy flooded through me.
Joy leapt through me.
Joy raced through me.
Joy rippled through me.
Joy settled my soul.
Joy stung my eyes.
Joy surged through me.
Joy swept through me.
Joy warmed my insides.
Joy washed through me.
Joy welled inside me.
Joy widened my eyes.
Joy broke over my face.
Joy clapped in my chest.
Joy flickered in my eyes.
Joy rang in my voice.
Joy rolled down my face.
Joy shone on my face.
Joy streamed down my cheeks.
Joy streamed down my face.
My body quivered with joy.
My eyebrows danced in joy.
My eyes beamed with joy.
My eyes danced with joy.
My eyes filled with joy.

My eyes gleamed with joy.
My eyes glittered in joy.
My eyes shimmered with joy.
My eyes shone with joy.
My eyes sparkled with joy.
My eyes twinkled with joy.
My eyes widened in joy.
My eyes widened with joy.
My face filled with joy.
My face flooded with joy.
My face glowed with joy.
My face lit with joy.
My head buzzed with joy.
My heart beat with joy.
My heart burst with joy.
My heart danced with joy.
My heart filled with joy.
My heart flipped with joy.
My heart fluttered with joy.
My heart leapt with joy.
My heart molten with joy.
My heart pinged with joy.
My voice brimmed with joy.
My voice quavered with joy.
My voice screeched with joy.
I felt a mixture of joy.
I felt a rush of joy.
I felt a surge of joy.
I felt a thrill of joy.
I gave a cry of joy.
I gave a shout of joy.
My eyebrows went up in joy.
My eyes were huge with joy.

My eyes were white with joy.
My eyes were wide with joy.
My face was brilliant with joy.
My heart was full of joy.
My nerves cried out in joy.

L

LOATHING

Definition: A feeling of intense dislike or disgust.
See HATRED

I shivered with loathing.
Loathing blurred my vision.
Loathing coursed through me.
Loathing simmered inside me.
Loathing twisted my features.
Loathing bubbled in my gut.
Loathing combusted behind my ribs.
Loathing crawled over my skin.
Loathing etched in my face.
Loathing etched on my face.
Loathing passed over my face.
Loathing rose in my gut.
Loathing rose in my throat.
Loathing smouldered in my eyes.
My body quivered with loathing.
My eyes brimmed with loathing.
My eyes bulged with loathing.
My eyes burned with loathing.
My eyes filled with loathing.
My eyes flared with loathing.
My eyes flashed with loathing.
My eyes flickered with loathing.
My eyes glared with loathing.
My eyes glazed in loathing.
My eyes gleamed with loathing.
My eyes glittered with loathing.
My eyes glowed with loathing.
My eyes locked in loathing.
My eyes narrowed as loathing.
My eyes narrowed in loathing.
My eyes narrowed with loathing.
My eyes seethed with loathing.
My face brimmed with loathing.
My face contorted with loathing.
My face darkened in loathing.
My face flushed with loathing.
My face loaded with loathing.
My face masked in loathing.
My face twisted in loathing.
My face twisted with loathing.
My heart filled with loathing.

My heart seethed with
loathing.
My mouth twisted in loathing.
My mouth twisted with
loathing.
My skin tingled with loathing.
My throat constricted with
loathing.
My voice filled with loathing.
My voice saturated with
loathing.
I felt a surge of loathing.
Loathing burned deep in my
soul.
My body was taut with
loathing.
My eyes were alive with
loathing.
My eyes were cold with
loathing.
My eyes were dead with
loathing.
My eyes were full of loathing.
My eyes were wide with
loathing.
My face was stiff with loathing.
My face was venomous with
loathing.
My heart was full of loathing.

LONELINESS

Definition: Sadness because one has no friends or company.
See SADNESS

Loneliness came over me.
Loneliness clouded my expression.
Loneliness crashed over me.
Loneliness crept over me.
Loneliness crossed my face.
Loneliness crossed my features.
Loneliness darkened my eyes.
Loneliness ebbed over me.
Loneliness entered my voice.
Loneliness filled my eyes.
Loneliness filled my voice.
Loneliness formed in me.
Loneliness howled through me.
Loneliness invaded my eyes.
Loneliness lined my face.
Loneliness rose off me.
Loneliness seeped into me.
Loneliness settled over me.
Loneliness sizzled through me.
Loneliness spiralled through me.
Loneliness squeezed my chest.
Loneliness swept through me.
Loneliness tinged my eyes.
Loneliness tinged my voice.
Loneliness tugged at me.
Loneliness washed over me.
Loneliness weighed on me.
Loneliness welled inside me.
Loneliness came into my eyes.
Loneliness came into my voice.

Loneliness crept into my expression.
Loneliness drifted across my face.
Loneliness flickered in my eyes.
Loneliness flickered in my face.
Loneliness lay in my heart.
Loneliness lingered in my eyes.
Loneliness passed over my face.
Loneliness seeped into my muscles.
Loneliness settled on my face.
Loneliness showed in my eyes.
Loneliness welled in my chest.
Loneliness welled in my eyes.
My eyes drooped with loneliness.
My eyes filled with loneliness.
My eyes haunted with loneliness.
My eyes shadowed in loneliness.
My face creased with loneliness.
My face crumpled with loneliness.
My face darkened with loneliness.
My face etched with loneliness.
My face filled with loneliness.
My face sagged with loneliness.
My tone laced with loneliness.

My tone shaded with
loneliness.
My tone softened with
loneliness.
My voice echoed with
loneliness.
My voice filled with loneliness.
My voice infused with
loneliness.
My voice laced with loneliness.
My voice tinged with
loneliness.
I felt a pang of loneliness.
I felt a sense of loneliness.
I felt a tug of loneliness.
My eyes were full of loneliness.
My face was heavy with
loneliness.
My tone was thick with
loneliness.
My voice was full of loneliness.
My voice was soft with
loneliness.
A touch of loneliness came
into my eyes.

LONGING

Definition: A yearning desire.
See DESIRE

Longing bubbled through me.
Longing caressed my mouth.
Longing clawed at me.
Longing coursed through me.
Longing crowded my chest.
Longing curled through me.
Longing darkened my irises.
Longing drifted through me.
Longing exploded inside me.
Longing flowed over me.
Longing flowed through me.
Longing fluttered inside me.
Longing glowed inside me.
Longing gushed through me.
Longing heated my blood.
Longing knifed through me.
Longing laced my voice.
Longing licked through me.
Longing made me melt.
Longing penetrated my heart.
Longing poured through me.
Longing pulsed through me.
Longing pumped through me.
Longing radiated from me.
Longing radiated through me.
Longing ravaged my face.
Longing rippled through me.
Longing rose from me.
Longing rose in me.
Longing shattered within me.
Longing slammed into me.
Longing sluiced through me.
Longing spiralled through me.

Longing splintered through me.
Longing sprouted inside me.
Longing surged through me.
Longing surged within me.
Longing swelled within me.
Longing swept through me.
Longing swirled through me.
Longing tightened inside me.
Longing tightened my features.
Longing tightened my throat.
Longing tugged at me.
Longing wafted through me.
Longing warmed my insides.
Longing went through me.
Longing banked in my eyes.
Longing combated in my brain.
Longing danced in my belly.
Longing flashed in my eyes.
Longing flickered in my expression.
Longing flickered in my eyes.
Longing nipped at my skin.
Longing swept through my body.
Longing throbbed against my belly.
My blood burned with longing.
My blood heated with longing.
My body burned with longing.

My body drugged with longing.
My body hardened with longing.
My body heated with longing.
My body hummed with longing.
My body jangled with longing.
My body shivered with longing.
My body stirred with longing.
My body throbbed with longing.
My body thrummed with longing.
My body twitched with longing.
My body unfurled with longing.
My chest clenched with longing.
My ears shut in longing.
My eyes blazed with longing.
My eyes danced with longing.
My eyes darkened with longing.
My eyes flared with longing.
My eyes flickered with longing.
My eyes gleamed with longing.
My eyes glittered with longing.
My eyes glowed with longing.
My eyes lit with longing.
My eyes narrowed with longing.
My eyes shimmered with longing.
My face filled with longing.
My face flushed with longing.

My heart burned with longing.
My heart filled with longing.
My heart fluttered with longing.
My heart swelled with longing.
My pulse raced with longing.
My skin flushed with longing.
My voice slurred with longing.
I felt a moment of longing.
I felt a pang of longing.
I felt a rush of longing.
I felt a sense of longing.
I felt a stab of longing.
I felt a twinge of longing.
I felt a wave of longing.
I felt an ache of longing.
Longing curled deep in my belly.
Longing pooled low in my belly.
My body was overwrought with longing.
My eyes went dark with longing.
My eyes were dark with longing.
My eyes were full of longing.
My eyes were hazy with longing.
My eyes were heavy with longing.
My eyes were unclouded with longing.
My face glazed over with longing.
My throat was thick with longing.

My voice sounded rough with
longing.
My voice was rough with
longing.
My voice was thick with
longing.

LOVE

Definition: An intense feeling of deep affection.

See AFFECTION

Love came over me.
Love crossed my face.
Love fell over me.
Love filled my eyes.
Love filled my mind.
Love flowed around me.
Love pierced my heart.
Love saturated my voice.
Love surged through me.
Love swept through me.
Love warred inside me.
Love washed over me.
Love washed through me.
Love welled inside me.
Love blazed in my eyes.
Love burned in my eyes.
Love crept into my voice.
Love gleamed in my eyes.
Love radiated from my face.
Love shimmered in my expression.
Love shone in my eyes.
Love shone through my tears.
Love stirred in my breast.
My chest squeezed with love.
My chest swelled with love.
My eyes brimmed with love.
My eyes darkened with love.
My eyes filled with love.
My eyes glowed with love.
My eyes moistened with love.
My eyes shone with love.
My eyes softened with love.

My face filled with love.
My face suffused with love.
My heart ached with love.
My heart engorged with love.
My heart filled with love.
My heart fluttered with love.
My heart looked for love.
My heart overflowed with love.
My heart soared with love.
My heart squeezed with love.
My heart swelled with love.
My heart swollen with love.
My heart warmed with love.
My throat tightened with love.
My tone filled with love.
My voice deepened with love.
My voice throbbed with love.
I felt a flush of love.
I felt a glow of love.
I felt a kind of love.
I felt a lot of love.
I felt a pang of love.
I felt a rush of love.
I felt a surge of love.
I felt a swell of love.
My eyes lit up with love.
My eyes were full of love.
My eyes were misty with love.
My eyes were warm with love.
My face was soft with love.
My heart was full of love.
My heart was heavy with love.

My voice was full of love.

LUST

Definition: Strong sexual desire.

See DESIRE

Lust bubbled through me.
Lust burned through me.
Lust caressed my mouth.
Lust clawed at me.
Lust coiled through me.
Lust coursed through me.
Lust crowded my chest.
Lust curled through me.
Lust darkened my irises.
Lust drifted through me.
Lust exploded inside me.
Lust flowed inside me.
Lust flowed over me.
Lust flowed through me.
Lust fluttered inside me.
Lust glowed inside me.
Lust gushed through me.
Lust heated my blood.
Lust knifed through me.
Lust laced my voice.
Lust licked through me.
Lust lit my eyes.
Lust made me melt.
Lust penetrated my heart.
Lust poured through me.
Lust pulsed through me.
Lust pumped through me.
Lust radiated from me.
Lust ravaged my face.
Lust rippled through me.
Lust rose from me.
Lust rose in me.
Lust shattered within me.

Lust sizzled through me.
Lust slammed into me.
Lust sluiced through me.
Lust spiralled through me.
Lust splintered through me.
Lust stirred inside me.
Lust surged through me.
Lust swelled within me.
Lust swept through me.
Lust swirled through me.
Lust tightened inside me.
Lust tightened my features.
Lust wafted through me.
Lust warmed my insides.
Lust went through me.
Lust banked in my eyes.
Lust burst in my centre.
Lust combated in my brain.
Lust danced in my belly.
Lust flashed in my eyes.
Lust flickered in my
expression.
Lust flickered in my eyes.
Lust nipped at my skin.
Lust pooled in my loins.
Lust throbbed against my
belly.
My blood burned with lust.
My blood heated with lust.
My body burned with lust.
My body drugged with lust.
My body hardened with lust.
My body heated with lust.

My body hummed with lust.
My body jangled with lust.
My body shivered with lust.
My body stirred with lust.
My body thrummed with lust.
My body twitched with lust.
My body unfurled with lust.
My ears shut in lust.
My eyes blazed with lust.
My eyes danced with lust.
My eyes darkened with lust.
My eyes flared with lust.
My eyes flickered with lust.
My eyes glazed with lust.
My eyes gleamed with lust.
My eyes glittered with lust.
My eyes glowed with lust.
My eyes lit with lust.
My eyes narrowed with lust.
My eyes shimmered with lust.
My eyes shone with lust.
My face flushed with lust.
My heart burned with lust.
My heart swelled with lust.
My pulse pounded with lust.
My pulse raced with lust.
My skin flushed with lust.
My voice slurred with lust.
I felt a bolt of lust.
I felt a flush of lust.
I felt a kick of lust.
I felt a prick of lust.
I felt a stab of lust.
I felt a surge of lust.
I felt a ton of lust.
I felt a wave of lust.
Lust curled deep in my belly.
Lust pooled low in my belly.

My blood was wild with lust.
My body was overwrought
with lust.
My eyes went dark with lust.
My eyes were dark with lust.
My eyes were full of lust.
My eyes were hazy with lust.
My eyes were heavy with lust.
My face glazed over with lust.
My throat was thick with lust.
My voice sounded rough with
lust.
My voice was coarse with lust.
My voice was rough with lust.
My voice was thick with lust.

M

MALAISE

Definition: A general feeling of discomfort, illness, or unease whose exact cause is difficult to identify.
See UNHAPPINESS

Malaise came over me.
Malaise clouded my expression.
Malaise crashed over me.
Malaise crept over me.
Malaise crossed my face.
Malaise crossed my features.
Malaise darkened my eyes.
Malaise ebbed over me.
Malaise entered my voice.
Malaise filled my eyes.
Malaise filled my voice.
Malaise howled through me.
Malaise invaded my eyes.
Malaise lined my face.
Malaise rose off me.
Malaise seeped into me.
Malaise settled over me.
Malaise sizzled through me.
Malaise spiralled through me.
Malaise squeezed my chest.
Malaise swept through me.
Malaise tinged my eyes.
Malaise tinged my voice.
Malaise tugged at me.
Malaise washed over me.

Malaise weighed on me.
Malaise welled inside me.
Malaise came into my eyes.
Malaise came into my voice.
Malaise crept into my expression.
Malaise drifted across my face.
Malaise flickered in my eyes.
Malaise flickered in my face.
Malaise lay in my heart.
Malaise lingered in my eyes.
Malaise passed over my face.
Malaise seeped into my muscles.
Malaise settled on my face.
Malaise showed in my eyes.
Malaise welled in my chest.
Malaise welled in my eyes.
My eyes drooped with malaise.
My eyes filled with malaise.
My eyes shadowed in malaise.
My face clenched with malaise.
My face creased with malaise.
My face crumpled with malaise.

My face darkened with
malaise.
My face etched with malaise.
My face filled with malaise.
My face sagged with malaise.
My tone laced with malaise.
My tone shaded with malaise.
My tone softened with
malaise.
My voice filled with malaise.
My voice infused with malaise.
My voice laced with malaise.
My voice tinged with malaise.
I felt a chill of malaise.
I felt a flash of malaise.
I felt a pang of malaise.
I felt a pinch of malaise.
I felt a sense of malaise.
I felt a swell of malaise.
I felt a touch of malaise.
I felt a twinge of malaise.
I felt a wave of malaise.
I gave a sigh of malaise.
My eyes were full of malaise.
My face was heavy with
malaise.
My tone was thick with
malaise.
My voice was full of malaise.
My voice was soft with
malaise.
A touch of malaise came into
my eyes.

MELANCHOLY

Definition: A feeling of pensive sadness, typically with no obvious cause.

See SADNESS

Melancholy came over me.
Melancholy clouded my expression.
Melancholy crashed over me.
Melancholy crept over me.
Melancholy crossed my face.
Melancholy crossed my features.
Melancholy darkened my eyes.
Melancholy ebbed over me.
Melancholy entered my voice.
Melancholy filled my eyes.
Melancholy filled my voice.
Melancholy howled through me.
Melancholy invaded my eyes.
Melancholy lined my face.
Melancholy rose off me.
Melancholy seeped into me.
Melancholy settled over me.
Melancholy settled upon me.
Melancholy sizzled through me.
Melancholy spiralled through me.
Melancholy squeezed my chest.
Melancholy swept through me.
Melancholy tinged my eyes.
Melancholy tinged my voice.
Melancholy tugged at me.
Melancholy washed over me.

Melancholy weighed on me.
Melancholy welled inside me.
Melancholy came into my eyes.
Melancholy came into my voice.
Melancholy crept into my expression.
Melancholy drifted across my face.
Melancholy flickered in my eyes.
Melancholy flickered in my face.
Melancholy lay in my heart.
Melancholy lingered in my eyes.
Melancholy passed over my face.
Melancholy seeped into my muscles.
Melancholy settled on my face.
Melancholy showed in my eyes.
Melancholy welled in my chest.
Melancholy welled in my eyes.
My eyes drooped with melancholy.
My eyes filled with melancholy.
My eyes shadowed in melancholy.

My face creased with
melancholy.
My face crumpled with
melancholy.
My face darkened with
melancholy.
My face etched with
melancholy.
My face filled with
melancholy.
My face sagged with
melancholy.
My tone laced with
melancholy.
My tone shaded with
melancholy.
My tone softened with
melancholy.
My voice broke with
melancholy.
My voice filled with
melancholy.
My voice infused with
melancholy.
My voice laced with
melancholy.
My voice tinged with
melancholy.
I felt a mixture of melancholy.
I felt a sense of melancholy.
I felt a touch of melancholy.
I felt a twinge of melancholy.
I felt a wave of melancholy.
My eyes were full of
melancholy.
My face was heavy with
melancholy.

My tone was thick with
melancholy.
My voice was full of
melancholy.
My voice was soft with
melancholy.
A touch of melancholy came
into my eyes.

MISERY

Definition: A state or feeling of great physical or mental distress or discomfort.

See UNHAPPINESS

I groaned in misery.
Misery clapped my hands.
Misery clawed at me.
Misery clogged my throat.
Misery crashed through me.
Misery crossed my face.
Misery crushed my chest.
Misery darkened my eyes.
Misery etched my face.
Misery exploded inside me.
Misery exploded through me.
Misery filled my body.
Misery filled my heart.
Misery filled my voice.
Misery fuelled my voice.
Misery ignited my nerves.
Misery lined my face.
Misery lined my features.
Misery paralysed my legs.
Misery pierced my body.
Misery pierced my sinuses.
Misery pulsed through me.
Misery ripped through me.
Misery robbed my breath.
Misery sang through me.
Misery stabbed my side.
Misery streaked my face.
Misery swept through me.
Misery throbbed inside me.
Misery tightened my features.
Misery tightened my throat.
Misery touched my heart.

Misery came into my eyes.
Misery came over my face.
Misery crawled around my mind.
Misery emanated from my body.
Misery etched on my face.
Misery exploded in my guts.
Misery flared from my fingertips.
Misery flared in my ribs.
Misery flared up my leg.
Misery flashed in my eyes.
Misery flickered in my eyes.
Misery froze in my throat.
Misery glazed in my eyes.
Misery grew in my face.
Misery radiated from my back.
Misery ripped across my face.
Misery ripped through my body.
Misery ripped through my head.
Misery rushed through my body.
Misery sat on my chest.
Misery seared through my leg.
Misery shrieked from my mouth.
Misery struck my nervous system.

Misery swept through my body.
Misery tore up my spine.
Misery washed down my cheeks.
Misery welled in my chest.
Misery welled into my eyes.
My body contorted in misery.
My body convulsed in misery.
My body creamed in misery.
My body exploded with misery.
My body paralyzed with misery.
My body screamed with misery.
My body shrieked in misery.
My body spasmed in misery.
My body throbbed in misery.
My body writhed in misery.
My chest heaved with misery.
My ears stabbed with misery.
My eyes closed in misery.
My eyes filled with misery.
My eyes flared with misery.
My eyes glazed in misery.
My eyes narrowed in misery.
My eyes rolled in misery.
My eyes swam with misery.
My eyes widened in misery.
My face clenched in misery.
My face clenched with misery.
My face contorted in misery.
My face contorted with misery.
My face crumbled with misery.
My face crumpled in misery.
My face etched in misery.

My face filled with misery.
My face lined with misery.
My face pinched in misery.
My face puckered in misery.
My face squeezed with misery.
My face twisted in misery.
My face twisted with misery.
My heart exploded with misery.
My lips tightened in misery.
My lips trembled in misery.
My mouth twisted with misery.
My nerves screamed in misery.
My shoulders sagged in misery.
My voice broke with misery.
My voice cracked with misery.
My voice filled with misery.
My voice grated with misery.
My voice rose in misery.
My voice twisted in misery.
My voice vibrated with misery.
I swallowed a ball of misery.
Misery lay heavy on my mind.
My body crumpled up in misery.
My eyes glowed red with misery.
My eyes opened wide with misery.
My eyes were bright with misery.
My eyes were dark with misery.
My eyes were full of misery.
My face screwed up in misery.
My face was full of misery.
My head hung low in misery.
My knees drew up in misery.

My mouth sagged open in
misery.
My throat closed up with
misery.
My voice trailed off in misery.
My voice was full of misery.
My voice was hoarse with
misery.
My voice was shrill with
misery.
A touch of misery came into
my eyes.

MORTIFICATION

Definition: Great embarrassment and shame.

See EMBARRASSMENT

I gasped in mortification.
I moaned in mortification.
Mortification burned my cheeks.
Mortification clouded my face.
Mortification coloured my face.
Mortification fell over me.
Mortification flicked at me.
Mortification flitted past me.
Mortification flooded my cheeks.
Mortification flooded through me.
Mortification heated my cheeks.
Mortification heated my face.
Mortification made me flush.
Mortification poured through me.
Mortification reddened my cheeks.
Mortification shuddered through me.
Mortification stained my cheeks.
Mortification stole through me.
Mortification swept over me.
Mortification swept through me.
Mortification tinged my voice.
Mortification warmed my face.

I grew hot with mortification.
I grew warm with mortification.
Mortification burned in my cheeks.
Mortification flickered on my face.
Mortification fluttered across my belly.
Mortification gnawed at my thoughts.
Mortification lodged in my throat.
Mortification rose in my cheeks.
Mortification rushed down my spine.
Mortification skated up my spine.
My cheeks burned with mortification.
My cheeks flushed with mortification.
My ears quivered with mortification.
My ears shifted in mortification.
My ears stiffened in mortification.
My ears stiffened with mortification.
My ears twitched with mortification.

My ears vibrated in
mortification.
My ears wriggled with
mortification.
My eyes closed in
mortification.
My eyes narrowed in
mortification.
My eyes warred with
mortification.
My face burned with
mortification.
My face coloured with
mortification.
My face flamed with
mortification.
My face flushed from
mortification.
My face flushed with
mortification.
My face fluttered from
mortification.
My face heated with
mortification.
My throat tightened with
mortification.
My tone edged with
mortification.
My tone softened with
mortification.
My voice coated with
mortification.
My body felt hot with
mortification.
My body went hot with
mortification.
My cheeks flushed red with
mortification.

My cheeks grew warm with
mortification.
My cheeks were warm with
mortification.
My face felt hot with
mortification.
My neck flushed red with
mortification.
My neck grew hot with
mortification.
My throat seized up with
mortification.
My voice was gruff with
mortification.
My voice was stiff with
mortification.
My voice was tight with
mortification.

N

NAUSEA

Definition: A feeling of loathing or disgust.

See DISGUST

I frowned in nausea.
I frowned with nausea.
I grimaced in nausea.
I grimaced with nausea.
I grunted in nausea.
I grunted with nausea.
I muttered in nausea.
I scowled in nausea.
I shuddered with nausea.
I sighed in nausea.
I sneered with nausea.
I sniffed in nausea.
I snorted in nausea.
I snorted with nausea.
I sobbed with nausea.
I spat in nausea.
I swallowed in nausea.
Nausea altered my face.
Nausea ate at me.
Nausea came over me.
Nausea choked my throat.
Nausea coloured my voice.
Nausea crossed my face.
Nausea filled my face.
Nausea flooded over me.
Nausea pervaded my tone.
Nausea puckered my lips.

Nausea ripped through me.
Nausea rippled through me.
Nausea rolled through me.
Nausea tinged my voice.
Nausea trickled over me.
My eyes widened in nausea.
My face clouded with nausea.
My face contorted in nausea.
My face creased with nausea.
My face filled with nausea.
My face grimaced in nausea.
My face twisted in nausea.
My face twisted with nausea.
My face wrinkled in nausea.
My face wrinkled with nausea.
My gut clenched with nausea.
My gut tightened with nausea.
My heart burned with nausea.
My lips curled in nausea.
My lips curled with nausea.
My lips snarled in nausea.
My lips twisted in nausea.
My mouth twisted in nausea.
My mouth twisted with
nausea.
My nose crinkled in nausea.
My nose wrinkled in nausea.

My nose wrinkled with nausea.
My skin tingled with nausea.
My stomach heaved with
nausea.
My tone filled with nausea.
My voice laced with nausea.
My voice thickened with
nausea.
My voice tightened with
nausea.
Nausea came across my face.
Nausea dripped in my tone.
Nausea flooded into my heart.
Nausea fought in my throat.
Nausea fought in my voice.
Nausea glowed in my eyes.
Nausea made my stomach
churn.
Nausea rose in my stomach.
Nausea seeped from my pores.
Nausea wiggled down my
frame.
I exhaled a breath of nausea.
I felt a rush of nausea.
I felt a surge of nausea.
I felt a wave of nausea.
I gave a grimace of nausea.
I gave a groan of nausea.
I gave a grunt of nausea.
I gave a huff of nausea.
I gave a shudder of nausea.
I gave a snort of nausea.
I gave a wave of nausea.
I muttered a sound of nausea.
I muttered a word of nausea.
My face creased up in nausea.
My face screwed up with
nausea.

My face was stiff with nausea.
My mouth cocked open in
nausea.
My mouth squashed up in
nausea.
My tone was harsh with
nausea.
My voice trailed off in nausea.
My voice was thick with
nausea.
My face was a mask of nausea.

NERVOUSNESS

Definition: The quality or state of being nervous.

See WORRY

Nervousness clouded my face.
Nervousness clouded my features.
Nervousness creased my forehead.
Nervousness crept through me.
Nervousness crinkled my features.
Nervousness crossed my face.
Nervousness darkened my eyes.
Nervousness edged my voice.
Nervousness etched my face.
Nervousness filled my senses.
Nervousness furrowed my brows.
Nervousness gnawed at me.
Nervousness grew inside me.
Nervousness knifed through me.
Nervousness knitted my brow.
Nervousness knitted my brows.
Nervousness knotted my belly.
Nervousness knotted my insides.
Nervousness lit my expression.
Nervousness mushroomed inside me.
Nervousness niggled at me.
Nervousness pinched my brows.

Nervousness raged inside me.
Nervousness ripped through me.
Nervousness rippled my jawline.
Nervousness seeped into me.
Nervousness slashed my face.
Nervousness tickled my spine.
Nervousness tightened my eyes.
Nervousness tightened my features.
Nervousness went through me.
My belly roiled with nervousness.
My brows creased in nervousness.
My brows etched with nervousness.
My brows furrowed with nervousness.
My brows knitted with nervousness.
My brows narrowed with nervousness.
My chest ached with nervousness.
My eyebrows scrunched in nervousness.
My eyes clouded with nervousness.
My eyes creased with nervousness.

My eyes darkened with nervousness.
My eyes faded with nervousness.
My eyes filled with nervousness.
My eyes flared with nervousness.
My eyes flickered with nervousness.
My eyes narrowed with nervousness.
My eyes pinched with nervousness.
My eyes shadowed with nervousness.
My face creased with nervousness.
My face crinkled in nervousness.
My face crinkled with nervousness.
My face crumpled with nervousness.
My face darkened with nervousness.
My face etched with nervousness.
My face gouged with nervousness.
My face lined with nervousness.
My face pinched with nervousness.
My face pouched with nervousness.
My face set in nervousness.

My face strained with nervousness.
My face swollen with nervousness.
My face twisted with nervousness.
My face twitched with nervousness.
My head ached with nervousness.
My head swam with nervousness.
My heart pounded with nervousness.
My insides churned with nervousness.
My insides scoured with nervousness.
My nerves jangled with nervousness.
My shoulders twitched with nervousness.
My voice cracked with nervousness.
My voice drooped with nervousness.
My voice trembled with nervousness.
Nervousness crumpled up my face.
Nervousness flickered in my expression.
Nervousness grew in my stomach.
Nervousness prickled across my nape.
Nervousness raced through my expression.

Nervousness scurried about
my mind.
Nervousness slid across my
face.
Nervousness slipped into my
voice.
Nervousness sneaked into my
voice.
I felt a pang of nervousness.
I felt a surge of nervousness.
I felt a twinge of nervousness.
I felt a twitch of nervousness.
My eyes were alive with
nervousness.
My eyes were dark with
nervousness.
My eyes were frantic with
nervousness.
My eyes were full of
nervousness.
My eyes were wide with
nervousness.
My face screwed up with
nervousness.
My face was full of
nervousness.
My face was taut with
nervousness.
My gut was full of nervousness.
My mouth was dry with
nervousness.
My mouth was a line of
nervousness.

NOSTALGIA

Definition: A sentimental longing or wistful affection for a period in the past.
See LONGING

Nostalgia bubbled through me.
Nostalgia came over me.
Nostalgia caressed my mouth.
Nostalgia clawed at me.
Nostalgia clouded my expression.
Nostalgia coursed through me.
Nostalgia crashed over me.
Nostalgia crept over me.
Nostalgia crossed my face.
Nostalgia crossed my features.
Nostalgia crowded my chest.
Nostalgia curled through me.
Nostalgia darkened my eyes.
Nostalgia darkened my irises.
Nostalgia drifted through me.
Nostalgia ebbed over me.
Nostalgia entered my voice.
Nostalgia exploded inside me.
Nostalgia filled my eyes.
Nostalgia filled my voice.
Nostalgia flowed over me.
Nostalgia flowed through me.
Nostalgia fluttered inside me.
Nostalgia glowed inside me.
Nostalgia gushed through me.
Nostalgia heated my blood.
Nostalgia howled through me.
Nostalgia invaded my eyes.
Nostalgia knifed through me.
Nostalgia laced my voice.
Nostalgia licked through me.

Nostalgia lined my face.
Nostalgia made me melt.
Nostalgia nagged at me.
Nostalgia painted my face.
Nostalgia passed through me.
Nostalgia penetrated my heart.
Nostalgia poured through me.
Nostalgia pulsed through me.
Nostalgia pumped through me.
Nostalgia radiated from me.
Nostalgia radiated through me.
Nostalgia ravaged my face.
Nostalgia rippled through me.
Nostalgia rose from me.
Nostalgia rose in me.
Nostalgia rose off me.
Nostalgia sang in me.
Nostalgia seeped into me.
Nostalgia settled over me.
Nostalgia shattered within me.
Nostalgia sizzled through me.
Nostalgia slammed into me.
Nostalgia sliced at me.
Nostalgia sluiced through me.
Nostalgia spiralled through me.
Nostalgia splintered through me.
Nostalgia sprouted inside me.
Nostalgia squeezed my chest.

Nostalgia surged through me.
Nostalgia surged within me.
Nostalgia swelled inside me.
Nostalgia swelled within me.
Nostalgia swept through me.
Nostalgia swirled through me.
Nostalgia tightened inside me.
Nostalgia tightened my chest.
Nostalgia tightened my features.
Nostalgia tightened my throat.
Nostalgia tinged my eyes.
Nostalgia tinged my voice.
Nostalgia tugged at me.
Nostalgia twisted my mouth.
Nostalgia wafted through me.
Nostalgia warmed my insides.
Nostalgia washed over me.
Nostalgia washed through me.
Nostalgia weighed on me.
Nostalgia welled inside me.
Nostalgia went through me.
My blood burned with nostalgia.
My blood heated with nostalgia.
My body burned with nostalgia.
My body drugged with nostalgia.
My body hardened with nostalgia.
My body heated with nostalgia.
My body hummed with nostalgia.
My body jangled with nostalgia.

My body shivered with nostalgia.
My body stirred with nostalgia.
My body throbbed with nostalgia.
My body thrummed with nostalgia.
My body twitched with nostalgia.
My body unfurled with nostalgia.
My chest clenched with nostalgia.
My ears shut in nostalgia.
My eyes blazed with nostalgia.
My eyes danced with nostalgia.
My eyes darkened with nostalgia.
My eyes drooped with nostalgia.
My eyes filled with nostalgia.
My eyes flared with nostalgia.
My eyes flickered with nostalgia.
My eyes gleamed with nostalgia.
My eyes glittered with nostalgia.
My eyes glowed with nostalgia.
My eyes lit with nostalgia.
My eyes narrowed with nostalgia.
My eyes shadowed in nostalgia.
My eyes shadowed with nostalgia.
My eyes shimmered with nostalgia.

My face creased with nostalgia.
My face crumpled with nostalgia.
My face darkened with nostalgia.
My face etched with nostalgia.
My face filled with nostalgia.
My face flushed with nostalgia.
My face sagged with nostalgia.
My heart burned with nostalgia.
My heart filled with nostalgia.
My heart flooded with nostalgia.
My heart fluttered with nostalgia.
My heart swelled with nostalgia.
My pulse raced with nostalgia.
My skin flushed with nostalgia.
My tone laced with nostalgia.
My tone shaded with nostalgia.
My tone softened with nostalgia.
My voice filled with nostalgia.
My voice infused with nostalgia.
My voice laced with nostalgia.
My voice poisoned with nostalgia.
My voice slurred with nostalgia.
My voice tinged with nostalgia.
Nostalgia banked in my eyes.
Nostalgia came into my eyes.
Nostalgia came into my voice.

Nostalgia combated in my brain.
Nostalgia crept into my expression.
Nostalgia danced in my belly.
Nostalgia drifted across my face.
Nostalgia flashed in my eyes.
Nostalgia flickered in my expression.
Nostalgia flickered in my eyes.
Nostalgia flickered in my face.
Nostalgia lay in my heart.
Nostalgia lingered in my eyes.
Nostalgia nipped at my skin.
Nostalgia passed over my face.
Nostalgia seeped into my muscles.
Nostalgia settled on my face.
Nostalgia showed in my eyes.
Nostalgia sounded in my voice.
Nostalgia surged through my head.
Nostalgia swept through my body.
Nostalgia throbbed against my belly.
Nostalgia welled in my chest.
Nostalgia welled in my eyes.
I felt a sense of nostalgia.
I felt a tug of nostalgia.
I felt a twist of nostalgia.
My body was overwrought with nostalgia.
My eyes went dark with nostalgia.
My eyes were dark with nostalgia.

My eyes were full of nostalgia.
My eyes were hazy with
nostalgia.
My eyes were heavy with
nostalgia.
My eyes were unclouded with
nostalgia.
My face glazed over with
nostalgia.
My face was heavy with
nostalgia.
My throat was thick with
nostalgia.
My tone was thick with
nostalgia.
My voice sounded rough with
nostalgia.
My voice was feeble with
nostalgia.
My voice was full of nostalgia.
My voice was rough with
nostalgia.
My voice was soft with
nostalgia.
My voice was thick with
nostalgia.
Nostalgia curled deep in my
belly.
Nostalgia pooled low in my
belly.
A touch of nostalgia came into
my eyes.

O

OPTIMISM

Definition: Hopefulness and confidence about the future or the success of something.
See HOPE

Optimism bloomed within me.
Optimism brightened my eyes.
Optimism brightened my face.
Optimism bubbled inside me.
Optimism filled my chest.
Optimism filled my eyes.
Optimism flared in me.
Optimism flared inside me.
Optimism flickered in me.
Optimism flooded my soul.
Optimism grew inside me.
Optimism kindled inside me.
Optimism laced my voice.
Optimism passed through me.
Optimism ran through me.
Optimism ripped through me.
Optimism rose in me.
Optimism rushed through me.
Optimism stirred inside me.
Optimism surged through me.
Optimism swelled inside me.
Optimism washed over me.
Optimism welled inside me.
Optimism went through me.
My chest filled with optimism.
My eyes brightened with optimism.
My eyes glimmered with optimism.
My eyes shone with optimism.
My eyes sparkled with optimism.
My eyes widened with optimism.
My face bloomed with optimism.
My face went from optimism.
My heart jumped with optimism.
My heart pounded with optimism.
My heart spiked with optimism.
My heart swelled with optimism.
My nerves vibrated with optimism.
Optimism bloomed in my chest.
Optimism blossomed in my heart.

Optimism blossomed in my mind.
Optimism budded in my chest.
Optimism budded in my heart.
Optimism came into my eyes.
Optimism dawned on my face.
Optimism exploded in my chest.
Optimism flared in my gaze.
Optimism flashed over my face.
Optimism flashed through my mind.
Optimism flicked across my face.
Optimism flickered across my face.
Optimism glimmered in my eyes.
Optimism glowed in my eyes.
Optimism quickened in my breast.
Optimism sprang in my face.
Optimism stirred in my heart.
Optimism surged in my breast.
Optimism swelled in my bosom.
Optimism swelled in my chest.
Optimism wormed through my chest.
I felt a flicker of optimism.
I felt a sense of optimism.
I felt a surge of optimism.
I felt a tinge of optimism.
My eyes burned incandescent with optimism.
My eyes lit up with optimism.
My eyes were full of optimism.
My eyes were shiny with optimism.
My eyes were wide with optimism.
My face lit up with optimism.
My face was alive with optimism.
My face was bright with optimism.

OUTRAGE

Definition: An extremely strong reaction of anger, shock, or indignation.
See INDIGNATION

I gasped in outrage.
I spluttered in outrage.
I stiffened in outrage.
Outrage burned inside me.
Outrage burned through me.
Outrage burned within me.
Outrage churned inside me.
Outrage churned through me.
Outrage clenched inside me.
Outrage clouded my face.
Outrage coiled inside me.
Outrage coloured my cheeks.
Outrage coursed through me.
Outrage crept into me.
Outrage entered my voice.
Outrage lit my eyes.
Outrage stained my cheeks.
Outrage suffused my cheeks.
Outrage swelled inside me.
Outrage tightened my jaw.
Outrage washed over me.
My body quivered with outrage.
My chest swelled with outrage.
My ears red with outrage.
My eyes blazed with outrage.
My eyes bulged in outrage.
My eyes burned with outrage.
My eyes filled with outrage.
My eyes flared in outrage.
My eyes glittered with outrage.
My eyes shone with outrage.
My eyes smouldered with outrage.
My eyes widened in outrage.
My eyes widened with outrage.
My face contorted in outrage.
My face contorted with outrage.
My face crumpled in outrage.
My face darkened with outrage.
My face flushed with outrage.
My face glowed with outrage.
My face reddened with outrage.
My face set with outrage.
My face strained in outrage.
My face tensed with outrage.
My face tightened in outrage.
My face tightened with outrage.
My face trembled with outrage.
My face twisted in outrage.
My face twisted with outrage.
My face twitched with outrage.
My head sang with outrage.
My heart filled with outrage.
My lips twisted with outrage.
My mouth clenched in outrage.
My stomach boiled with outrage.

My throat burned with outrage.
My tone tinged with outrage.
My voice boomed in outrage.
My voice crackled with outrage.
My voice edged with outrage.
My voice ragged with outrage.
My voice rattled with outrage.
My voice shook with outrage.
My voice trembled with outrage.
Outrage burned in my chest.
Outrage burned in my eyes.
Outrage came into my voice.
Outrage chattered in my head.
Outrage churned in my gut.
Outrage churned through my belly.
Outrage coiled in my belly.
Outrage coursed through my veins.
Outrage crackled in my eyes.
Outrage crept into my tone.
Outrage crept into my voice.
Outrage curdled inside my belly.
Outrage etched in my face.
Outrage flared in my heart.
Outrage sprouted in my gut.
Outrage surged through my veins.
Outrage swelled in my throat.
I felt a sense of outrage.
I felt a zip of outrage.
My eyebrows shot up in outrage.
My eyes went wide in outrage.

My eyes went wide with outrage.
My eyes were wide with outrage.
My face screwed up in outrage.
My face turned flush with outrage.
My face turned red with outrage.
My face turned rosy with outrage.
My face was full of outrage.
My face was ruddy with outrage.
My face went dark with outrage.
My mouth dropped open in outrage.
My voice was alive with outrage.
My voice was shrill with outrage.
My voice was thick with outrage.
Outrage burned bright in my eyes.

P

PANIC

Definition: Sudden uncontrollable fear or anxiety, often causing wildly unthinking behaviour.

See ANXIETY

Panic blanketed my mind.
Panic breathed through me.
Panic charged through me.
Panic clawed at me.
Panic clenched my chest.
Panic clenched my muscles.
Panic closed my throat.
Panic clouded my eyes.
Panic clouded my mind.
Panic crashed over me.
Panic creased my face.
Panic crossed my face.
Panic curled through me.
Panic darted through me.
Panic distorted my features.
Panic distorted my voice.
Panic dulled my senses.
Panic filled my chest.
Panic filled my eyes.
Panic filled my throat.
Panic filled my voice.
Panic flooded through me.
Panic gnawed at me.
Panic grabbed at me.
Panic jolted through me.
Panic knifed through me.

Panic leaped through me.
Panic lit my face.
Panic made me tremble.
Panic mushroomed inside me.
Panic overshadowed my mind.
Panic painted my face.
Panic passed through me.
Panic raced through me.
Panic rippled through me.
Panic rolled over me.
Panic rolled through me.
Panic rose in me.
Panic rose inside me.
Panic rushed through me.
Panic settled over me.
Panic sharpened my senses.
Panic shot through me.
Panic shrieked at me.
Panic simmered inside me.
Panic slammed into me.
Panic slapped at me.
Panic spurted through me.
Panic stabbed at me.
Panic stole my breath.
Panic stole over me.
Panic stopped my breath.

Panic streaked my face.
Panic streaked through me.
Panic streamed past me.
Panic surged through me.
Panic swept my heart.
Panic swept over me.
Panic swept through me.
Panic swirled around me.
Panic thrummed through me.
Panic tightened my face.
Panic tightened my stomach.
Panic tinged my voice.
Panic touched my mind.
Panic washed over me.
Panic weakened my legs.
Panic welled inside me.
Panic welled within me.
Panic went through me.
Panic widened my eyes.
My body rushed with panic.
My body tensed with panic.
My body went into panic.
My eyes filled with panic.
My eyes flared with panic.
My eyes flashed with panic.
My eyes lit with panic.
My eyes rolled in panic.
My eyes widened in panic.
My eyes widened with panic.
My face constricted with
panic.
My face contorted in panic.
My face flitted with panic.
My heart jolted in panic.
My voice cracked in panic.
My voice cracked with panic.
My voice edged with panic.
My voice fractured with panic.

My voice rang with panic.
My voice rose in panic.
My voice shook with panic.
My voice shrilled with panic.
Panic ballooned in my chest.
Panic blew across my mind.
Panic bloomed on my
forehead.
Panic bubbled in my chest.
Panic caught in my throat.
Panic clawed at my stomach.
Panic closed up my throat.
Panic crept into my voice.
Panic flared between my
temples.
Panic flared in my eyes.
Panic flashed across my face.
Panic flashed in my eyes.
Panic flickered across my eyes.
Panic flickered in my eyes.
Panic flickered through my
gut.
Panic fluttered in my chest.
Panic knifed through my arms.
Panic lodged in my windpipe.
Panic raced through my body.
Panic raced through my
system.
Panic rang within my skull.
Panic rippled across my face.
Panic rose in my chest.
Panic rose in my face.
Panic rose in my gut.
Panic rose in my stomach.
Panic rose in my throat.
Panic rose in my voice.
Panic seeped into my mind.
Panic showed in my voice.

Panic sifted through my mind.
Panic slashed across my face.
Panic slid down my spine.
Panic slid through my
stomach.
Panic stabbed at my chest.
Panic started in my eyes.
Panic stuck in my throat.
Panic surfaced in my eyes.
Panic swirled in my stomach.
Panic tightened around my
stomach.
Panic tightened in my chest.
Panic welled in my chest.
I felt a bubble of panic.
I felt a burst of panic.
I felt a chill of panic.
I felt a dart of panic.
I felt a flash of panic.
I felt a flicker of panic.
I felt a flush of panic.
I felt a flutter of panic.
I felt a jolt of panic.
I felt a level of panic.
I felt a moment of panic.
I felt a punch of panic.
I felt a rush of panic.
I felt a rustle of panic.
I felt a sense of panic.
I felt a shock of panic.
I felt a shot of panic.
I felt a shudder of panic.
I felt a spasm of panic.
I felt a stab of panic.
I felt a surge of panic.
I felt a swell of panic.
I felt a tickle of panic.
I felt a trickle of panic.

I felt a twinge of panic.
I felt a wave of panic.
I felt an edge of panic.
I felt an instant of panic.
I swallowed a rush of panic.
My eyes flew open as panic.
My eyes were bright with
panic.
My eyes were wide in panic.
My eyes were wide with panic.
My eyes were wild with panic.
My head jerked up in panic.
My voice was hoarse with
panic.
My voice was thin with panic.
Panic sat thick in my throat.

PASSION

Definition: An intense desire or enthusiasm for something.
See DESIRE

Passion boiled inside me.
Passion bubbled through me.
Passion caressed my mouth.
Passion clawed at me.
Passion clouded my mind.
Passion coursed through me.
Passion crowded my chest.
Passion curled through me.
Passion darkened my eyes.
Passion darkened my irises.
Passion dilated my eyes.
Passion drifted through me.
Passion entered my voice.
Passion exploded inside me.
Passion exploded within me.
Passion filled my head.
Passion flowed over me.
Passion flowed through me.
Passion fluttered inside me.
Passion glowed inside me.
Passion gushed through me.
Passion heated my blood.
Passion knifed through me.
Passion laced my voice.
Passion licked through me.
Passion made me melt.
Passion penetrated my heart.
Passion poured through me.
Passion pulsed through me.
Passion pumped through me.
Passion radiated from me.
Passion ravaged my face.
Passion rippled through me.

Passion rose from me.
Passion rose in me.
Passion shattered within me.
Passion slammed into me.
Passion sluiced through me.
Passion spiralled through me.
Passion splintered through me.
Passion surged through me.
Passion swelled within me.
Passion swept through me.
Passion swirled through me.
Passion thickened my voice.
Passion tightened inside me.
Passion tightened my features.
Passion wafted through me.
Passion warmed my insides.
Passion washed through me.
Passion went through me.
My blood burned with passion.
My blood heated with passion.
My body burned with passion.
My body drugged with passion.
My body hardened with passion.
My body heated with passion.
My body hummed with passion.
My body jangled with passion.
My body shivered with passion.
My body stirred with passion.

My body thrummed with passion.
My body twitched with passion.
My body unfurled with passion.
My body vibrated with passion.
My ears shut in passion.
My eyes blazed with passion.
My eyes danced with passion.
My eyes darkened with passion.
My eyes dilated with passion.
My eyes filled with passion.
My eyes flared with passion.
My eyes flickered with passion.
My eyes glazed with passion.
My eyes gleamed with passion.
My eyes glittered with passion.
My eyes glowed with passion.
My eyes hooded with passion.
My eyes lit with passion.
My eyes narrowed with passion.
My eyes shimmered with passion.
My eyes sparkled with passion.
My face filled with passion.
My face flushed with passion.
My face mottled with passion.
My heart burned with passion.
My heart swelled with passion.
My pulse raced with passion.
My skin blushed with passion.
My skin flushed with passion.
My voice sang with passion.
My voice shook with passion.

My voice slurred with passion.
Passion banked in my eyes.
Passion combated in my brain.
Passion danced in my belly.
Passion exploded in my chest.
Passion flamed in my expression.
Passion flared in my eyes.
Passion flashed in my eyes.
Passion flashed into my eyes.
Passion flickered in my expression.
Passion flickered in my eyes.
Passion glittered in my eyes.
Passion nipped at my skin.
Passion throbbed against my belly.
My body was overwrought with passion.
My eyes grew hazy with passion.
My eyes went dark with passion.
My eyes were bloodshot with passion.
My eyes were bright with passion.
My eyes were dark with passion.
My eyes were full of passion.
My eyes were hazy with passion.
My eyes were heavy with passion.
My face glazed over with passion.
My throat was thick with passion.

My voice was rough with
passion.
My voice was thick with
passion.
Passion curled deep in my
belly.
Passion pooled low in my
belly.

PESSIMISM

Definition: A tendency to see the worst aspect of things or believe that the worst will happen.

See GLOOM

Pessimism came over me.
Pessimism clouded my expression.
Pessimism crashed over me.
Pessimism crept over me.
Pessimism crossed my face.
Pessimism crossed my features.
Pessimism darkened my eyes.
Pessimism descended on me.
Pessimism descended over me.
Pessimism ebbed over me.
Pessimism entered my voice.
Pessimism filled my eyes.
Pessimism filled my voice.
Pessimism hovered over me.
Pessimism howled through me.
Pessimism invaded my eyes.
Pessimism lined my face.
Pessimism obscured my vision.
Pessimism ravaged my body.
Pessimism rose off me.
Pessimism seeped into me.
Pessimism settled on me.
Pessimism settled over me.
Pessimism sizzled through me.
Pessimism spiralled through me.
Pessimism squeezed my chest.
Pessimism swept over me.
Pessimism swept through me.
Pessimism tinged my eyes.

Pessimism tinged my voice.
Pessimism tugged at me.
Pessimism washed over me.
Pessimism weighed on me.
Pessimism welled inside me.
My eyes drooped with pessimism.
My eyes filled with pessimism.
My eyes shadowed in pessimism.
My face clenched with pessimism.
My face creased with pessimism.
My face crumpled with pessimism.
My face darkened with pessimism.
My face descended with pessimism.
My face drawn in pessimism.
My face etched with pessimism.
My face filled with pessimism.
My face sagged with pessimism.
My face sunk in pessimism.
My mind beset with pessimism.
My tone laced with pessimism.
My tone shaded with pessimism.

My tone softened with
pessimism.
My voice filled with
pessimism.
My voice infused with
pessimism.
My voice laced with
pessimism.
My voice tinged with
pessimism.
Pessimism came into my eyes.
Pessimism came into my voice.
Pessimism crept into my
expression.
Pessimism drifted across my
face.
Pessimism flickered in my eyes.
Pessimism flickered in my face.
Pessimism lay in my heart.
Pessimism lingered in my eyes.
Pessimism passed over my face.
Pessimism ran down my spine.
Pessimism seeped into my
muscles.
Pessimism settled in my heart.
Pessimism settled on my face.
Pessimism settled on my
shoulders.
Pessimism showed in my eyes.
Pessimism welled in my chest.
Pessimism welled in my eyes.
My eyes were full of pessimism.
My face was heavy with
pessimism.
My tone was thick with
pessimism.
My voice was full of
pessimism.

My voice was heavy with
pessimism.
My voice was soft with
pessimism.
A touch of pessimism came
into my eyes.

PITY

Definition: The feeling of sorrow and compassion caused by the sufferings and misfortunes of others.

See COMPASSION

Pity clouded my eyes.
Pity coloured my words.
Pity crossed my face.
Pity darkened my eyes.
Pity filled my eyes.
Pity flooded my heart.
Pity rippled through me.
Pity rolled through me.
Pity seeped through me.
Pity softened my expression.
Pity stirred in me.
Pity surged through me.
Pity touched my eyes.
Pity touched my voice.
Pity tugged at me.
Pity warred inside me.
Pity welled inside me.
My chest squeezed with pity.
My chest tightened in pity.
My eyes brimmed with pity.
My eyes darkened with pity.
My eyes filled with pity.
My eyes flickered with pity.
My eyes glowed with pity.
My eyes moistened with pity.
My eyes softened with pity.
My eyes warmed with pity.
My face burned in pity.
My face filled with pity.
My face throbbed in pity.
My face twisted with pity.
My head throbbed in pity.

My heart ached with pity.
My heart clenched with pity.
My heart filled with pity.
My heart lurched in pity.
My heart overflowed with pity.
My heart sank with pity.
My heart squeezed in pity.
My heart swelled with pity.
My heart twisted with pity.
My lips twitched in pity.
My mouth parted in pity.
My stomach growled in pity.
My stomach gurgled in pity.
My stomach knotted with pity.
My stomach murmured in pity.
My stomach rumbled in pity.
My stomach tightened in pity.
My tone filled with pity.
My voice dripped with pity.
My voice filled with pity.
My voice laced with pity.
My voice throbbed with pity.
Pity blazed in my eyes.
Pity crept into my voice.
Pity registered in my eyes.
Pity rolled into my head.
Pity shone in my eyes.
Pity shone in my face.
Pity showed on my face.
Pity stirred in my gut.
Pity welled in my chest.

I felt a jolt of pity.
I felt a kind of pity.
I felt a mixture of pity.
I felt a moment of pity.
I felt a pang of pity.
I felt a rush of pity.
I felt a stab of pity.
I felt a sting of pity.
I felt a surge of pity.
I felt a touch of pity.
I felt a tug of pity.
I felt a twinge of pity.
I felt a twist of pity.
I felt a wave of pity.
My eyes were full of pity.
My eyes were warm with pity.
My eyes were wide with pity.
My face was full of pity.
My face was soft with pity.
My mouth turned down in
pity.
My mouth went soft with pity.
My voice pitched low with
pity.
My voice was full of pity.

PLEASURE

Definition: A feeling of happy satisfaction and enjoyment.

See HAPPINESS

I beamed with pleasure.
I blushed with pleasure.
I flushed with pleasure.
I gasped as pleasure.
I gasped in pleasure.
I gasped with pleasure.
I grinned with pleasure.
I groaned in pleasure.
I groaned with pleasure.
I grunted in pleasure.
I grunted with pleasure.
I moaned with pleasure.
I sighed with pleasure.
I smiled with pleasure.
Pleasure coursed through me.
Pleasure crashed through me.
Pleasure crawled over me.
Pleasure encircled my head.
Pleasure exploded within me.
Pleasure filled my chest.
Pleasure filled my lungs.
Pleasure flowed through me.
Pleasure hummed through me.
Pleasure licked through me.
Pleasure melted my bones.
Pleasure moved through me.
Pleasure pierced my brain.
Pleasure poured through me.
Pleasure raced through me.
Pleasure radiated through me.
Pleasure ran through me.
Pleasure ripped through me.
Pleasure rippled through me.

Pleasure roared through me.
Pleasure rocked through me.
Pleasure seared my senses.
Pleasure shot through me.
Pleasure shuddered through me.
Pleasure sliced through me.
Pleasure spiked through me.
Pleasure splintered my brain.
Pleasure stole through me.
Pleasure swept through me.
Pleasure touched my face.
Pleasure washed over me.
Pleasure washed through me.
My body jerked in pleasure.
My body sighed in pleasure.
My body teemed with pleasure.
My eyes closed in pleasure.
My eyes closed with pleasure.
My eyes crinkled with pleasure.
My eyes flashed with pleasure.
My eyes glazed with pleasure.
My eyes glowed with pleasure.
My eyes rolled with pleasure.
My eyes shut with pleasure.
My eyes sparkled with pleasure.
My eyes widened with pleasure.
My face danced with pleasure.
My face flushed with pleasure.

My face lit with pleasure.
My heart sighed with pleasure.
My lips twitched with pleasure.
My mouth opened in pleasure.
My skin mottled with pleasure.
Pleasure appeared on my face.
Pleasure burned in my stomach.
Pleasure flowed from my lips.
Pleasure glided through my body.
Pleasure infused in my expression.
Pleasure raced down my spine.
Pleasure ran through my voice.
Pleasure rocked through my body.
Pleasure rumbled from my throat.
Pleasure shimmied down my spine.
Pleasure skittered down my body.
Pleasure sparked through my system.
Pleasure swept across my face.
Pleasure vibrated along my skin.
Pleasure washed over my body.
I felt a bolt of pleasure.
I felt a flush of pleasure.
I felt a glow of pleasure.
I felt a jolt of pleasure.
I felt a quiver of pleasure.
I felt a rush of pleasure.
I felt a shock of pleasure.
I felt a stab of pleasure.

I felt a surge of pleasure.
I felt a swell of pleasure.
I felt a thrill of pleasure.
I felt a tingle of pleasure.
I felt a twist of pleasure.
I felt a wave of pleasure.
I gave a cry of pleasure.
I gave a gasp of pleasure.
I gave a shudder of pleasure.
I gave a sigh of pleasure.
I sighed an oooohhh of pleasure.
My eyes slid shut in pleasure.
My face grew radiant with pleasure.
My face was aglow with pleasure.
My face was rapt with pleasure.

PRIDE

Definition: A feeling or deep pleasure or satisfaction derived from one's own achievements.

See PLEASURE

I beamed with pride.
I flushed with pride.
I grinned with pride.
I smiled with pride.
I swelled with pride.
Pride burned inside me.
Pride coursed through me.
Pride crashed through me.
Pride crawled over me.
Pride encircled my head.
Pride entered my voice.
Pride exploded within me.
Pride filled my chest.
Pride filled my lungs.
Pride flowed through me.
Pride glowed from me.
Pride hummed through me.
Pride licked through me.
Pride melted my bones.
Pride moved through me.
Pride pierced my brain.
Pride poured through me.
Pride raced through me.
Pride radiated through me.
Pride ran through me.
Pride ripped through me.
Pride rippled through me.
Pride roared through me.
Pride rocked through me.
Pride seared my senses.
Pride shot through me.
Pride shuddered through me.

Pride sliced through me.
Pride spiked through me.
Pride splintered my brain.
Pride stirred inside me.
Pride stole through me.
Pride swept through me.
Pride touched my face.
Pride washed over me.
Pride washed through me.
My body jerked in pride.
My body sighed in pride.
My body teemed with pride.
My chest choked with pride.
My chest expanded with pride.
My chest puffed with pride.
My chest swelled with pride.
My eyes burned with pride.
My eyes closed in pride.
My eyes closed with pride.
My eyes crinkled with pride.
My eyes filled with pride.
My eyes flashed with pride.
My eyes glazed with pride.
My eyes gleamed with pride.
My eyes glistened with pride.
My eyes glowed with pride.
My eyes rolled with pride.
My eyes shone with pride.
My eyes shut with pride.
My eyes sparkled with pride.
My eyes widened with pride.
My face beamed with pride.

My face danced with pride.
My face flushed with pride.
My face lit with pride.
My heart burned with pride.
My heart burst with pride.
My heart glowed with pride.
My heart sighed with pride.
My heart swelled with pride.
My lips twitched with pride.
My mouth opened in pride.
My skin mottled with pride.
My voice filled with pride.
My voice oozed with pride.
My voice rose with pride.
My voice tinged with pride.
Pride appeared on my face.
Pride broke through my tears.
Pride burned in my stomach.
Pride flowed from my lips.
Pride glided through my body.
Pride infused in my expression.
Pride mushroomed in my
chest.
Pride oozed through my veins.
Pride raced down my spine.
Pride ran through my voice.
Pride rocked through my
body.
Pride rose up my throat.
Pride rumbled from my throat.
Pride shimmied down my
spine.
Pride shone in my eyes.
Pride skittered down my body.
Pride sparked through my
system.
Pride swept across my face.
Pride vibrated along my skin.

Pride washed over my body.
I felt a burst of pride.
I felt a flash of pride.
I felt a flush of pride.
I felt a lilt of pride.
I felt a measure of pride.
I felt a moment of pride.
I felt a pang of pride.
I felt a prick of pride.
I felt a prickle of pride.
I felt a rush of pride.
I felt a sense of pride.
I felt a spike of pride.
I felt a squeeze of pride.
I felt a surge of pride.
I felt a swell of pride.
I felt a thrill of pride.
I felt a tinge of pride.
I felt a touch of pride.
I felt a twinge of pride.
I felt an amount of pride.
My chest puffed out with
pride.
My chest puffed up with pride.
My eyes lit up with pride.
My eyes slid shut in pride.
My face grew radiant with
pride.
My face was aglow with pride.
My face was rapt with pride.

R

RAGE
Definition: Violent uncontrollable anger.
See ANGER

I bellowed with rage.
I burned with rage.
I moaned in rage.
I simmered with rage.
Rage ate at me.
Rage ate my soul.
Rage bloomed inside me.
Rage boiled inside me.
Rage boiled within me.
Rage broke over me.
Rage bubbled in me.
Rage bubbled inside me.
Rage built inside me.
Rage buried inside me.
Rage burned within me.
Rage came over me.
Rage churned through me.
Rage clawed at me.
Rage coursed through me.
Rage curled in me.
Rage darkened my eyes.
Rage distorted my face.
Rage engorged my face.
Rage erupted from me.
Rage erupted inside me.
Rage expanded my insides.
Rage filled my ears.

Rage filled my throat.
Rage filled my voice.
Rage flared in me.
Rage flashed over me.
Rage flew through me.
Rage fuelled my blood.
Rage grew inside me.
Rage hardened my tone.
Rage heated my blood.
Rage heated my bloodstream.
Rage hung over me.
Rage iced my tone.
Rage poured off me.
Rage poured through me.
Rage pulsed through me.
Rage pummelled my insides.
Rage roared through me.
Rage roiled inside me.
Rage rose in me.
Rage rose inside me.
Rage seared my eyes.
Rage seared my face.
Rage seethed inside me.
Rage seized my body.
Rage shook my body.
Rage shot through me.
Rage shrilled my voice.

Rage surged through me.
Rage swelled inside me.
Rage swelled within me.
Rage swept through me.
Rage tightened my face.
Rage tore through me.
Rage trembled through me.
Rage twisted my face.
Rage twisted my features.
Rage volleyed through me.
Rage washed through me.
My body seethed with rage.
My body shook with rage.
My body steeped in rage.
My body trembled with rage.
My chest tightened with rage.
My eyes blazed with rage.
My eyes bulged with rage.
My eyes burned with rage.
My eyes danced with rage.
My eyes filled with rage.
My eyes flared with rage.
My eyes flashed with rage.
My eyes flickered with rage.
My eyes glinted with rage.
My eyes glittered with rage.
My eyes narrowed with rage.
My eyes rolled with rage.
My eyes seethed with rage.
My eyes shimmered with rage.
My eyes slitted with rage.
My eyes squinted with rage.
My eyes widened with rage.
My face contorted in rage.
My face contorted with rage.
My face distorted with rage.
My face filled with rage.
My face flushed with rage.

My face knotted with rage.
My face reddened with rage.
My face suffused with rage.
My face swollen with rage.
My face twisted in rage.
My face twisted with rage.
My face writhed with rage.
My heart filled with rage.
My heart pounded with rage.
My heart swelled with rage.
My lips contorted in rage.
My lips tightened with rage.
My lips trembled with rage.
My mouth tightened in rage.
My mouth twisted in rage.
My mouth twisted with rage.
My neck pulsed with rage.
My skin flushed with rage.
My vision blurred with rage.
My voice choked with rage.
My voice filled with rage.
My voice ragged with rage.
My voice seared with rage.
My voice trembled with rage.
My voice vibrated with rage.
Rage ate at my gut.
Rage ate at my soul.
Rage balled inside my stomach.
Rage boiled in my belly.
Rage burned in my eyes.
Rage burned in my stomach.
Rage burned on my face.
Rage chained in my eyes.
Rage circulated in my blood.
Rage coursed through my
veins.
Rage exploded in my chest.
Rage flared in my chest.

Rage flared in my eyes.
Rage flared on my face.
Rage flashed in my eyes.
Rage glowed from my eyes.
Rage rippled through my blood.
Rage rose in my chest.
Rage rose in my gut.
Rage rose in my throat.
Rage seeped into my voice.
Rage seethed in my eyes.
Rage sparked in my eyes.
Rage splintered through my blood.
Rage swept through my veins.
Rage swirled behind my eyes.
Rage welled in my eyes.
I felt a bolt of rage.
I felt a burst of rage.
I felt a flash of rage.
I felt a flood of rage.
I felt a flush of rage.
I felt a pinch of rage.
I felt a shock of rage.
I felt a spurt of rage.
I felt a surge of rage.
I felt a tremor of rage.
I felt a wash of rage.
I felt a wave of rage.
I felt an upwelling of rage.
I gave a scream of rage.
I uttered a cry of rage.
I uttered a snarl of rage.
My eyes flashed hot with rage.
My eyes glazed over with rage.
My eyes were black with rage.
My eyes were dark with rage.
My eyes were dull with rage.

My eyes were full of rage.
My eyes were insane with rage.
My eyes were wide in rage.
My eyes were wide with rage.
My eyes were wild with rage.
My face screwed up with rage.
My face shaded white with rage.
My face turned crimson with rage.
My face turned purple with rage.
My face turned red in rage.
My face turned red with rage.
My face turned white with rage.
My face was purple with rage.
My face was red with rage.
My face was unrecognizable with rage.
My face was white with rage.
My face was wild with rage.
My face went red with rage.
My heart was full of rage.
My voice was full of rage.

RAPTURE

Definition: A feeling of intense pleasure or joy.

See PLEASURE

Rapture coursed through me.
Rapture crashed through me.
Rapture crawled over me.
Rapture encircled my head.
Rapture exploded within me.
Rapture filled my chest.
Rapture filled my lungs.
Rapture flowed through me.
Rapture hummed through me.
Rapture licked through me.
Rapture melted my bones.
Rapture moved through me.
Rapture pierced my brain.
Rapture poured through me.
Rapture raced through me.
Rapture radiated through me.
Rapture ran through me.
Rapture ripped through me.
Rapture rippled through me.
Rapture roared through me.
Rapture rocked through me.
Rapture seared my senses.
Rapture shot through me.
Rapture shuddered through me.
Rapture sliced through me.
Rapture spiked through me.
Rapture splintered my brain.
Rapture stole through me.
Rapture swept through me.
Rapture touched my face.
Rapture washed over me.
Rapture washed through me.

My body jerked in rapture.
My body sighed in rapture.
My body teemed with rapture.
My eyes closed in rapture.
My eyes closed with rapture.
My eyes crinkled with rapture.
My eyes flashed with rapture.
My eyes glazed with rapture.
My eyes glowed with rapture.
My eyes rolled with rapture.
My eyes shut with rapture.
My eyes sparkled with rapture.
My eyes widened with rapture.
My face danced with rapture.
My face flushed with rapture.
My face lit with rapture.
My face stunned with rapture.
My heart sighed with rapture.
My lips twitched with rapture.
My mouth opened in rapture.
My skin mottled with rapture.
Rapture appeared on my face.
Rapture burned in my stomach.
Rapture came over my face.
Rapture flowed from my lips.
Rapture glided through my body.
Rapture infused in my expression.
Rapture raced down my spine.
Rapture ran through my voice.

Rapture rocked through my
body.
Rapture rumbled from my
throat.
Rapture shimmied down my
spine.
Rapture skittered down my
body.
Rapture sparked through my
system.
Rapture swept across my face.
Rapture vibrated along my
skin.
Rapture washed over my body.
My eyes slid shut in rapture.
My face grew radiant with
rapture.
My face was aglow with
rapture.
My face was rapt with rapture.

REGRET

Definition: A feeling of sadness, repentance, or disappointment over an occurrence or something that one has done or failed to do.
See SADNESS

I sighed with regret.
Regret came over me.
Regret clouded my expression.
Regret crashed over me.
Regret crept over me.
Regret crossed my face.
Regret crossed my features.
Regret darkened my eyes.
Regret ebbed over me.
Regret entered my voice.
Regret filled my eyes.
Regret filled my voice.
Regret howled through me.
Regret invaded my eyes.
Regret laced my voice.
Regret lined my face.
Regret nagged at me.
Regret painted my face.
Regret rose off me.
Regret sang in me.
Regret seeped into me.
Regret settled over me.
Regret sizzled through me.
Regret slammed into me.
Regret sliced at me.
Regret spiralled through me.
Regret squeezed my chest.
Regret swelled inside me.
Regret swept through me.
Regret tightened my chest.
Regret tinged my eyes.
Regret tinged my voice.

Regret tugged at me.
Regret twisted my mouth.
Regret washed over me.
Regret washed through me.
Regret weighed on me.
Regret welled inside me.
My eyes drooped with regret.
My eyes filled with regret.
My eyes shadowed in regret.
My eyes shadowed with regret.
My face creased with regret.
My face crumpled with regret.
My face darkened with regret.
My face etched with regret.
My face filled with regret.
My face sagged with regret.
My heart flooded with regret.
My tone laced with regret.
My tone shaded with regret.
My tone softened with regret.
My voice filled with regret.
My voice infused with regret.
My voice laced with regret.
My voice poisoned with regret.
My voice tinged with regret.
Regret came into my eyes.
Regret came into my voice.
Regret crept into my
expression.
Regret drifted across my face.
Regret flashed in my eyes.
Regret flickered in my eyes.

Regret flickered in my face.
Regret lay in my heart.
Regret lingered in my eyes.
Regret passed over my face.
Regret seeped into my muscles.
Regret settled on my face.
Regret showed in my eyes.
Regret sounded in my voice.
Regret surged through my
head.
Regret welled in my chest.
Regret welled in my eyes.
I exhaled a sigh of regret.
I felt a flash of regret.
I felt a mix of regret.
I felt a moment of regret.
I felt a pang of regret.
I felt a qualm of regret.
I felt a rush of regret.
I felt a sense of regret.
I felt a stab of regret.
I felt a surge of regret.
I felt a tinge of regret.
I felt a tug of regret.
I felt a twinge of regret.
I felt a wave of regret.
I felt an ounce of regret.
My eyes were full of regret.
My face was heavy with regret.
My tone was thick with regret.
My voice was feeble with
regret.
My voice was full of regret.
My voice was soft with regret.
A touch of regret came into
my eyes.

RELIEF

Definition: A feeling of reassurance and relaxation following release from anxiety or distress.

I exhaled in relief.
I exhaled with relief.
I gasped with relief.
I grinned in relief.
I grinned with relief.
I groaned with relief.
I grunted with relief.
I sighed in relief.
I sighed with relief.
I smiled in relief.
I smiled with relief.
I sobbed with relief.
I swallowed with relief.
Relief came over me.
Relief coursed through me.
Relief crashed over me.
Relief crossed my face.
Relief filled my face.
Relief flooded my body.
Relief flooded my face.
Relief flooded over me.
Relief flooded through me.
Relief flowed through me.
Relief lightened my heart.
Relief niggled at me.
Relief passed my face.
Relief passed over me.
Relief passed through me.
Relief poured through me.
Relief pulsed through me.
Relief roared through me.
Relief rushed over me.
Relief rushed through me.

Relief settled over me.
Relief shuddered through me.
Relief slid my fingers.
Relief softened my eyes.
Relief softened my face.
Relief softened my features.
Relief softened my mood.
Relief spilled over me.
Relief spilled through me.
Relief spread my face.
Relief stilled my tongue.
Relief stole over me.
Relief surged through me.
Relief swept over me.
Relief swept through me.
Relief warmed my gut.
Relief washed over me.
Relief washed through me.
Relief weakened my knees.
Relief wet my cheeks.
Relief whirled inside me.
Relief whispered through me.
Relief whooshed through me.
My body deflated in relief.
My body sagged with relief.
My chest eased with relief.
My chest heaved with relief.
My eyes filled with relief.
My eyes widened in relief.
My face lit with relief.
My face melted with relief.
My face mixed with relief.
My face sagged with relief.

My face shone with relief.
My face suffused with relief.
My heart bounded with relief.
My heart filled with relief.
My heart pounded with relief.
My shoulders drooped with relief.
My shoulders dropped in relief.
My shoulders heaved with relief.
My shoulders relaxed in relief.
My shoulders sagged in relief.
My shoulders sagged with relief.
My shoulders sank in relief.
My shoulders slumped in relief.
My shoulders slumped with relief.
My skin exhaled in relief.
My voice cracked with relief.
My voice flooded with relief.
My voice lifted with relief.
Relief bloomed on my face.
Relief crept across my face.
Relief echoed in my sigh.
Relief flashed in my eyes.
Relief flickered in my eyes.
Relief flooded through my body.
Relief flooded through my mind.
Relief loosened up my shoulder.
Relief plastered on my face.
Relief showed in my eyes.
Relief showed on my face.

Relief spilled across my features.
Relief streamed down my cheeks.
Relief streamed through my body.
Relief travelled down my spine.
Relief washed down my back.
Relief washed over my face.
Relief washed through my mind.
Relief whistled through my lips.
I exhaled a breath of relief.
I exhaled a sigh of relief.
I felt a bit of relief.
I felt a current of relief.
I felt a flicker of relief.
I felt a flood of relief.
I felt a flush of relief.
I felt a gust of relief.
I felt a hint of relief.
I felt a jolt of relief.
I felt a kind of relief.
I felt a leap of relief.
I felt a lift of relief.
I felt a lurch of relief.
I felt a measure of relief.
I felt a mixture of relief.
I felt a moment of relief.
I felt a pang of relief.
I felt a rush of relief.
I felt a sense of relief.
I felt a shudder of relief.
I felt a spike of relief.
I felt a stir of relief.
I felt a surge of relief.

I felt a swell of relief.
I felt a twinge of relief.
I felt a wash of relief.
I felt a wave of relief.
I felt an amount of relief.
I gave a gasp of relief.
I gave a laugh of relief.
I gave a shudder of relief.
I gave a sigh of relief.
I gave a sob of relief.
I gave an exclamation of relief.
I grinned a sigh of relief.
I sighed a sigh of relief.
I uttered a gasp of relief.
I uttered a sigh of relief.
My body was flaccid with
relief.
My eyes lit up with relief.
My face lit up with relief.
My face was full of relief.
My knees went weak with
relief.
My voice turned husky with
relief.

REMORSE

Definition: Deep regret or guilt for a wrong committed.

See REGRET

Remorse came over me.
Remorse clouded my expression.
Remorse clutched my heart.
Remorse crashed over me.
Remorse crept over me.
Remorse crossed my face.
Remorse crossed my features.
Remorse darkened my eyes.
Remorse ebbed over me.
Remorse entered my voice.
Remorse filled my eyes.
Remorse filled my voice.
Remorse flooded through me.
Remorse howled through me.
Remorse invaded my eyes.
Remorse laced my voice.
Remorse lined my face.
Remorse nagged at me.
Remorse painted my face.
Remorse rose off me.
Remorse sang in me.
Remorse seeped into me.
Remorse settled over me.
Remorse shot through me.
Remorse sizzled through me.
Remorse slammed into me.
Remorse sliced at me.
Remorse spiralled through me.
Remorse squeezed my chest.
Remorse squeezed my soul.
Remorse swelled inside me.
Remorse swept through me.

Remorse tightened my chest.
Remorse tinged my eyes.
Remorse tinged my voice.
Remorse tugged at me.
Remorse twisted my mouth.
Remorse washed over me.
Remorse washed through me.
Remorse weighed on me.
Remorse welled inside me.
My eyes drooped with remorse.
My eyes filled with remorse.
My eyes shadowed in remorse.
My eyes shadowed with remorse.
My face creased with remorse.
My face crumpled with remorse.
My face darkened with remorse.
My face etched with remorse.
My face filled with remorse.
My face sagged with remorse.
My heart flooded with remorse.
My tone laced with remorse.
My tone shaded with remorse.
My tone softened with remorse.
My voice filled with remorse.
My voice infused with remorse.
My voice laced with remorse.

My voice poisoned with remorse.
My voice tinged with remorse.
Remorse came into my eyes.
Remorse came into my voice.
Remorse crept into my expression.
Remorse drifted across my face.
Remorse flashed in my eyes.
Remorse flickered in my eyes.
Remorse flickered in my face.
Remorse lay in my heart.
Remorse lingered in my eyes.
Remorse passed over my face.
Remorse seeped into my muscles.
Remorse settled on my face.
Remorse showed in my eyes.
Remorse sounded in my voice.
Remorse surged through my head.
Remorse welled in my chest.
Remorse welled in my eyes.
I felt a pang of remorse.
I felt a smidge of remorse.
I felt a spasm of remorse.
I felt a stab of remorse.
I felt a sting of remorse.
I felt a twinge of remorse.
I felt a wave of remorse.
I felt an ounce of remorse.
My eyes were full of remorse.
My eyes were hot with remorse.
My face was heavy with remorse.

My shoulders weighted down with remorse.
My tone was thick with remorse.
My voice was feeble with remorse.
My voice was full of remorse.
My voice was soft with remorse.
A touch of remorse came into my eyes.

RESENTMENT

Definition: Bitter indignation at having been treated unfairly.

See BITTERNESS

Resentment burned inside me.
Resentment burned through me.
Resentment burned within me.
Resentment churned inside me.
Resentment churned through me.
Resentment clenched inside me.
Resentment clouded my face.
Resentment coiled inside me.
Resentment coloured my cheeks.
Resentment coursed through me.
Resentment crept into me.
Resentment entered my voice.
Resentment filled my throat.
Resentment laced my humour.
Resentment laced my voice.
Resentment lit my eyes.
Resentment poured over me.
Resentment stained my cheeks.
Resentment suffused my cheeks.
Resentment swelled inside me.
Resentment tightened my jaw.
Resentment washed over me.
My body quickened in resentment.
My body quivered with resentment.
My chest swelled with resentment.
My eyebrows climbed in resentment.
My eyes blazed with resentment.
My eyes dazzled in resentment.
My eyes filled with resentment.
My eyes glittered with resentment.
My eyes shone with resentment.
My eyes smouldered with resentment.
My eyes widened with resentment.
My face crumpled in resentment.
My face darkened with resentment.
My face filled with resentment.
My face flushed with resentment.
My face reddened with resentment.
My face set with resentment.
My face strained in resentment.
My face tensed with resentment.

My face tightened in resentment.
My face tightened with resentment.
My face trembled with resentment.
My face twisted in resentment.
My face twisted with resentment.
My face twitched with resentment.
My head ached in resentment.
My head sang with resentment.
My heart filled with resentment.
My heart seethed with resentment.
My lips twisted with resentment.
My stomach boiled with resentment.
My tone drenched with resentment.
My tone laden with resentment.
My tone reeked of resentment.
My voice crackled with resentment.
My voice edged with resentment.
My voice laced with resentment.
My voice ragged with resentment.
My voice rattled with resentment.

My voice sank with resentment.
My voice shook with resentment.
My voice tinged with resentment.
Resentment burned in my chest.
Resentment burned in my eyes.
Resentment came into my voice.
Resentment chattered in my head.
Resentment churned in my gut.
Resentment churned through my belly.
Resentment coiled in my belly.
Resentment coursed through my veins.
Resentment crackled in my eyes.
Resentment crept into my tone.
Resentment crept into my voice.
Resentment curdled inside my belly.
Resentment edged into my voice.
Resentment flared in my heart.
Resentment rose in my throat.
Resentment shone in my eyes.
Resentment sprouted in my gut.
Resentment swelled in my throat.

I felt a spot of resentment.
I felt a stab of resentment.
I felt a surge of resentment.
I felt a touch of resentment.
I felt a twinge of resentment.
I felt a twist of resentment.
My eyes were wide with
resentment.
My face screwed up in
resentment.
My face turned flush with
resentment.
My face turned red with
resentment.
My face turned rosy with
resentment.
My face was ruddy with
resentment.
My face went dark with
resentment.
My voice trailed off in
resentment.
My voice was alive with
resentment.
My voice was shrill with
resentment.
Resentment burned bright in
my eyes.

REVULSION

Definition: A sense of disgust and loathing.
See DISGUST

I shuddered in revulsion.
I shuddered with revulsion.
Revulsion altered my face.
Revulsion ate at me.
Revulsion came over me.
Revulsion choked my throat.
Revulsion coloured my voice.
Revulsion crossed my face.
Revulsion filled my face.
Revulsion flooded over me.
Revulsion pervaded my tone.
Revulsion puckered my lips.
Revulsion ripped through me.
Revulsion rippled through me.
Revulsion rolled through me.
Revulsion tinged my voice.
Revulsion trickled over me.
My eyes widened in revulsion.
My face clouded with
revulsion.
My face contorted in
revulsion.
My face creased with revulsion.
My face filled with revulsion.
My face grimaced in revulsion.
My face twisted in revulsion.
My face twisted with
revulsion.
My face wrinkled in revulsion.
My face wrinkled with
revulsion.
My gut clenched with
revulsion.

My gut tightened with
revulsion.
My heart burned with
revulsion.
My lips curled in revulsion.
My lips curled with revulsion.
My lips snarled in revulsion.
My lips twisted in revulsion.
My mouth twisted in
revulsion.
My mouth twisted with
revulsion.
My nose crinkled in revulsion.
My nose wrinkled in revulsion.
My nose wrinkled with
revulsion.
My skin tingled with
revulsion.
My stomach heaved with
revulsion.
My tone filled with revulsion.
My voice laced with revulsion.
My voice thickened with
revulsion.
My voice tightened with
revulsion.
Revulsion came across my face.
Revulsion dripped in my tone.
Revulsion flooded into my
heart.
Revulsion fought in my throat.
Revulsion fought in my voice.
Revulsion glowed in my eyes.

Revulsion made my stomach
churn.
Revulsion rose in my stomach.
Revulsion seeped from my
pores.
Revulsion wiggled down my
frame.
I felt a cramp of revulsion.
I felt a sense of revulsion.
I felt a shiver of revulsion.
I felt a spasm of revulsion.
I felt a wave of revulsion.
I gave a cry of revulsion.
I uttered a cry of revulsion.
My face creased up in
revulsion.
My face screwed up with
revulsion.
My face was stiff with
revulsion.
My mouth cocked open in
revulsion.
My mouth squashed up in
revulsion.
My tone was harsh with
revulsion.
My voice trailed off in
revulsion.
My voice was thick with
revulsion.
My face was a mask of
revulsion.

S

SADNESS

Definition: The condition or quality of being sad.

See UNHAPPINESS

Sadness came over me.
Sadness clouded my expression.
Sadness crashed over me.
Sadness crept over me.
Sadness crossed my face.
Sadness crossed my features.
Sadness darkened my eyes.
Sadness ebbed over me.
Sadness entered my voice.
Sadness filled my eyes.
Sadness filled my voice.
Sadness howled through me.
Sadness invaded my eyes.
Sadness lined my face.
Sadness rose off me.
Sadness seeped into me.
Sadness settled over me.
Sadness sizzled through me.
Sadness spiralled through me.
Sadness squeezed my chest.
Sadness swept through me.
Sadness tinged my eyes.
Sadness tinged my voice.
Sadness tugged at me.
Sadness washed over me.
Sadness weighed on me.

Sadness welled inside me.
My eyes drooped with sadness.
My eyes filled with sadness.
My eyes shadowed in sadness.
My face clenched with sadness.
My face creased with sadness.
My face crumpled with sadness.
My face darkened with sadness.
My face etched with sadness.
My face filled with sadness.
My face sagged with sadness.
My tone laced with sadness.
My tone shaded with sadness.
My tone softened with sadness.
My voice filled with sadness.
My voice infused with sadness.
My voice laced with sadness.
My voice tinged with sadness.
Sadness came into my eyes.
Sadness came into my voice.
Sadness crept into my expression.
Sadness drifted across my face.
Sadness flickered in my eyes.

Sadness flickered in my face.
Sadness lay in my heart.
Sadness lingered in my eyes.
Sadness passed over my face.
Sadness seeped into my
muscles.
Sadness settled on my face.
Sadness showed in my eyes.
Sadness welled in my chest.
Sadness welled in my eyes.
I felt a chill of sadness.
I felt a flash of sadness.
I felt a pang of sadness.
I felt a pinch of sadness.
I felt a sense of sadness.
I felt a swell of sadness.
I felt a touch of sadness.
I felt a twinge of sadness.
I felt a wave of sadness.
I gave a sigh of sadness.
My eyes were full of sadness.
My face was heavy with
sadness.
My tone was thick with
sadness.
My voice was full of sadness.
My voice was soft with
sadness.
A touch of sadness came into
my eyes.

SATISFACTION

Definition: Fulfilment of one's wishes, expectations, or needs, or the pleasure derived from this.

See CONTENTMENT

I grinned with satisfaction.
I grunted in satisfaction.
I grunted with satisfaction.
I sighed in satisfaction.
I sighed with satisfaction.
I smiled in satisfaction.
I smiled with satisfaction.
I snorted with satisfaction.
Satisfaction battered my brain.
Satisfaction came over me.
Satisfaction coursed through me.
Satisfaction crashed through me.
Satisfaction crawled over me.
Satisfaction creased my lips.
Satisfaction encircled my head.
Satisfaction exploded within me.
Satisfaction filled my chest.
Satisfaction filled my frame.
Satisfaction filled my lungs.
Satisfaction flowed through me.
Satisfaction hummed through me.
Satisfaction licked through me.
Satisfaction lit my face.
Satisfaction lit my features.
Satisfaction melted my bones.
Satisfaction moved through me.

Satisfaction passed through me.
Satisfaction pierced my brain.
Satisfaction poured through me.
Satisfaction raced through me.
Satisfaction radiated through me.
Satisfaction ran through me.
Satisfaction ripped through me.
Satisfaction rippled through me.
Satisfaction roared through me.
Satisfaction rocked through me.
Satisfaction seared my senses.
Satisfaction seeped through me.
Satisfaction settled over me.
Satisfaction shot through me.
Satisfaction shuddered through me.
Satisfaction sliced through me.
Satisfaction spiked through me.
Satisfaction splintered my brain.
Satisfaction stole through me.
Satisfaction swelled within me.
Satisfaction swept through me.

Satisfaction tinged my voice.
Satisfaction touched my face.
Satisfaction washed over me.
Satisfaction washed through me.
My body jerked in satisfaction.
My body sighed in satisfaction.
My body teemed with satisfaction.
My eyes closed in satisfaction.
My eyes closed with satisfaction.
My eyes crinkled with satisfaction.
My eyes flashed with satisfaction.
My eyes glazed with satisfaction.
My eyes gleamed in satisfaction.
My eyes glinted with satisfaction.
My eyes glowed with satisfaction.
My eyes rolled with satisfaction.
My eyes set with satisfaction.
My eyes shut with satisfaction.
My eyes sparkled with satisfaction.
My eyes widened with satisfaction.
My face beamed with satisfaction.
My face danced with satisfaction.
My face flushed with satisfaction.

My face gleamed with satisfaction.
My face lit with satisfaction.
My heart glowed with satisfaction.
My heart hummed with satisfaction.
My heart sighed with satisfaction.
My lips twitched with satisfaction.
My mouth opened in satisfaction.
My skin mottled with satisfaction.
My voice filled with satisfaction.
Satisfaction appeared on my face.
Satisfaction burned in my stomach.
Satisfaction crept over my face.
Satisfaction flickered in my eyes.
Satisfaction flowed from my lips.
Satisfaction flowed through my body.
Satisfaction glided through my body.
Satisfaction infused in my expression.
Satisfaction raced down my spine.
Satisfaction radiated from my expression.
Satisfaction ran through my voice.

Satisfaction rivered through my body.
Satisfaction rocked through my body.
Satisfaction rumbled from my throat.
Satisfaction shimmied down my spine.
Satisfaction shone on my face.
Satisfaction skittered down my body.
Satisfaction sparked through my system.
Satisfaction swept across my face.
Satisfaction vibrated along my skin.
Satisfaction washed over my body.
I exhaled a breath of satisfaction.
I felt a burst of satisfaction.
I felt a flicker of satisfaction.
I felt a glow of satisfaction.
I felt a kind of satisfaction.
I felt a measure of satisfaction.
I felt a sense of satisfaction.
I felt a stab of satisfaction.
I felt a surge of satisfaction.
I felt a thrill of satisfaction.
I felt a tingle of satisfaction.
I felt a trace of satisfaction.
I felt a twinge of satisfaction.
I felt a warmth of satisfaction.
I felt a wave of satisfaction.
I felt an amount of satisfaction.
I gave a chuckle of satisfaction.

I gave a grunt of satisfaction.
I gave a murmur of satisfaction.
I gave a nod of satisfaction.
I gave a shout of satisfaction.
I gave a sigh of satisfaction.
My eyes slid shut in satisfaction.
My eyes were bright with satisfaction.
My face grew radiant with satisfaction.
My face was aglow with satisfaction.
My face was rapt with satisfaction.
My head was high with satisfaction.

SCEPTICISM

Definition: A sceptical attitude.
See DOUBT

I darkened with scepticism.
My face registered scepticism.
Scepticism came over me.
Scepticism chewed at me.
Scepticism clouded my
expression.
Scepticism clouded my
features.
Scepticism covered my
expression.
Scepticism crashed over me.
Scepticism crept over me.
Scepticism crossed my face.
Scepticism crossed my features.
Scepticism darkened my eyes.
Scepticism darkened my face.
Scepticism descended on me.
Scepticism descended over me.
Scepticism ebbed over me.
Scepticism entered my voice.
Scepticism filled my eyes.
Scepticism filled my voice.
Scepticism hovered over me.
Scepticism howled through
me.
Scepticism invaded my eyes.
Scepticism lined my face.
Scepticism obscured my vision.
Scepticism ravaged my body.
Scepticism rose off me.
Scepticism seeped into me.
Scepticism settled on me.
Scepticism settled over me.

Scepticism sizzled through me.
Scepticism spiralled through
me.
Scepticism squeezed my chest.
Scepticism swept over me.
Scepticism swept through me.
Scepticism tinged my eyes.
Scepticism tinged my voice.
Scepticism tugged at me.
Scepticism washed over me.
Scepticism weighed on me.
Scepticism welled inside me.
I was paralyzed with
scepticism.
My eyes drooped with
scepticism.
My eyes filled with scepticism.
My eyes shadowed in
scepticism.
My face clenched with
scepticism.
My face creased with
scepticism.
My face crumpled with
scepticism.
My face darkened with
scepticism.
My face descended with
scepticism.
My face drawn in scepticism.
My face etched with
scepticism.
My face filled with scepticism.

My face sagged with scepticism.
My face sunk in scepticism.
My mind beset with scepticism.
My tone laced with scepticism.
My tone shaded with scepticism.
My tone softened with scepticism.
My voice filled with scepticism.
My voice infused with scepticism.
My voice laced with scepticism.
My voice laden with scepticism.
My voice tinged with scepticism.
Scepticism came into my eyes.
Scepticism came into my voice.
Scepticism crept into my expression.
Scepticism drifted across my face.
Scepticism flickered in my eyes.
Scepticism flickered in my face.
Scepticism flickered in my mind.
Scepticism flickered through my mind.
Scepticism lay in my heart.
Scepticism lingered in my eyes.
Scepticism passed over my face.

Scepticism ran down my spine.
Scepticism seeped into my muscles.
Scepticism settled in my heart.
Scepticism settled on my face.
Scepticism settled on my shoulders.
Scepticism shone in my face.
Scepticism showed in my eyes.
Scepticism welled in my chest.
Scepticism welled in my eyes.
My eyes were full of scepticism.
My face was heavy with scepticism.
My tone was thick with scepticism.
My voice was full of scepticism.
My voice was heavy with scepticism.
My voice was soft with scepticism.
A touch of scepticism came into my eyes.

SCORN

Definition: A feeling and expression of contempt or disdain for someone or something.
See CONTEMPT

Scorn clawed at me.
Scorn crossed my face.
Scorn curled my lips.
Scorn darkened my eyes.
Scorn edged my voice.
Scorn filled my body.
Scorn filled my voice.
Scorn tinged my voice.
Scorn touched my voice.
My brows slanted in scorn.
My eyes blazed with scorn.
My eyes filled with scorn.
My eyes flashed with scorn.
My eyes flickered with scorn.
My eyes glowed with scorn.
My eyes narrowed in scorn.
My eyes narrowed with scorn.
My eyes shone with scorn.
My face contorted in scorn.
My face contorted with scorn.
My face filled with scorn.
My face flushed with scorn.
My face twisted in scorn.
My face twisted with scorn.
My face wrinkled with scorn.
My face written with scorn.
My heart filled with scorn.
My lip curled in scorn.
My lips curled in scorn.
My lips curled with scorn.
My lips twisted in scorn.
My lips twisted with scorn.

My mouth curled in scorn.
My mouth twisted in scorn.
My nose flared in scorn.
My tone laced with scorn.
My voice dripped with scorn.
My voice filled with scorn.
My voice jagged with scorn.
My voice laced with scorn.
My voice loaded with scorn.
My voice quavered with scorn.
My voice rang with scorn.
My voice sharpened with scorn.
My voice touched with scorn.
My voice vibrated with scorn.
Scorn etched on my face.
Scorn flashed in my eyes.
Scorn flickered in my eyes.
Scorn poured from my mouth.
My brows were tight in scorn.
My eyes were full of scorn.
My face screwed up in scorn.
My face was full of scorn.
My voice was thick with scorn.
Scorn lay thick in my voice.

SHAME

Definition: A painful feeling of humiliation or distress caused by the consciousness of wrong or foolish behaviour.
See HUMILIATION

I blushed with shame.
I burned with shame.
Shame ate at me.
Shame burned my face.
Shame burned through me.
Shame clawed at me.
Shame coiled inside me.
Shame crossed my face.
Shame curdled in me.
Shame distorted my expression.
Shame filled my face.
Shame flooded my cheeks.
Shame heated my cheeks.
Shame heated my face.
Shame pricked my skin.
Shame rose inside me.
Shame rushed through me.
Shame scorched my face.
Shame seared my cheeks.
Shame seeped through me.
Shame slammed into me.
Shame slashed my cheeks.
Shame squeezed my heart.
Shame stung my face.
Shame swept over me.
Shame warmed my face.
Shame washed over me.
Shame washed through me.
I grew hot with shame.
I grew warm with shame.
My eyes burned with shame.

My eyes dropped with shame.
My eyes stung with shame.
My eyes weighted with shame.
My face burned with shame.
My face flamed with shame.
My face flushed with shame.
My face fluttered from shame.
My face heated with shame.
My heart sank with shame.
My heart smouldered with shame.
My shoulders drooped in shame.
My shoulders rounded in shame.
My throat seized with shame.
My throat tightened with shame.
My tone edged with shame.
My tone filled with shame.
My voice choked with shame.
Shame ate at my soul.
Shame burned in my cheeks.
Shame raced along my nerves.
Shame ran down my cheeks.
Shame streamed from my eyes.
I felt a flash of shame.
I felt a flush of shame.
I felt a kind of shame.
I felt a knife of shame.
I felt a moment of shame.
I felt a prick of shame.

I felt a quiver of shame.
I felt a sense of shame.
I felt a spike of shame.
I felt a stab of shame.
I felt a tinge of shame.
I felt a twinge of shame.
I felt a wave of shame.
I felt an ounce of shame.
I uttered a scream of shame.
My eyes cast down in shame.
My eyes were red with shame.
My face grew hot with shame.
My face grew red in shame.
My face turned hot with
shame.
My neck flushed red with
shame.
My neck grew hot with shame.
My voice was gruff with
shame.
My voice was thick with
shame.
My voice was tight with
shame.
Shame pulled taut in my
stomach.

SHOCK

Definition: A feeling of disturbed surprise resulting from a sudden upsetting event.
See SURPRISE

I froze in shock.
I gasped in shock.
I gasped with shock.
I muttered in shock.
Shock ate at me.
Shock crashed through me.
Shock crossed my face.
Shock filled my mind.
Shock flooded my emotions.
Shock flooded my face.
Shock froze my face.
Shock glazed my irises.
Shock hardened my voice.
Shock jarred my arms.
Shock jarred my shoulders.
Shock jolted through me.
Shock muffled my words.
Shock passed through me.
Shock raced through me.
Shock ran through me.
Shock ripped through me.
Shock robbed my voice.
Shock rolled over me.
Shock rolled through me.
Shock rounded my eyes.
Shock slammed into me.
Shock stalled my mind.
Shock strained my features.
Shock strained my lungs.
Shock struck my face.
Shock surged through me.
Shock tightened my belly.

Shock twisted my features.
Shock went through me.
Shock widened my eyes.
My body convulsed with shock.
My body jerked in shock.
My body reeled with shock.
My body went into shock.
My eyebrows rose in shock.
My eyes bulged in shock.
My eyes bulged with shock.
My eyes filled with shock.
My eyes flared in shock.
My eyes flared with shock.
My eyes flashed in shock.
My eyes flickered from shock.
My eyes glazed with shock.
My eyes opened in shock.
My eyes opened with shock.
My eyes rounded in shock.
My eyes stared in shock.
My eyes widened in shock.
My eyes widened with shock.
My face dropped with shock.
My face frozen in shock.
My face lined with shock.
My face paled in shock.
My face paled with shock.
My face strained with shock.
My face twisted from shock.
My head jerked in shock.
My head reeled in shock.

My heart jumped with shock.
My jaw dropped in shock.
My jaw trembled with shock.
My knees weakened in shock.
My lips parted in shock.
My mouth opened in shock.
My mouth parted in shock.
My mouth shut in shock.
My stomach boiled in shock.
My voice blurred with shock.
My voice hushed with shock.
My voice ragged with shock.
My voice rose with shock.
My voice shook with shock.
Shock etched in my face.
Shock etched on my face.
Shock flared in my eyes.
Shock flashed in my eyes.
Shock pulsed through my body.
Shock registered on my face.
Shock settled on my face.
Shock showed in my face.
Shock showed on my face.
Shock sizzled down my back.
Shock squeezed at my insides.
Shock went through my body.
I felt a bolt of shock.
I felt a prickle of shock.
I felt a punch of shock.
I felt a ripple of shock.
I felt a sensation of shock.
I felt a sense of shock.
I felt a spike of shock.
I felt a thrust of shock.
I felt a tingle of shock.
I felt a tremor of shock.
I felt a wave of shock.

I felt a wrench of shock.
I gave a grunt of shock.
My body went rigid in shock.
My ears went rigid with shock.
My ears went stiff with shock.
My eyes flew open in shock.
My eyes flew wide with shock.
My eyes grew wide with shock.
My eyes opened wide with shock.
My eyes popped wide with shock.
My eyes went wide in shock.
My eyes went wide with shock.
My eyes were blank with shock.
My eyes were huge with shock.
My eyes were large with shock.
My eyes were wide in shock.
My eyes were wide with shock.
My face turned yellow with shock.
My face was blank with shock.
My lips went white with shock.
My mouth dropped open in shock.
My mouth dropped open with shock.
My mouth fell open in shock.
My mouth gaped open in shock.
My mouth hung open in shock.
My mouth slacked open in shock.
My throat seized up in shock.
My voice was dull with shock.

My voice was harsh with
shock.
My voice was small with shock.
My voice was vague with
shock.

SORROW

Definition: A feeling of deep distress caused by loss, disappointment, or other misfortune suffered by oneself or others.
See SADNESS

I smiled with sorrow.
Sorrow brushed my face.
Sorrow came over me.
Sorrow clenched my chest.
Sorrow clouded my expression.
Sorrow crashed over me.
Sorrow crept over me.
Sorrow crossed my brow.
Sorrow crossed my face.
Sorrow crossed my features.
Sorrow darkened my eyes.
Sorrow ebbed over me.
Sorrow entered my voice.
Sorrow filled my eyes.
Sorrow filled my face.
Sorrow filled my voice.
Sorrow howled through me.
Sorrow infiltrated my smile.
Sorrow invaded my eyes.
Sorrow lined my face.
Sorrow rose off me.
Sorrow seeped into me.
Sorrow settled over me.
Sorrow shadowed my eyes.
Sorrow sizzled through me.
Sorrow spiralled through me.
Sorrow squeezed my chest.
Sorrow swept through me.
Sorrow tinged my eyes.
Sorrow tinged my voice.
Sorrow tugged at me.
Sorrow washed over me.

Sorrow weighed on me.
Sorrow welled inside me.
My eyes drooped with sorrow.
My eyes dulled with sorrow.
My eyes filled with sorrow.
My eyes haunted with sorrow.
My eyes shaded with sorrow.
My eyes shadowed in sorrow.
My face contorted with sorrow.
My face creased with sorrow.
My face crumpled with sorrow.
My face darkened with sorrow.
My face etched with sorrow.
My face filled with sorrow.
My face frozen in sorrow.
My face sagged with sorrow.
My head bowed in sorrow.
My heart filled with sorrow.
My heart submerged in sorrow.
My tone laced with sorrow.
My tone shaded with sorrow.
My tone softened with sorrow.
My voice filled with sorrow.
My voice infused with sorrow.
My voice laced with sorrow.
My voice tinged with sorrow.
Sorrow came into my eyes.
Sorrow came into my voice.

Sorrow coursed through my
body.
Sorrow crept into my
expression.
Sorrow drifted across my face.
Sorrow flickered in my eyes.
Sorrow flickered in my face.
Sorrow lay in my heart.
Sorrow lingered in my eyes.
Sorrow passed over my face.
Sorrow radiated from my eyes.
Sorrow rose from my skin.
Sorrow seeped into my
muscles.
Sorrow settled on my face.
Sorrow showed in my eyes.
Sorrow surfaced through my
skin.
Sorrow welled in my chest.
Sorrow welled in my eyes.
I felt a gust of sorrow.
I felt a kind of sorrow.
I felt a moment of sorrow.
I felt a pang of sorrow.
I felt a rush of sorrow.
I felt a sense of sorrow.
I felt a stab of sorrow.
I felt a wave of sorrow.
I uttered a word of sorrow.
My eyes were black with
sorrow.
My eyes were full of sorrow.
My eyes were vacant with
sorrow.
My face was heavy with
sorrow.
My tone was thick with
sorrow.

My voice was full of sorrow.
My voice was soft with sorrow.
A touch of sorrow came into
my eyes.

SPITE

Definition: A desire to hurt, annoy, or offend someone.
See BITTERNESS

I blushed in spite.
I chuckled in spite.
I flushed in spite.
I grinned in spite.
I shivered in spite.
I sighed in spite.
I smiled in spite.
Spite burned inside me.
Spite burned through me.
Spite burned within me.
Spite churned inside me.
Spite churned through me.
Spite clenched inside me.
Spite clouded my face.
Spite coiled inside me.
Spite coloured my cheeks.
Spite coursed through me.
Spite crept into me.
Spite entered my voice.
Spite filled my throat.
Spite laced my humour.
Spite laced my voice.
Spite lit my eyes.
Spite poured over me.
Spite stained my cheeks.
Spite suffused my cheeks.
Spite swelled inside me.
Spite tightened my jaw.
Spite washed over me.
My body quickened in spite.
My body quivered with spite.
My chest swelled with spite.
My eyebrows climbed in spite.

My eyes blazed with spite.
My eyes dazzled in spite.
My eyes filled with spite.
My eyes glittered with spite.
My eyes shone with spite.
My eyes smouldered with spite.
My eyes widened with spite.
My face crumpled in spite.
My face darkened with spite.
My face filled with spite.
My face flushed with spite.
My face reddened with spite.
My face set with spite.
My face strained in spite.
My face tensed with spite.
My face tightened in spite.
My face tightened with spite.
My face trembled with spite.
My face twisted in spite.
My face twisted with spite.
My face twitched with spite.
My head ached in spite.
My head sang with spite.
My heart filled with spite.
My heart seethed with spite.
My lips twisted with spite.
My stomach boiled with spite.
My tone drenched with spite.
My tone laden with spite.
My tone reeked of spite.
My voice crackled with spite.
My voice edged with spite.

My voice laced with spite.
My voice ragged with spite.
My voice rattled with spite.
My voice sank with spite.
My voice shook with spite.
My voice tinged with spite.
Spite burned in my chest.
Spite burned in my eyes.
Spite came into my voice.
Spite chattered in my head.
Spite churned in my gut.
Spite churned through my
belly.
Spite coiled in my belly.
Spite coursed through my
veins.
Spite crackled in my eyes.
Spite crept into my tone.
Spite crept into my voice.
Spite curdled inside my belly.
Spite edged into my voice.
Spite flared in my heart.
Spite rose in my throat.
Spite shone in my eyes.
Spite sprouted in my gut.
Spite swelled in my throat.
I snorted a laugh in spite.
My eyes were wide with spite.
My face screwed up in spite.
My face turned flush with
spite.
My face turned red with spite.
My face turned rosy with spite.
My face was ruddy with spite.
My face went dark with spite.
My voice trailed off in spite.
My voice was alive with spite.
My voice was shrill with spite.

Spite burned bright in my eyes.

SUFFERING

Definition: The state of undergoing pain, distress, or hardship.

See DISTRESS

Suffering ate into me.
Suffering churned inside me.
Suffering clawed at me.
Suffering coursed through me.
Suffering crossed my face.
Suffering filled my voice.
Suffering flooded over me.
Suffering knotted my gut.
Suffering knotted my insides.
Suffering knotted my shoulders.
Suffering knotted my stomach.
Suffering lined my face.
Suffering pinched my lips.
Suffering pumped my heart.
Suffering ran through me.
Suffering rushed through me.
Suffering scraped my spine.
Suffering slipped from me.
Suffering squeezed my belly.
Suffering swept over me.
Suffering swept through me.
Suffering swirled through me.
Suffering tightened my breath.
Suffering tightened my features.
Suffering tightened my shoulders.
Suffering touched my heart.
Suffering tugged at me.
Suffering washed over me.
Suffering washed through me.
Suffering weighed on me.

Suffering went through me.
Suffering wormed through me.
My body hummed with suffering.
My eyebrows furrowed in suffering.
My eyes clouded with suffering.
My eyes flared with suffering.
My eyes widened in suffering.
My face creased in suffering.
My face creased with suffering.
My face crumpled in suffering.
My face etched in suffering.
My face flooded with suffering.
My face flushed with suffering.
My face lined with suffering.
My face pinched with suffering.
My face twisted with suffering.
My face wisped with suffering.
My head throbbed with suffering.
My jaw worked with suffering.
My mouth puckered with suffering.
My nose quivered with suffering.
My shoulders knotted with suffering.
My stomach clenched in suffering.

My stomach cramped with suffering.
My stomach knotted with suffering.
My voice broken with suffering.
My voice cracked with suffering.
My voice marbled with suffering.
My voice rose in suffering.
My voice strained with suffering.
My voice tinged with suffering.
Suffering came into my eyes.
Suffering churned in my gut.
Suffering coursed through my veins.
Suffering crawled up my back.
Suffering crept into my voice.
Suffering crept up my spine.
Suffering emanated from my body.
Suffering etched across my face.
Suffering flickered in my eyes.
Suffering glazed in my eyes.
Suffering nagged at my mind.
Suffering plucked at my chest.
Suffering pressed against my chest.
Suffering pulsed through my body.
Suffering pumped through my veins.
Suffering roared in my head.
Suffering roiled in my gut.
Suffering rose in my throat.

Suffering slithered up my spine.
Suffering spilled through my guts.
Suffering sprinted across my eyes.
Suffering swept through my body.
Suffering trembled in my stomach.
Suffering whispered in my gut.
My eyes opened wide with suffering.
My eyes were bright with suffering.
My face was full of suffering.
My mouth was dry with suffering.
My spine went cold with suffering.
My voice was shrill with suffering.
My voice was taut with suffering.
My voice was thin with suffering.
Suffering caused my throat to tighten.

SURPRISE

Definition: A feeling of mild astonishment or shock caused by something unexpected.

See ASTONISHMENT

I flinched in surprise.
I flinched with surprise.
I froze with surprise.
I gasped in surprise.
I grimaced in surprise.
I grunted in surprise.
I grunted with surprise.
I smiled in surprise.
I stiffened in surprise.
I stuttered with surprise.
I yelped in surprise.
Surprise brightened my gaze.
Surprise coloured my voice.
Surprise crossed my face.
Surprise flared inside me.
Surprise jolted through me.
Surprise lit my eyes.
Surprise lit my face.
Surprise lit my features.
Surprise parted my lips.
Surprise snaked through me.
Surprise twisted my gut.
My brows arched in surprise.
My brows climbed in surprise.
My brows lifted in surprise.
My brows raised in surprise.
My brows rose in surprise.
My ears flickered in surprise.
My eyebrows arched in surprise.
My eyebrows arched with surprise.

My eyebrows lifted in surprise.
My eyebrows raised in surprise.
My eyebrows rose in surprise.
My eyebrows rose with surprise.
My eyes blinked in surprise.
My eyes blinked with surprise.
My eyes bloomed with surprise.
My eyes brightened with surprise.
My eyes filled with surprise.
My eyes flared in surprise.
My eyes flared with surprise.
My eyes flashed from surprise.
My eyes flashed with surprise.
My eyes flickered with surprise.
My eyes fluttered in surprise.
My eyes opened in surprise.
My eyes popped in surprise.
My eyes rounded in surprise.
My eyes scrunched in surprise.
My eyes shut in surprise.
My eyes twinkled with surprise.
My eyes widened in surprise.
My eyes widened with surprise.
My face altered from surprise.
My face contorted with surprise.
My face relaxed with surprise.

My face scrunched in surprise.
My face twisted in surprise.
My face winced in surprise.
My head cocked in surprise.
My head jerked in surprise.
My head shook in surprise.
My head throbbed with surprise.
My jaw dropped in surprise.
My lips parted in surprise.
My lips rounded in surprise.
My mouth opened in surprise.
My skin deepened with surprise.
Surprise edged into my voice.
Surprise flashed on my face.
Surprise flickered across my face.
Surprise flitted across my face.
Surprise lit up my face.
Surprise passed across my face.
Surprise passed over my face.
Surprise plastered across my face.
Surprise played across my face.
Surprise registered on my face.
Surprise settled on my face.
Surprise settled over my face.
Surprise showed in my eyes.
Surprise sounded in my voice.
I arched an eyebrow in surprise.
I felt a flash of surprise.
I felt a hitch of surprise.
I felt a jolt of surprise.
I felt a kick of surprise.
I felt a punch of surprise.
I felt a quality of surprise.

I felt a ripple of surprise.
I felt a sense of surprise.
I felt a shock of surprise.
I felt a spike of surprise.
I felt a tremor of surprise.
I gave a cry of surprise.
I gave a gasp of surprise.
I gave a grunt of surprise.
I gave a hiss of surprise.
I gave a jolt of surprise.
I gave a laugh of surprise.
I gave a look of surprise.
I gave a murmur of surprise.
I gave a squeak of surprise.
I gave a squeal of surprise.
I gave a start of surprise.
I gave a twitch of surprise.
I gave a whistle of surprise.
I gave a yip of surprise.
I gave an exclamation of surprise.
I uttered a cry of surprise.
My body was motionless with surprise.
My brows shot up in surprise.
My eyebrows shot up in surprise.
My eyebrows went up in surprise.
My eyes bloomed wide with surprise.
My eyes flew open in surprise.
My eyes grew huge with surprise.
My eyes lit up in surprise.
My eyes opened wide with surprise.
My eyes shot up in surprise.

My eyes were luminous with
surprise.
My eyes were wide in surprise.
My eyes were wide with
surprise.
My face lit up in surprise.
My face screwed up in surprise.
My face was blank with
surprise.
My face was full of surprise.
My face was wide with
surprise.
My head was abuzz with
surprise.
My head whipped around in
surprise.
My mouth dropped open in
surprise.
My mouth fell open in
surprise.
My mouth hung open in
surprise.
My mouth was agape in
surprise.

SUSPICION

Definition: Cautious distrust.
See DOUBT

I darkened with suspicion.
My face registered suspicion.
Suspicion came over me.
Suspicion chewed at me.
Suspicion clouded my
expression.
Suspicion clouded my features.
Suspicion covered my
expression.
Suspicion crashed over me.
Suspicion crept over me.
Suspicion crossed my face.
Suspicion crossed my features.
Suspicion darkened my eyes.
Suspicion darkened my face.
Suspicion descended on me.
Suspicion descended over me.
Suspicion ebbed over me.
Suspicion entered my voice.
Suspicion filled my eyes.
Suspicion filled my voice.
Suspicion hovered over me.
Suspicion howled through me.
Suspicion invaded my eyes.
Suspicion lined my face.
Suspicion obscured my vision.
Suspicion ravaged my body.
Suspicion rose off me.
Suspicion seeped into me.
Suspicion settled on me.
Suspicion settled over me.
Suspicion sizzled through me.

Suspicion spiralled through
me.
Suspicion squeezed my chest.
Suspicion swept over me.
Suspicion swept through me.
Suspicion tinged my eyes.
Suspicion tinged my voice.
Suspicion tugged at me.
Suspicion washed over me.
Suspicion weighed on me.
Suspicion welled inside me.
I was paralyzed with suspicion.
My eyes drooped with
suspicion.
My eyes filled with suspicion.
My eyes shadowed in
suspicion.
My face clenched with
suspicion.
My face creased with
suspicion.
My face crumpled with
suspicion.
My face darkened with
suspicion.
My face descended with
suspicion.
My face drew in suspicion.
My face etched with suspicion.
My face filled with suspicion.
My face sagged with suspicion.
My face sunk in suspicion.
My mind beset with suspicion.

My tone laced with suspicion.
My tone shaded with
suspicion.
My tone softened with
suspicion.
My voice filled with suspicion.
My voice infused with
suspicion.
My voice laced with suspicion.
My voice laden with suspicion.
My voice tinged with
suspicion.
Suspicion came into my eyes.
Suspicion came into my voice.
Suspicion crept into my
expression.
Suspicion drifted across my
face.
Suspicion flickered in my eyes.
Suspicion flickered in my face.
Suspicion flickered in my
mind.
Suspicion flickered through
my mind.
Suspicion lay in my heart.
Suspicion lingered in my eyes.
Suspicion passed over my face.
Suspicion ran down my spine.
Suspicion seeped into my
muscles.
Suspicion settled in my heart.
Suspicion settled on my face.
Suspicion settled on my
shoulders.
Suspicion shone in my face.
Suspicion showed in my eyes.
Suspicion welled in my chest.
Suspicion welled in my eyes.

My eyes were full of suspicion.
My face was heavy with
suspicion.
My tone was thick with
suspicion.
My voice was full of suspicion.
My voice was heavy with
suspicion.
My voice was soft with
suspicion.
A touch of suspicion came into
my eyes.

SYMPATHY

Definition: Feelings of pity and sorrow for someone else's misfortune.
See PITY

I frowned with sympathy.
I sighed in sympathy.
I smiled in sympathy.
Sympathy came from me.
Sympathy clouded my eyes.
Sympathy coloured my words.
Sympathy crossed my face.
Sympathy darkened my eyes.
Sympathy filled my eyes.
Sympathy flooded my heart.
Sympathy rippled through me.
Sympathy rolled through me.
Sympathy seeped through me.
Sympathy softened my
expression.
Sympathy stirred in me.
Sympathy touched my eyes.
Sympathy touched my voice.
Sympathy tugged at me.
My chest tightened in
sympathy.
My eyes filled with sympathy.
My eyes flickered with
sympathy.
My eyes glowed with
sympathy.
My eyes warmed with
sympathy.
My face burned in sympathy.
My face filled with sympathy.
My face throbbed in sympathy.
My face twisted with
sympathy.

My head throbbed in
sympathy.
My heart ached with
sympathy.
My heart clenched with
sympathy.
My heart filled with sympathy.
My heart lurched in sympathy.
My heart overflowed with
sympathy.
My heart sank with sympathy.
My heart squeezed in
sympathy.
My heart swelled with
sympathy.
My heart twisted with
sympathy.
My lips twitched in sympathy.
My mouth parted in sympathy.
My stomach growled in
sympathy.
My stomach gurgled in
sympathy.
My stomach knotted with
sympathy.
My stomach murmured in
sympathy.
My stomach rumbled in
sympathy.
My stomach tightened in
sympathy.
My voice dripped with
sympathy.

My voice filled with sympathy.
My voice laced with sympathy.
Sympathy registered in my
eyes.
Sympathy rolled into my head.
Sympathy shone in my eyes.
Sympathy shone in my face.
Sympathy showed on my face.
Sympathy stirred in my gut.
Sympathy welled in my chest.
I felt a deal of sympathy.
I felt a flash of sympathy.
I felt a measure of sympathy.
I felt a moment of sympathy.
I felt a pang of sympathy.
I felt a shot of sympathy.
I felt a stab of sympathy.
I felt a surge of sympathy.
I felt a touch of sympathy.
I felt a twinge of sympathy.
I felt a twist of sympathy.
I gave a nod of sympathy.
My eyes were full of sympathy.
My eyes were warm with
sympathy.
My eyes were wide with
sympathy.
My face was full of sympathy.
My mouth turned down in
sympathy.
My mouth went soft with
sympathy.
My voice pitched low with
sympathy.
My voice was full of sympathy.

T

TENDERNESS
Definition: Feelings of deep affection.
See AFFECTION

Tenderness came over me.
Tenderness clouded my eyes.
Tenderness crossed my face.
Tenderness fell over me.
Tenderness filled my eyes.
Tenderness filled my mind.
Tenderness flowed around me.
Tenderness pierced my heart.
Tenderness saturated my voice.
Tenderness surged through me.
Tenderness swept through me.
Tenderness warred inside me.
Tenderness washed over me.
Tenderness washed through me.
Tenderness welled inside me.
My chest squeezed with tenderness.
My chest swelled with tenderness.
My eyes brimmed with tenderness.
My eyes darkened with tenderness.
My eyes filled with tenderness.
My eyes glistened with tenderness.
My eyes glowed with tenderness.
My eyes moistened with tenderness.
My eyes shone with tenderness.
My eyes softened with tenderness.
My face filled with tenderness.
My face suffused with tenderness.
My heart ached with tenderness.
My heart engorged with tenderness.
My heart filled with tenderness.
My heart fluttered with tenderness.
My heart looked for tenderness.
My heart overflowed with tenderness.
My heart soared with tenderness.

My heart squeezed with tenderness.
My heart swelled with tenderness.
My heart swollen with tenderness.
My heart warmed with tenderness.
My throat tightened as tenderness.
My tone filled with tenderness.
My voice deepened with tenderness.
My voice throbbed with tenderness.
Tenderness blazed in my eyes.
Tenderness burned in my eyes.
Tenderness crept into my voice.
Tenderness gleamed in my eyes.
Tenderness radiated from my face.
Tenderness shimmered in my expression.
Tenderness shone in my eyes.
Tenderness shone through my tears.
Tenderness sparkled in my eyes.
Tenderness stirred in my breast.
I felt a rush of tenderness.
I felt a wave of tenderness.
My eyes lit up with tenderness.
My eyes were full of tenderness.

My eyes were misty with tenderness.
My eyes were warm with tenderness.
My face was soft with tenderness.
My heart was full of tenderness.
My heart was heavy with tenderness.
My voice was full of tenderness.

TENSION

Definition: Mental or emotional strain.

See ANXIETY

Tension built inside me.
Tension climbed my spine.
Tension clipped my words.
Tension coiled inside me.
Tension coiled within me.
Tension coursed through me.
Tension crackled through me.
Tension emanated from me.
Tension escalated inside me.
Tension filled my body.
Tension filled my stomach.
Tension fled my body.
Tension grew within me.
Tension heightened my senses.
Tension knotted my muscles.
Tension knotted my neck.
Tension knotted my
shoulders.
Tension lined my face.
Tension made me shudder.
Tension marked my brow.
Tension mounted inside me.
Tension pulled my muscles.
Tension raced between me.
Tension racked my body.
Tension radiated from me.
Tension rippled through me.
Tension rose in me.
Tension rose inside me.
Tension rose within me.
Tension spiralled through me.
Tension stiffened my body.

Tension strummed through
me.
Tension strung through me.
Tension thrummed through
me.
Tension tightened my body.
Tension tightened my posture.
Tension tightened my throat.
Tension vibrated through me.
My body ached from tension.
My body coiled with tension.
My body hummed with
tension.
My body knotted in tension.
My body knotted with
tension.
My body racked with tension.
My eyes pinched with tension.
My face etched with tension.
My face lined with tension.
My face rippled with tension.
My face set with tension.
My face twitched with tension.
My jaw popped with tension.
My jaw rippled with tension.
My jaw set with tension.
My mouth dimpled with
tension.
My neck ached from tension.
My nerves hummed with
tension.
My shoulders ached with
tension.

My shoulders bulged with tension.
My shoulders burned with tension.
My shoulders cramped with tension.
My shoulders hunched with tension.
My shoulders knotted with tension.
My shoulders locked with tension.
My shoulders rose in tension.
My shoulders stiffened with tension.
My stomach clenched with tension.
My tone tinged with tension.
My voice broke with tension.
My voice burred with tension.
My voice choked with tension.
My voice edged with tension.
Tension bled from my neck.
Tension clawed at my muscles.
Tension coiled in my gut.
Tension crept into my voice.
Tension crept up my spine.
Tension curled in my gut.
Tension etched on my face.
Tension exploded across my neck.
Tension exploded in my stomach.
Tension flooded through my body.
Tension grew in my belly.
Tension knotted in my stomach.
Tension made my voice crack.
Tension made my voice hoarse.
Tension made my voice shrill.
Tension moved through my body.
Tension pulled at my mouth.
Tension pulled at my muscles.
Tension radiated from my body.
Tension rippled through my body.
Tension rippled through my shoulders.
Tension rose in my chest.
Tension rose in my gut.
Tension rose in my throat.
Tension sparked in my eyes.
Tension surged in my belly.
Tension tightened in my belly.
I felt a bit of tension.
I felt a cord of tension.
I felt a crick of tension.
I felt a frisson of tension.
I felt a knot of tension.
I felt a layer of tension.
I felt a release of tension.
I felt a sense of tension.
I felt a surge of tension.
I felt an ache of tension.
My body was rigid with tension.
My body was taut with tension.
My face was puffy with tension.
My shoulders were rigid with tension.

Tension made my voice sound
strangled.
My body language was riddled
with tension.

TERROR

Definition: Extreme fear.
See FEAR

I froze in terror.
I froze with terror.
I gasped in terror.
I shivered in terror.
Terror came at me.
Terror came upon me.
Terror clawed at me.
Terror clogged my throat.
Terror clutched at me.
Terror coursed through me.
Terror crashed over me.
Terror crossed my face.
Terror cut through me.
Terror darkened my eyes.
Terror darkened my face.
Terror distorted my features.
Terror filled my eyes.
Terror filled my insides.
Terror flashed through me.
Terror froze my body.
Terror froze my heart.
Terror grew in me.
Terror gripped my throat.
Terror knifed at me.
Terror knotted my stomach.
Terror leaped in me.
Terror leaped inside me.
Terror leaped through me.
Terror pierced my chest.
Terror pulsed inside me.
Terror ripped from me.
Terror ripped through me.
Terror rippled through me.

Terror rolled through me.
Terror rushed through me.
Terror shot through me.
Terror shuddered through me.
Terror slammed into me.
Terror spiked through me.
Terror spiralled through me.
Terror streaked through me.
Terror surged through me.
Terror swept over me.
Terror swirled through me.
Terror tore through me.
Terror turned my face.
Terror twisted my face.
Terror washed over me.
Terror washed through me.
Terror widened my eyes.
My body flooded with terror.
My body screamed in terror.
My ears popped in terror.
My eyes blazed with terror.
My eyes bulged in terror.
My eyes bulged with terror.
My eyes filled with terror.
My eyes glittered with terror.
My eyes rolled in terror.
My eyes rolled with terror.
My eyes shone with terror.
My eyes widened in terror.
My eyes widened with terror.
My face contorted in terror.
My face contorted with terror.
My face convulsed with terror.

My face creased in terror.
My face distorted in terror.
My face pinched with terror.
My face twisted in terror.
My face twitched in terror.
My heart clutched with terror.
My heart fluttered with terror.
My heart pounded in terror.
My heart pounded with terror.
My heart thudded with terror.
My heart thumped in terror.
My mouth opened in terror.
My mouth opened with terror.
My stomach curdled in terror.
My throat closed with terror.
My voice faltered in terror.
My voice quivered with terror.
Terror emptied into my veins.
Terror etched on my face.
Terror etched upon my face.
Terror evaporated from my
countenance.
Terror leaped into my throat.
Terror raced down my spine.
Terror raced through my
blood.
Terror ran through my body.
Terror rose in my mind.
Terror rose in my throat.
Terror rose into my throat.
Terror settled in my belly.
Terror shot down my spine.
Terror sprang from my lips.
Terror stencilled across my
face.
Terror twisted around my
muscles.
Terror weighed down my legs.

I felt a burst of terror.
I felt a fist of terror.
I felt a lurch of terror.
I felt a shaft of terror.
I felt a slice of terror.
I felt a spike of terror.
I felt a stab of terror.
I felt a surge of terror.
I felt a thrill of terror.
I felt an instant of terror.
I gave a cry of terror.
I gave a whimper of terror.
I swallowed a ball of terror.
My eyes came alive with terror.
My eyes clouded over with
terror.
My eyes were bright with
terror.
My eyes were brilliant with
terror.
My eyes were buggy with
terror.
My eyes were full of terror.
My eyes were glassy with
terror.
My eyes were huge with terror.
My eyes were stark with terror.
My eyes were wide in terror.
My eyes were wide with terror.
My eyes were wild with terror.
My heart iced over with terror.
My heart was full of terror.
My voice was hoarse with
terror.
My voice was incoherent with
terror.
My voice was sharp with
terror.

My voice was thick with terror.
Terror knifed deep into my
soul.

THRILL

Definition: A sudden feeling of excitement and pleasure.

See EXCITEMENT

Thrill brightened my face.
Thrill coiled in me.
Thrill coursed through me.
Thrill crossed my face.
Thrill entered my voice.
Thrill flowed through me.
Thrill grew inside me.
Thrill heated my blood.
Thrill jabbed my brain.
Thrill mounted inside me.
Thrill moved through me.
Thrill painted my features.
Thrill pulsed through me.
Thrill quickened my breath.
Thrill raced through me.
Thrill ran through me.
Thrill rippled through me.
Thrill rose in me.
Thrill rose inside me.
Thrill rose within me.
Thrill rushed through me.
Thrill skittered through me.
Thrill stirred in me.
Thrill swept over me.
Thrill swept through me.
Thrill tickled my stomach.
Thrill touched my voice.
Thrill washed over me.
Thrill went through me.
A thrill came upon me.
A thrill moved through me.
A thrill raced through me.
A thrill ran through me.

A thrill shot through me.
A thrill swept through me.
A thrill went through me.
A thrill whipped through me.
My blood heated with thrill.
My body quivered with thrill.
My chest bubbled with thrill.
My chest pounded with thrill.
My ears flapped in thrill.
My ears fluttered with thrill.
My ears quivered with thrill.
My eyes blazed with thrill.
My eyes burned with thrill.
My eyes danced with thrill.
My eyes flashed in thrill.
My eyes flashed with thrill.
My eyes gleamed with thrill.
My eyes glinted with thrill.
My eyes glistened with thrill.
My eyes glittered with thrill.
My eyes shone in thrill.
My eyes shone with thrill.
My eyes sparkled with thrill.
My eyes twinkled with thrill.
My eyes widened in thrill.
My eyes widened with thrill.
My face filled with thrill.
My face flickered with thrill.
My face flushed with thrill.
My face glowed with thrill.
My face polished with thrill.
My face shone with thrill.
My face swelled with thrill.

My face tingled with thrill.
My head bobbed in thrill.
My head twitched with thrill.
My heart beat with thrill.
My heart filled with thrill.
My heart fluttered with thrill.
My heart pounded with thrill.
My heart quickened in thrill.
My heart quickened with
thrill.
My heart raced with thrill.
My heart thumped with thrill.
My lips quivered with thrill.
My mouth twitched with
thrill.
My nose twitched in thrill.
My pulse kicked with thrill.
My pulse pounded with thrill.
My pulse raced with thrill.
My skin glowed with thrill.
My stomach churned with
thrill.
My stomach squirmed with
thrill.
My voice cracked with thrill.
My voice filled with thrill.
My voice rang with thrill.
My voice rose in thrill.
My voice rose with thrill.
My voice shook with thrill.
My voice squeaked with thrill.
My voice tinged with thrill.
My voice trembled with thrill.
Thrill blazed in my eyes.
Thrill bubbled in my voice.
Thrill budded in my chest.
Thrill burgeoned in my loins.
Thrill closed on my chest.

Thrill coursed through my
veins.
Thrill crept down my back.
Thrill crept into my voice.
Thrill fizzed in my chest.
Thrill flashed into my bones.
Thrill gleamed in my eyes.
Thrill played across my face.
Thrill poked at my belly.
Thrill ran up my spine.
Thrill rippled through my
veins.
Thrill rose in my chest.
Thrill rose in my voice.
Thrill stirred along my nerve.
Thrill welled in my breast.
A thrill ran through my veins.
A thrill shot up my spine.
A thrill swept through my
veins.
A thrill went up my spine.
My eyes burned bright with
thrill.
My eyes grew big with thrill.
My eyes lit up in thrill.
My eyes lit up with thrill.
My eyes were alight with thrill.
My eyes were alive with thrill.
My eyes were big with thrill.
My eyes were bright with
thrill.
My eyes were brilliant with
thrill.
My eyes were fierce with thrill.
My eyes were frantic with
thrill.
My eyes were full of thrill.
My eyes were wide with thrill.

My face flushed grey with
thrill.
My face lit up with thrill.
My face was bright with thrill.
My neck felt prickly with
thrill.
My skin was clammy with
thrill.
My skin was electric with
thrill.
My stomach screwed up with
thrill.
My voice was full of thrill.
My voice was hoarse with
thrill.
Thrill caused my voice to rise.

TORMENT

Definition: Severe physical or mental suffering.
See AGONY

Torment clapped my hands.
Torment crashed through me.
Torment exploded inside me.
Torment exploded through
me.
Torment ignited my nerves.
Torment overlay my face.
Torment paralysed my legs.
Torment pierced my body.
Torment pierced my sinuses.
Torment pulsed through me.
Torment ripped through me.
Torment stabbed my side.
Torment washed over me.
My body contorted in
torment.
My body convulsed in
torment.
My body creamed in torment.
My body exploded with
torment.
My body screamed in torment.
My body screamed with
torment.
My body shrieked in torment.
My body spasmed in torment.
My body throbbed in torment.
My body writhed in torment.
My ears stabbed with torment.
My eyes closed in torment.
My eyes filled with torment.
My eyes glazed in torment.
My eyes narrowed in torment.

My eyes rolled in torment.
My eyes shut in torment.
My face clenched in torment.
My face contorted in torment.
My face contorted with
torment.
My face etched in torment.
My face lined with torment.
My face twisted in torment.
My face twisted with torment.
My lips tightened in torment.
My nerves screamed in
torment.
My voice choked with
torment.
Torment came over my face.
Torment crawled around my
mind.
Torment etched on my face.
Torment etched on my faces.
Torment exploded in my guts.
Torment flared from my
fingertips.
Torment flared in my ribs.
Torment flared up my leg.
Torment flashed on my face.
Torment froze in my throat.
Torment radiated from my
back.
Torment raged inside my
body.
Torment ripped across my
face.

Torment ripped through my
body.
Torment ripped through my
head.
Torment rushed through my
body.
Torment seared through my
leg.
Torment shrieked from my
mouth.
Torment struck my nervous
system.
Torment swept through my
body.
Torment tore up my spine.
Torment welled into my eyes.
My body crumpled up in
torment.
My eyes glowed red with
torment.
My eyes opened wide with
torment.
My eyes were full of torment.
My face screwed up in
torment.
My head hung low in torment.
My knees drew up in torment.
My mouth sagged open in
torment.
My voice was hoarse with
torment.

TREPIDATION

Definition: A feeling of fear or anxiety about something that may happen.

See FEAR

I filled with trepidation.
I fluttered with trepidation.
I froze with trepidation.
I gasped in trepidation.
I muttered in trepidation.
I shivered from trepidation.
I shivered in trepidation.
I shuddered with trepidation.
I yelped with trepidation.
Trepidation arced through me.
Trepidation ate at me.
Trepidation ate into me.
Trepidation bled into me.
Trepidation blurred my vision.
Trepidation boiled inside me.
Trepidation bubbled in me.
Trepidation burned my nostrils.
Trepidation chilled my spine.
Trepidation clawed at me.
Trepidation clenched my stomach.
Trepidation clogged my thoughts.
Trepidation clogged my throat.
Trepidation clouded my brain.
Trepidation clouded my expression.
Trepidation clouded my eyes.
Trepidation clutched my heart.

Trepidation coated my mouth.
Trepidation consumed my face.
Trepidation coursed through me.
Trepidation cramped my chest.
Trepidation crashed into me.
Trepidation crashed through me.
Trepidation crawled through me.
Trepidation crept over me.
Trepidation crossed my face.
Trepidation crowded my chest.
Trepidation crowded my throat.
Trepidation cut through me.
Trepidation darkened my eyes.
Trepidation darkened my face.
Trepidation darted through me.
Trepidation dried my mouth.
Trepidation exploded inside me.
Trepidation fell over me.
Trepidation filled my eyes.
Trepidation filled my face.
Trepidation filled my mind.
Trepidation flared in me.
Trepidation flooded into me.

Trepidation flooded my mind.
Trepidation flooded my veins.
Trepidation flowed into me.
Trepidation grabbed at me.
Trepidation grew within me.
Trepidation gripped my gut.
Trepidation gripped my heart.
Trepidation gripped my soul.
Trepidation gripped my
stomach.
Trepidation gripped my
throat.
Trepidation iced my veins.
Trepidation jack-knifed
through me.
Trepidation jolted through
me.
Trepidation knifed through
me.
Trepidation knotted my
insides.
Trepidation laced my voice.
Trepidation lanced through
me.
Trepidation leaped through
me.
Trepidation licked at me.
Trepidation lined my face.
Trepidation lit inside me.
Trepidation lit my eyes.
Trepidation lit my nerves.
Trepidation made me sweat.
Trepidation moved through
me.
Trepidation mushroomed
inside me.
Trepidation nagged at me.
Trepidation painted my face.

Trepidation plucked at me.
Trepidation poured through
me.
Trepidation pricked my spine.
Trepidation prodded my
mind.
Trepidation pulsed through
me.
Trepidation pumped through
me.
Trepidation raced through me.
Trepidation racked my body.
Trepidation radiated from me.
Trepidation raged inside me.
Trepidation raked through
me.
Trepidation ran over me.
Trepidation ran through me.
Trepidation rifled through me.
Trepidation ripped through
me.
Trepidation rippled through
me.
Trepidation rode through me.
Trepidation roiled inside me.
Trepidation roiled through
me.
Trepidation rolled through
me.
Trepidation rose in me.
Trepidation rose inside me.
Trepidation rushed through
me.
Trepidation seized my chest.
Trepidation seized my
stomach.
Trepidation shivered through
me.

Trepidation shot through me.
Trepidation shuddered
through me.
Trepidation skimmed my
nerves.
Trepidation slammed into me.
Trepidation slithered through
me.
Trepidation snaked through
me.
Trepidation soured my
stomach.
Trepidation spiralled inside
me.
Trepidation spiralled through
me.
Trepidation squeezed my
chest.
Trepidation squeezed my
heart.
Trepidation squeezed my
lungs.
Trepidation stabbed through
me.
Trepidation stilled my fingers.
Trepidation streaked my face.
Trepidation streaked through
me.
Trepidation struck through
me.
Trepidation surged through
me.
Trepidation swelled inside me.
Trepidation swept over me.
Trepidation swept through
me.
Trepidation swirled through
me.

Trepidation thundered
through me.
Trepidation tied my stomach.
Trepidation tightened around
me.
Trepidation tightened my
chest.
Trepidation tightened my
lungs.
Trepidation tightened my
nerves.
Trepidation tightened my
skin.
Trepidation tinged my words.
Trepidation travelled through
me.
Trepidation trickled over me.
Trepidation turned my
stomach.
Trepidation washed my face.
Trepidation washed over me.
Trepidation washed through
me.
Trepidation went through me.
Trepidation whipped through
me.
Trepidation widened my eyes.
Trepidation wormed through
me.
My body convulsed in
trepidation.
My body pulsed with
trepidation.
My body quivered with
trepidation.
My body shook with
trepidation.

My body shuddered with trepidation.
My body trembled in trepidation.
My body trembled with trepidation.
My body vibrated with trepidation.
My chest clenched with trepidation.
My chest seized with trepidation.
My eyes blazed with trepidation.
My eyes brimmed with trepidation.
My eyes bulged in trepidation.
My eyes bulged with trepidation.
My eyes clouded with trepidation.
My eyes darkened with trepidation.
My eyes darted in trepidation.
My eyes dilated with trepidation.
My eyes filled with trepidation.
My eyes flashed with trepidation.
My eyes flickered with trepidation.
My eyes glazed with trepidation.
My eyes glittered with trepidation.
My eyes inked with trepidation.

My eyes marbled with trepidation.
My eyes popped with trepidation.
My eyes protruded with trepidation.
My eyes rolled in trepidation.
My eyes shone with trepidation.
My eyes simmered with trepidation.
My eyes touched with trepidation.
My eyes widened in trepidation.
My eyes widened with trepidation.
My face contorted with trepidation.
My face distorted with trepidation.
My face drawn in trepidation.
My face etched with trepidation.
My face filled with trepidation.
My face frozen in trepidation.
My face frozen with trepidation.
My face pinched with trepidation.
My face tightened with trepidation.
My face twisted in trepidation.
My face twisted with trepidation.
My face twitched with trepidation.

My heart banged with trepidation.
My heart clutched in trepidation.
My heart drummed with trepidation.
My heart filled with trepidation.
My heart frozen with trepidation.
My heart hammered with trepidation.
My heart pounded in trepidation.
My heart pounded with trepidation.
My heart protested in trepidation.
My heart sank with trepidation.
My heart seized with trepidation.
My heart squeezed with trepidation.
My heart thudded with trepidation.
My heartbeat stuttered in trepidation.
My lips compressed in trepidation.
My mouth contorted with trepidation.
My mouth writhed with trepidation.
My nerves jangled with trepidation.
My skin chilled with trepidation.

My skin pricked with trepidation.
My skin prickled with trepidation.
My throat clamped with trepidation.
My throat clogged with trepidation.
My throat constricted in trepidation.
My throat constricted with trepidation.
My throat dried in trepidation.
My throat parched from trepidation.
My throat tightened with trepidation.
My tone laced with trepidation.
My voice chattered with trepidation.
My voice choked with trepidation.
My voice cracked from trepidation.
My voice cracked with trepidation.
My voice edged with trepidation.
My voice hushed with trepidation.
My voice laced with trepidation.
My voice muted with trepidation.
My voice quavered with trepidation.

My voice quivered with trepidation.
My voice ragged with trepidation.
My voice rose in trepidation.
My voice shook with trepidation.
My voice tinged with trepidation.
My voice trembled with trepidation.
My voice vibrated with trepidation.
My voice whined with trepidation.
Trepidation blew through my heart.
Trepidation bloomed in my face.
Trepidation blossomed in my belly.
Trepidation burned in my throat.
Trepidation burrowed into my spine.
Trepidation caught in my throat.
Trepidation churned in my gut.
Trepidation clamped around my neck.
Trepidation clawed at my chest.
Trepidation clawed at my heart.
Trepidation clawed at my insides.
Trepidation clawed at my throat.
Trepidation clawed up my spine.
Trepidation closed around my heart.
Trepidation closed up my throat.
Trepidation coursed through my body.
Trepidation crawled along my collar.
Trepidation crawled on my skin.
Trepidation crawled through my limbs.
Trepidation crawled up my spine.
Trepidation crept down my spine.
Trepidation crept into my expression.
Trepidation crept through my body.
Trepidation crept up my spine.
Trepidation etched in my eyes.
Trepidation etched into my expression.
Trepidation etched into my eyes.
Trepidation etched on my face.
Trepidation etched on my features.
Trepidation fell across my eyes.
Trepidation flashed in my eyes.

Trepidation flickered in my eyes.

Trepidation fluttered through my breast.

Trepidation grew in my eyes.

Trepidation grew in my gut.

Trepidation jammed in my throat.

Trepidation knotted in my belly.

Trepidation lifted from my heart.

Trepidation lingered in my voice.

Trepidation lumped in my throat.

Trepidation made my chest tight.

Trepidation made my knees weak.

Trepidation made my throat sore.

Trepidation oozed from my pores.

Trepidation played across my face.

Trepidation played over my face.

Trepidation poured through my body.

Trepidation pressed against my heart.

Trepidation pried open my heart.

Trepidation ran down my spine.

Trepidation ran through my bowels.

Trepidation ran through my veins.

Trepidation ran up my spine.

Trepidation reflected in my eyes.

Trepidation reflected in my face.

Trepidation registered in my eyes.

Trepidation ripped through my stomach.

Trepidation rippled across my skin.

Trepidation rolled down my cheeks.

Trepidation rolled through my stomach.

Trepidation rose in my gut.

Trepidation rose in my throat.

Trepidation seeped into my mind.

Trepidation settled in my stomach.

Trepidation shone from my eyes.

Trepidation shone in my eyes.

Trepidation shot down my spine.

Trepidation shot up my spine.

Trepidation showed in my eyes.

Trepidation showed on my face.

Trepidation slammed into my brain.

Trepidation sliced through my midsection.

Trepidation slid down my
spine.
Trepidation slithered along my
skin.
Trepidation slithered through
my belly.
Trepidation slithered up my
spine.
Trepidation smouldered in my
stomach.
Trepidation snaked along my
spine.
Trepidation snatched at my
heart.
Trepidation streamed down
my face.
Trepidation surged through
my gut.
Trepidation swirled in my
stomach.
Trepidation tightened
between my shoulders.
Trepidation tightened in my
stomach.
Trepidation traipsed up my
spine.
Trepidation trembled down
my spine.
Trepidation tugged at my legs.
Trepidation wafted up my
spine.
Trepidation washed through
my mouth.
I felt a burst of trepidation.
I felt a chill of trepidation.
I felt a flash of trepidation.
I felt a flutter of trepidation.
I felt a goad of trepidation.

I felt a jab of trepidation.
I felt a jolt of trepidation.
I felt a knife of trepidation.
I felt a knot of trepidation.
I felt a lancet of trepidation.
I felt a mixture of trepidation.
I felt a moment of trepidation.
I felt a note of trepidation.
I felt a pang of trepidation.
I felt a prickle of trepidation.
I felt a pulse of trepidation.
I felt a quiver of trepidation.
I felt a ridge of trepidation.
I felt a ripple of trepidation.
I felt a rush of trepidation.
I felt a sense of trepidation.
I felt a shaft of trepidation.
I felt a shiver of trepidation.
I felt a shudder of trepidation.
I felt a slick of trepidation.
I felt a spark of trepidation.
I felt a spasm of trepidation.
I felt a spike of trepidation.
I felt a spurt of trepidation.
I felt a stab of trepidation.
I felt a surge of trepidation.
I felt a swell of trepidation.
I felt a thrill of trepidation.
I felt a tingle of trepidation.
I felt a tremor of trepidation.
I felt a twinge of trepidation.
I felt a whisper of trepidation.
I felt a whorl of trepidation.
I felt an ache of trepidation.
I felt an icicle of trepidation.
I gave a tremor of trepidation.
I sniffed a sliver of trepidation.

I swallowed a lump of
trepidation.
My body was electric with
trepidation.
My eyes grew huge with
trepidation.
My eyes grew wide with
trepidation.
My eyes opened wide in
trepidation.
My eyes opened wide with
trepidation.
My eyes snapped wide with
trepidation.
My eyes squeezed shut with
trepidation.
My eyes were big with
trepidation.
My eyes were black with
trepidation.
My eyes were blind with
trepidation.
My eyes were bright with
trepidation.
My eyes were crazy with
trepidation.
My eyes were dark with
trepidation.
My eyes were full of
trepidation.
My eyes were glassy with
trepidation.
My eyes were grey with
trepidation.
My eyes were huge with
trepidation.
My eyes were large with
trepidation.

My eyes were wide with
trepidation.
My eyes were wild with
trepidation.
My face was ashen with
trepidation.
My face was crazy with
trepidation.
My face was frantic with
trepidation.
My heart became cold with
trepidation.
My heart was full of
trepidation.
My mouth fell open in
trepidation.
My mouth grew dry with
trepidation.
My mouth hung open in
trepidation.
My mouth was dry with
trepidation.
My shoulders were tense with
trepidation.
My stomach turned sick with
trepidation.
My throat was raw with
trepidation.
My throat was thick with
trepidation.
My voice pitched high with
trepidation.
My voice was shrill with
trepidation.

TRIUMPH

Definition: Joy or satisfaction resulting from a success or victory.
See JOY

I beamed in triumph.
I grinned in triumph.
I smiled in triumph.
I yelped in triumph.
Triumph brightened my eyes.
Triumph coursed through me.
Triumph darkened my eyes.
Triumph engorged my heart.
Triumph engulfed my face.
Triumph filled my heart.
Triumph flashed through me.
Triumph flooded through me.
Triumph leapt through me.
Triumph lit my eyes.
Triumph raced through me.
Triumph rippled through me.
Triumph settled my soul.
Triumph stung my eyes.
Triumph surged through me.
Triumph swept through me.
Triumph warmed my insides.
Triumph washed through me.
Triumph welled inside me.
Triumph widened my eyes.
My body quivered with triumph.
My chest swelled with triumph.
My eyebrows danced in triumph.
My eyes beamed with triumph.
My eyes burned with triumph.
My eyes danced with triumph.

My eyes filled with triumph.
My eyes flashed in triumph.
My eyes gleamed with triumph.
My eyes glittered in triumph.
My eyes glowed in triumph.
My eyes shimmered with triumph.
My eyes shone with triumph.
My eyes sparkled with triumph.
My eyes twinkled with triumph.
My eyes widened in triumph.
My eyes widened with triumph.
My face filled with triumph.
My face flooded with triumph.
My face glowed with triumph.
My face lit with triumph.
My face written with triumph.
My head buzzed with triumph.
My heart beat with triumph.
My heart burst with triumph.
My heart danced with triumph.
My heart filled with triumph.
My heart flipped with triumph.
My heart fluttered with triumph.
My heart leapt with triumph.

My heart molten with
triumph.
My heart pinged with
triumph.
My voice brimmed with
triumph.
My voice crackled with
triumph.
My voice quavered with
triumph.
My voice screeched with
triumph.
Triumph broke over my face.
Triumph clapped in my chest.
Triumph flashed across my
face.
Triumph flickered in my eyes.
Triumph flitted across my
face.
Triumph gleamed in my eyes.
Triumph glistened in my eyes.
Triumph rang in my voice.
Triumph rolled down my face.
Triumph shone on my face.
Triumph streamed down my
cheeks.
Triumph streamed down my
face.
I felt a burst of triumph.
I felt a flash of triumph.
I felt a glow of triumph.
I felt a kind of triumph.
I felt a moment of triumph.
I felt a sense of triumph.
I felt a surge of triumph.
I gave a cry of triumph.
I gave a punch of triumph.
I gave a roar of triumph.

I uttered a cry of triumph.
My eyebrows went up in
triumph.
My eyes lit up with triumph.
My eyes were cold with
triumph.
My eyes were huge with
triumph.
My eyes were white with
triumph.
My eyes were wide with
triumph.
My face lit up in triumph.
My face was brilliant with
triumph.
My heart was full of triumph.
My nerves cried out in
triumph.

U

UNEASINESS
Definition: A feeling of anxiety or discomfort.
See ANXIETY

Uneasiness ate into me.
Uneasiness churned inside me.
Uneasiness clawed at me.
Uneasiness coursed through me.
Uneasiness crossed my face.
Uneasiness fell over me.
Uneasiness filled my voice.
Uneasiness flicked at me.
Uneasiness flitted past me.
Uneasiness flooded over me.
Uneasiness knotted my gut.
Uneasiness knotted my insides.
Uneasiness knotted my shoulders.
Uneasiness knotted my stomach.
Uneasiness lined my face.
Uneasiness pinched my lips.
Uneasiness pumped my heart.
Uneasiness ran through me.
Uneasiness rushed through me.
Uneasiness scraped my spine.
Uneasiness slipped from me.
Uneasiness squeezed my belly.

Uneasiness stole through me.
Uneasiness swept over me.
Uneasiness swept through me.
Uneasiness swirled through me.
Uneasiness tightened my breath.
Uneasiness tightened my shoulders.
Uneasiness tugged at me.
Uneasiness washed over me.
Uneasiness washed through me.
Uneasiness weighed on me.
Uneasiness went through me.
Uneasiness wormed through me.
My body hummed with uneasiness.
My eyebrows furrowed in uneasiness.
My eyes clouded with uneasiness.
My eyes widened in uneasiness.
My face creased in uneasiness.

My face creased with
uneasiness.
My face flooded with
uneasiness.
My face flushed with
uneasiness.
My face fluttered from
uneasiness.
My face pinched with
uneasiness.
My face twisted with
uneasiness.
My face wisped with
uneasiness.
My head throbbed with
uneasiness.
My jaw worked with
uneasiness.
My mouth puckered with
uneasiness.
My nose quivered with
uneasiness.
My shoulders knotted with
uneasiness.
My stomach clenched in
uneasiness.
My stomach cramped with
uneasiness.
My stomach knotted with
uneasiness.
My tone edged with
uneasiness.
My tone softened with
uneasiness.
My voice broken with
uneasiness.
My voice marbled with
uneasiness.

My voice strained with
uneasiness.
My voice tinged with
uneasiness.
Uneasiness came into my eyes.
Uneasiness churned in my gut.
Uneasiness coursed through
my veins.
Uneasiness crawled up my
back.
Uneasiness crept into my
voice.
Uneasiness crept up my spine.
Uneasiness etched across my
face.
Uneasiness flickered in my
eyes.
Uneasiness gnawed at my
thoughts.
Uneasiness nagged at my
mind.
Uneasiness plucked at my
chest.
Uneasiness pressed against my
chest.
Uneasiness pulsed through my
body.
Uneasiness pumped through
my veins.
Uneasiness roared in my head.
Uneasiness roiled in my gut.
Uneasiness rose in my throat.
Uneasiness rushed down my
spine.
Uneasiness skated up my
spine.
Uneasiness slithered up my
spine.

Uneasiness spilled through my guts.
Uneasiness sprinted across my eyes.
Uneasiness swept through my body.
Uneasiness trembled in my stomach.
Uneasiness whispered in my gut.
I felt a chill of uneasiness.
I felt a flutter of uneasiness.
I felt a moment of uneasiness.
I felt a ripple of uneasiness.
I felt a sense of uneasiness.
I felt a stab of uneasiness.
I felt a surge of uneasiness.
I felt a trace of uneasiness.
I felt a tremor of uneasiness.
I felt a twinge of uneasiness.
My face was full of uneasiness.
My mouth was dry with uneasiness.
My spine went cold with uneasiness.
My voice was taut with uneasiness.
My voice was thin with uneasiness.
Uneasiness caused my throat to tighten.

UNHAPPINESS

Definition: The feeling of not being happy.
See SADNESS

Unhappiness came over me.
Unhappiness clouded my expression.
Unhappiness crashed over me.
Unhappiness crept over me.
Unhappiness crossed my face.
Unhappiness crossed my features.
Unhappiness darkened my eyes.
Unhappiness ebbed over me.
Unhappiness entered my voice.
Unhappiness filled my eyes.
Unhappiness filled my voice.
Unhappiness howled through me.
Unhappiness invaded my eyes.
Unhappiness lined my face.
Unhappiness rose off me.
Unhappiness seeped into me.
Unhappiness settled over me.
Unhappiness sizzled through me.
Unhappiness spiralled through me.
Unhappiness squeezed my chest.
Unhappiness swept through me.
Unhappiness tinged my eyes.
Unhappiness tinged my voice.
Unhappiness tugged at me.

Unhappiness washed over me.
Unhappiness weighed on me.
Unhappiness welled inside me.
My eyes drooped with unhappiness.
My eyes filled with unhappiness.
My eyes shadowed in unhappiness.
My face clenched with unhappiness.
My face creased with unhappiness.
My face crumpled with unhappiness.
My face darkened with unhappiness.
My face etched with unhappiness.
My face filled with unhappiness.
My face sagged with unhappiness.
My tone laced with unhappiness.
My tone shaded with unhappiness.
My tone softened with unhappiness.
My voice filled with unhappiness.
My voice infused with unhappiness.

My voice laced with
unhappiness.
My voice tinged with
unhappiness.
Unhappiness came into my
eyes.
Unhappiness came into my
voice.
Unhappiness crept into my
expression.
Unhappiness drifted across my
face.
Unhappiness flickered in my
eyes.
Unhappiness flickered in my
face.
Unhappiness lay in my heart.
Unhappiness lingered in my
eyes.
Unhappiness passed over my
face.
Unhappiness seeped into my
muscles.
Unhappiness settled on my
face.
Unhappiness showed in my
eyes.
Unhappiness welled in my
chest.
Unhappiness welled in my
eyes.
I felt a chill of unhappiness.
I felt a flash of unhappiness.
I felt a pang of unhappiness.
I felt a pinch of unhappiness.
I felt a sense of unhappiness.
I felt a swell of unhappiness.
I felt a touch of unhappiness.

I felt a twinge of unhappiness.
I felt a wave of unhappiness.
I gave a sigh of unhappiness.
My eyes were full of
unhappiness.
My face was heavy with
unhappiness.
My tone was thick with
unhappiness.
My voice was full of
unhappiness.
My voice was soft with
unhappiness.
A touch of unhappiness came
into my eyes.

WOE

Definition: Great sorrow or distress.

See MISERY

I groaned in woe.
Woe clapped my hands.
Woe clawed at me.
Woe clogged my throat.
Woe crashed through me.
Woe crossed my face.
Woe crushed my chest.
Woe darkened my eyes.
Woe etched my face.
Woe exploded inside me.
Woe exploded through me.
Woe filled my body.
Woe filled my heart.
Woe filled my voice.
Woe fuelled my voice.
Woe ignited my nerves.
Woe lined my face.
Woe lined my features.
Woe paralysed my legs.
Woe pierced my body.
Woe pierced my sinuses.
Woe pulsed through me.
Woe ripped through me.
Woe robbed my breath.
Woe sang through me.
Woe stabbed my side.
Woe streaked my face.

Woe swept through me.
Woe throbbed inside me.
Woe tightened my features.
Woe tightened my throat.
Woe touched my heart.
My body contorted in woe.
My body convulsed in woe.
My body creamed in woe.
My body exploded with woe.
My body paralyzed with woe.
My body screamed with woe.
My body shrieked in woe.
My body spasmed in woe.
My body throbbed in woe.
My body writhed in woe.
My chest heaved with woe.
My ears stabbed with woe.
My eyes closed in woe.
My eyes filled with woe.
My eyes flared with woe.
My eyes glazed in woe.
My eyes narrowed in woe.
My eyes rolled in woe.
My eyes swam with woe.
My eyes widened in woe.
My face clenched in woe.
My face clenched with woe.

My face contorted in woe.
My face contorted with woe.
My face crumbled with woe.
My face crumpled in woe.
My face etched in woe.
My face filled with woe.
My face lined with woe.
My face pinched in woe.
My face puckered in woe.
My face squeezed with woe.
My face twisted in woe.
My face twisted with woe.
My heart exploded with woe.
My lips tightened in woe.
My lips trembled in woe.
My mouth twisted with woe.
My nerves screamed in woe.
My shoulders sagged in woe.
My voice broke with woe.
My voice cracked with woe.
My voice filled with woe.
My voice grated with woe.
My voice rose in woe.
My voice twisted in woe.
My voice vibrated with woe.
Woe came into my eyes.
Woe came over my face.
Woe crawled around my mind.
Woe emanated from my body.
Woe etched on my face.
Woe exploded in my guts.
Woe flared from my fingertips.
Woe flared in my ribs.
Woe flared up my leg.
Woe flashed in my eyes.
Woe flickered in my eyes.
Woe froze in my throat.
Woe glazed in my eyes.

Woe grew in my face.
Woe radiated from my back.
Woe ripped across my face.
Woe ripped through my body.
Woe ripped through my head.
Woe rushed through my body.
Woe sat on my chest.
Woe seared through my leg.
Woe shrieked from my mouth.
Woe struck my nervous
system.
Woe swept through my body.
Woe tore up my spine.
Woe washed down my cheeks.
Woe welled in my chest.
Woe welled into my eyes.
I swallowed a ball of woe.
My body crumpled up in woe.
My eyes glowed red with woe.
My eyes opened wide with
woe.
My eyes were bright with woe.
My eyes were dark with woe.
My eyes were full of woe.
My face screwed up in woe.
My face was full of woe.
My head hung low in woe.
My knees drew up in woe.
My mouth sagged open in woe.
My throat closed up with woe.
My voice trailed off in woe.
My voice was full of woe.
My voice was hoarse with woe.
My voice was shrill with woe.
Woe lay heavy on my mind.
A touch of woe came into my
eyes.

WONDER

Definition: A feeling of amazement and admiration, caused by something beautiful, remarkable, or unfamiliar.
See AWE

I grunted in wonder.
Wonder brightened my gaze.
Wonder coloured my voice.
Wonder crept over me.
Wonder crossed my face.
Wonder flared inside me.
Wonder jolted through me.
Wonder lit my eyes.
Wonder lit my face.
Wonder lit my features.
Wonder made me gasp.
Wonder parted my lips.
Wonder rose within me.
Wonder snaked through me.
Wonder twisted my gut.
My brows arched in wonder.
My brows climbed in wonder.
My brows lifted in wonder.
My brows raised in wonder.
My brows rose in wonder.
My ears flickered in wonder.
My eyebrows arched in wonder.
My eyebrows arched with wonder.
My eyebrows lifted in wonder.
My eyebrows raised in wonder.
My eyebrows rose in wonder.
My eyebrows rose with wonder.
My eyes blinked in wonder.
My eyes blinked with wonder.

My eyes bloomed with wonder.
My eyes brightened with wonder.
My eyes filled with wonder.
My eyes flared in wonder.
My eyes flared with wonder.
My eyes flashed from wonder.
My eyes flashed with wonder.
My eyes flickered with wonder.
My eyes fluttered in wonder.
My eyes opened in wonder.
My eyes popped in wonder.
My eyes popped with wonder.
My eyes rounded in wonder.
My eyes scrunched in wonder.
My eyes shut in wonder.
My eyes stared in wonder.
My eyes twinkled with wonder.
My eyes widened in wonder.
My eyes widened with wonder.
My face altered from wonder.
My face collapsed in wonder.
My face contorted with wonder.
My face frozen in wonder.
My face relaxed with wonder.
My face scrunched in wonder.
My face twisted in wonder.
My face winced in wonder.
My head cocked in wonder.

My head jerked in wonder.
My head shook in wonder.
My head throbbed with wonder.
My jaw dropped in wonder.
My jaw gaped in wonder.
My lips parted in wonder.
My lips rounded in wonder.
My mouth dropped in wonder.
My mouth gaped in wonder.
My mouth opened in wonder.
My mouth parted in wonder.
My skin deepened with wonder.
My voice filled with wonder.
Wonder came over my face.
Wonder edged into my voice.
Wonder flashed on my face.
Wonder flickered across my face.
Wonder flickered over my face.
Wonder flitted across my face.
Wonder lit up my face.
Wonder passed across my face.
Wonder passed over my face.
Wonder plastered across my face.
Wonder played across my face.
Wonder reflected in my eyes.
Wonder registered on my face.
Wonder settled on my face.
Wonder settled over my face.
Wonder showed in my eyes.
Wonder sounded in my voice.
I felt a shiver of wonder.
I felt a tinge of wonder.

I gave a whistle of wonder.
My body was motionless with wonder.
My brows shot up in wonder.
My eyebrows shot up in wonder.
My eyebrows went up in wonder.
My eyes bloomed wide with wonder.
My eyes flew open in wonder.
My eyes grew huge with wonder.
My eyes grew wide with wonder.
My eyes lit up in wonder.
My eyes opened wide in wonder.
My eyes opened wide with wonder.
My eyes shot up in wonder.
My eyes were full of wonder.
My eyes were luminous with wonder.
My eyes were wide in wonder.
My eyes were wide with wonder.
My face lit up in wonder.
My face screwed up in wonder.
My face was alive with wonder.
My face was blank with wonder.
My face was full of wonder.
My face was wide with wonder.
My head was abuzz with wonder.

My head whipped around in
wonder.
My mouth dropped open in
wonder.
My mouth fell open in
wonder.
My mouth hung open in
wonder.
My mouth was agape in
wonder.
My mouth was wide in
wonder.
My voice was soft with
wonder.

WONDERMENT

Definition: A state of awed admiration or respect.

See AWE

I grunted in wonderment.
Wonderment brightened my gaze.
Wonderment coloured my voice.
Wonderment crept over me.
Wonderment crossed my face.
Wonderment flared inside me.
Wonderment jolted through me.
Wonderment lit my eyes.
Wonderment lit my face.
Wonderment lit my features.
Wonderment made me gasp.
Wonderment parted my lips.
Wonderment rose within me.
Wonderment snaked through me.
Wonderment twisted my gut.
My brows arched in wonderment.
My brows climbed in wonderment.
My brows lifted in wonderment.
My brows raised in wonderment.
My brows rose in wonderment.
My ears flickered in wonderment.
My eyebrows arched in wonderment.

My eyebrows arched with wonderment.
My eyebrows lifted in wonderment.
My eyebrows raised in wonderment.
My eyebrows rose in wonderment.
My eyebrows rose with wonderment.
My eyes blinked in wonderment.
My eyes blinked with wonderment.
My eyes bloomed with wonderment.
My eyes brightened with wonderment.
My eyes filled with wonderment.
My eyes flared in wonderment.
My eyes flared with wonderment.
My eyes flashed from wonderment.
My eyes flashed with wonderment.
My eyes flickered with wonderment.
My eyes fluttered in wonderment.
My eyes opened in wonderment.

My eyes popped in
wonderment.
My eyes popped with
wonderment.
My eyes rounded in
wonderment.
My eyes scrunched in
wonderment.
My eyes shut in wonderment.
My eyes stared in
wonderment.
My eyes twinkled with
wonderment.
My eyes widened in
wonderment.
My eyes widened with
wonderment.
My face altered from
wonderment.
My face collapsed in
wonderment.
My face contorted with
wonderment.
My face frozen in
wonderment.
My face relaxed with
wonderment.
My face scrunched in
wonderment.
My face twisted in
wonderment.
My face winced in
wonderment.
My head cocked in
wonderment.
My head jerked in
wonderment.

My head shook in
wonderment.
My head throbbed with
wonderment.
My jaw dropped in
wonderment.
My jaw gaped in wonderment.
My lips parted in wonderment.
My lips rounded in
wonderment.
My mouth dropped in
wonderment.
My mouth gaped in
wonderment.
My mouth opened in
wonderment.
My mouth parted in
wonderment.
My skin deepened with
wonderment.
My voice filled with
wonderment.
Wonderment came over my
face.
Wonderment edged into my
voice.
Wonderment flashed on my
face.
Wonderment flickered across
my face.
Wonderment flickered over
my face.
Wonderment flitted across my
face.
Wonderment lit up my face.
Wonderment passed across my
face.

Wonderment passed over my face.
Wonderment plastered across my face.
Wonderment played across my face.
Wonderment reflected in my eyes.
Wonderment registered on my face.
Wonderment settled on my face.
Wonderment settled over my face.
Wonderment showed in my eyes.
Wonderment sounded in my voice.
I felt a shiver of wonderment.
I felt a tinge of wonderment.
I gave a whistle of wonderment.
My body was motionless with wonderment.
My brows shot up in wonderment.
My eyebrows shot up in wonderment.
My eyebrows went up in wonderment.
My eyes bloomed wide with wonderment.
My eyes flew open in wonderment.
My eyes grew huge with wonderment.
My eyes grew wide with wonderment.

My eyes lit up in wonderment.
My eyes opened wide in wonderment.
My eyes opened wide with wonderment.
My eyes shot up in wonderment.
My eyes were full of wonderment.
My eyes were luminous with wonderment.
My eyes were wide in wonderment.
My eyes were wide with wonderment.
My face lit up in wonderment.
My face screwed up in wonderment.
My face was alive with wonderment.
My face was blank with wonderment.
My face was full of wonderment.
My face was wide with wonderment.
My head was abuzz with wonderment.
My head whipped around in wonderment.
My mouth dropped open in wonderment.
My mouth fell open in wonderment.
My mouth hung open in wonderment.
My mouth was agape in wonderment.

My mouth was wide in
wonderment.
My voice was soft with
wonderment.

WORRY

Definition: The state of being anxious and troubled over actual or potential problems.
See ANXIETY

I bubbled with worry.
I filled with worry.
I frowned in worry.
Worry clouded my face.
Worry clouded my features.
Worry creased my forehead.
Worry crinkled my features.
Worry crossed my face.
Worry darkened my eyes.
Worry edged my voice.
Worry etched my face.
Worry filled my senses.
Worry furrowed my brows.
Worry gnawed at me.
Worry knifed through me.
Worry knitted my brow.
Worry knitted my brows.
Worry knotted my belly.
Worry knotted my insides.
Worry lit my expression.
Worry mushroomed inside me.
Worry niggled at me.
Worry pinched my brows.
Worry rippled my jawline.
Worry seeped into me.
Worry slashed my face.
Worry tickled my spine.
Worry tightened my eyes.
Worry tightened my features.
Worry went through me.
My brows creased in worry.

My brows etched with worry.
My brows furrowed with worry.
My brows knitted with worry.
My brows narrowed with worry.
My chest ached with worry.
My eyebrows scrunched in worry.
My eyes clouded with worry.
My eyes creased with worry.
My eyes darkened with worry.
My eyes faded with worry.
My eyes filled with worry.
My eyes flared with worry.
My eyes flickered with worry.
My eyes narrowed with worry.
My eyes pinched with worry.
My eyes shadowed with worry.
My face creased with worry.
My face crinkled in worry.
My face crinkled with worry.
My face crumpled with worry.
My face darkened with worry.
My face etched with worry.
My face gouged with worry.
My face lined with worry.
My face pinched with worry.
My face pouched with worry.
My face set in worry.
My face strained with worry.
My face swollen with worry.

My face twisted with worry.
My head ached with worry.
My head swam with worry.
My heart pounded with worry.
My insides churned with
worry.
My insides scoured with
worry.
My nerves jangled with worry.
My voice drooped with worry.
My voice trembled with worry.
Worry crumpled up my face.
Worry flickered in my
expression.
Worry grew in my stomach.
Worry raced through my
expression.
Worry scurried about my
mind.
Worry slid across my face.
Worry slipped into my voice.
I felt a stab of worry.
I felt a twinge of worry.
I swallowed a tickle of worry.
My eyes were alive with worry.
My eyes were dark with worry.
My eyes were frantic with
worry.
My eyes were full of worry.
My eyes were wide with worry.
My face screwed up with
worry.
My face was full of worry.
My face was taut with worry.
My gut was full of worry.
My mouth was a line of worry.

WRATH

Definition: Extreme anger.
See ANGER

Wrath battled inside me.
Wrath boiled in me.
Wrath boiled inside me.
Wrath boiled within me.
Wrath brightened my eyes.
Wrath broke within me.
Wrath bubbled inside me.
Wrath bubbled within me.
Wrath built inside me.
Wrath burned inside me.
Wrath burned through me.
Wrath burned within me.
Wrath churned inside me.
Wrath churned through me.
Wrath clenched inside me.
Wrath clouded my face.
Wrath coiled inside me.
Wrath coursed through me.
Wrath crept into me.
Wrath crossed my brow.
Wrath crossed my eyes.
Wrath crossed my face.
Wrath crowded my throat.
Wrath darkened my
complexion.
Wrath darkened my eyes.
Wrath dimmed my eyes.
Wrath emanated from me.
Wrath engulfed my body.
Wrath entered my voice.
Wrath etched my face.
Wrath festered inside me.
Wrath filled my eyes.

Wrath flared in me.
Wrath flared inside me.
Wrath flared through me.
Wrath flashed in me.
Wrath flickered in me.
Wrath flooded my face.
Wrath flooded my soul.
Wrath flooded through me.
Wrath flushed through me.
Wrath grew inside me.
Wrath grew within me.
Wrath hardened my face.
Wrath hardened my insides.
Wrath hardened my tone.
Wrath hardened my voice.
Wrath hardened my words.
Wrath heated my blood.
Wrath hissed inside me.
Wrath knotted my insides.
Wrath knotted my stomach.
Wrath mottled my face.
Wrath mounted inside me.
Wrath mushroomed inside
me.
Wrath opened my eyes.
Wrath overpowered my
instinct.
Wrath painted my face.
Wrath passed over me.
Wrath pumped through me.
Wrath raced through me.
Wrath radiated from me.
Wrath railed through me.

Wrath ran through me.
Wrath reddened my cheeks.
Wrath reddened my chief.
Wrath reddened my face.
Wrath roared in me.
Wrath roared through me.
Wrath robbed my smile.
Wrath rode through me.
Wrath roiled inside me.
Wrath roiled within me.
Wrath rose in me.
Wrath rose inside me.
Wrath rose within me.
Wrath rumbled through me.
Wrath rushed through me.
Wrath seared my eyes.
Wrath seeped through me.
Wrath seethed through me.
Wrath sharpened my eyes.
Wrath sheened my eyes.
Wrath shot through me.
Wrath slashed my features.
Wrath smoldered inside me.
Wrath smoldered within me.
Wrath smouldered inside me.
Wrath sparked inside me.
Wrath sparked my adrenaline.
Wrath spiked in me.
Wrath spiked through me.
Wrath spiralled through me.
Wrath splintered through me.
Wrath stung my eyes.
Wrath surged inside me.
Wrath surged through me.
Wrath swelled inside me.
Wrath swept over me.
Wrath swirled through me.
Wrath swirled within me.

Wrath tainted my voice.
Wrath tightened my face.
Wrath tightened my lips.
Wrath tightened my mouth.
Wrath tightened my throat.
Wrath tinged my voice.
Wrath tinged my words.
Wrath tore through me.
Wrath touched my voice.
Wrath trembled through me.
Wrath twisted my face.
Wrath washed over me.
Wrath welled within me.
Wrath went through me.
My blood boiled with wrath.
My body quaked with wrath.
My body quivered with wrath.
My body shook with wrath.
My body teemed with wrath.
My chest throbbed with wrath.
My ears warm with wrath.
My eyebrows knitted in wrath.
My eyes blazed with wrath.
My eyes bulged in wrath.
My eyes bulged with wrath.
My eyes burned with wrath.
My eyes clouded with wrath.
My eyes filled with wrath.
My eyes fixed with wrath.
My eyes flared in wrath.
My eyes flared with wrath.
My eyes flashed in wrath.
My eyes flashed with wrath.
My eyes flickered with wrath.
My eyes glinted with wrath.
My eyes glittered with wrath.
My eyes glowed with wrath.
My eyes hardened with wrath.

My eyes narrowed in wrath.
My eyes narrowed with wrath.
My eyes shone with wrath.
My eyes shrank with wrath.
My eyes simmered with wrath.
My eyes smouldered with
wrath.
My eyes snapped with wrath.
My eyes sparkled with wrath.
My eyes widened in wrath.
My face blackened with wrath.
My face blanched with wrath.
My face burned with wrath.
My face contorted in wrath.
My face contorted with wrath.
My face creased with wrath.
My face darkened in wrath.
My face darkened with wrath.
My face flared with wrath.
My face flashed with wrath.
My face flushed in wrath.
My face flushed with wrath.
My face reddened in wrath.
My face reddened with wrath.
My face set with wrath.
My face strained in wrath.
My face tensed with wrath.
My face tightened in wrath.
My face tightened with wrath.
My face twisted in wrath.
My face twisted with wrath.
My face twitched with wrath.
My head sang with wrath.
My heart pounded with wrath.
My jaw bunched with wrath.
My jaw clenched in wrath.
My jaw clenched with wrath.
My jaw fixed in wrath.

My jaw flexed with wrath.
My jaw pulsed with wrath.
My jaw set in wrath.
My jaw squared in wrath.
My jaw twitched with wrath.
My lips curled with wrath.
My lips flattened with wrath.
My lips pinched in wrath.
My lips pursed in wrath.
My lips tightened in wrath.
My mouth pinched in wrath.
My mouth pinched with
wrath.
My mouth pursed in wrath.
My mouth thinned in wrath.
My mouth tightened in wrath.
My neck bulged in wrath.
My neck pulsed in wrath.
My nose flared with wrath.
My skin flushed with wrath.
My stomach churned with
wrath.
My stomach knotted in wrath.
My throat tightened with
wrath.
My tone edged toward wrath.
My voice bristled with wrath.
My voice cracked with wrath.
My voice deepened with
wrath.
My voice filled with wrath.
My voice hardened with
wrath.
My voice laced with wrath.
My voice pitched with wrath.
My voice quaked with wrath.
My voice quivered with wrath.
My voice raised in wrath.

My voice rasped with wrath.
My voice rose in wrath.
My voice rose with wrath.
My voice seethed in wrath.
My voice seethed with wrath.
My voice shook with wrath.
My voice smoldered with
wrath.
My voice steeped in wrath.
My voice stiffened with wrath.
My voice tinged with wrath.
My voice trembled with wrath.
My voice vibrated in wrath.
My voice vibrated with wrath.
Wrath blossomed in my chest.
Wrath blossomed in my face.
Wrath boiled beneath my skin.
Wrath boiled in my chest.
Wrath boiled in my gut.
Wrath boiled in my veins.
Wrath braided around my
spine.
Wrath bubbled up my throat.
Wrath burned in my belly.
Wrath burned in my chest.
Wrath came into my voice.
Wrath chattered in my head.
Wrath churned in my gut.
Wrath churned through my
belly.
Wrath coiled in my belly.
Wrath coursed through my
veins.
Wrath crackled in my eyes.
Wrath crept into my tone.
Wrath crept into my voice.
Wrath dashed across my face.
Wrath etched into my face.

Wrath expanded in my chest.
Wrath expanded in my gut.
Wrath exploded through my
veins.
Wrath festered in my chest.
Wrath flared in my breast.
Wrath flared in my eyes.
Wrath flared in my gaze.
Wrath flared on my face.
Wrath flashed across my face.
Wrath flashed in my
expression.
Wrath flashed in my eyes.
Wrath flashed in my face.
Wrath flashed through my
mind.
Wrath flickered across my
face.
Wrath flickered in my eyes.
Wrath flitted across my
expression.
Wrath flowed through my
veins.
Wrath flushed through my
face.
Wrath glittered in my eyes.
Wrath grew in my shoulders.
Wrath hummed through my
system.
Wrath lit up my insides.
Wrath lodged in my throat.
Wrath mounted in my voice.
Wrath raced across my
features.
Wrath raged in my eyes.
Wrath registered in my eyes.
Wrath rippled across my face.

Wrath rippled through my
body.
Wrath roared in my ears.
Wrath rose in my gut.
Wrath rose in my throat.
Wrath rose in my voice.
Wrath rose up my neck.
Wrath seeped into my body.
Wrath seeped into my voice.
Wrath seethed in my eyes.
Wrath shone in my eyes.
Wrath showed on my face.
Wrath simmered in my breast.
Wrath simmered in my eyes.
Wrath sizzled in my eyes.
Wrath slammed into my mind.
Wrath smoldered in my breast.
Wrath smoldered in my eyes.
Wrath sparked in my eyes.
Wrath surfaced in my tone.
Wrath surged through my
body.
Wrath surged through my
veins.
Wrath swelled in my chest.
Wrath swirled through my
insides.
Wrath tightened up my face.
Wrath tore at my heart.
Wrath vibrated in my voice.
Wrath washed over my mind.
My ears burned hot from
wrath.
My eyes glazed over with
wrath.
My eyes lit up with wrath.
My eyes opened wide with
wrath.

My eyes rimmed red with
wrath.
My eyes turned hot with
wrath.
My eyes were bright with
wrath.
My eyes were dark with wrath.
My eyes were fierce with
wrath.
My eyes were narrow in wrath.
My eyes were wide with wrath.
My eyes were wild with wrath.
My face grew heavy with
wrath.
My face grew hot with wrath.
My face screwed up in wrath.
My face turned flush with
wrath.
My face turned red with
wrath.
My face turned rosy with
wrath.
My face was fierce with wrath.
My face was hot with wrath.
My face was livid with wrath.
My face was mobile with
wrath.
My face was puffy with wrath.
My face was red with wrath.
My face was ruddy with wrath.
My lips were taut with wrath.
My neck flushed crimson with
wrath.
My skin turned red with
wrath.
My vision went red with
wrath.

My voice boomed out in
wrath.
My voice was full of wrath.
My voice was harsh with
wrath.
My voice was hot with wrath.
My voice was taut with wrath.
My voice was terse with wrath.
My voice was thick with
wrath.
Wrath flared red in my vision.

Y

YEARNING

Definition: A feeling of intense longing for something.
See LONGING

Yearning bubbled through me.
Yearning caressed my mouth.
Yearning clawed at me.
Yearning coursed through me.
Yearning crowded my chest.
Yearning curled through me.
Yearning darkened my irises.
Yearning drifted through me.
Yearning exploded inside me.
Yearning flowed over me.
Yearning flowed through me.
Yearning fluttered inside me.
Yearning glowed inside me.
Yearning gushed through me.
Yearning heated my blood.
Yearning knifed through me.
Yearning laced my voice.
Yearning licked through me.
Yearning made me melt.
Yearning penetrated my heart.
Yearning poured through me.
Yearning pulsed through me.
Yearning pumped through me.
Yearning radiated from me.
Yearning radiated through me.
Yearning ravaged my face.
Yearning rippled through me.

Yearning rose from me.
Yearning rose in me.
Yearning shattered within me.
Yearning slammed into me.
Yearning sluiced through me.
Yearning spiralled through me.
Yearning splintered through
me.
Yearning sprouted inside me.
Yearning surged through me.
Yearning surged within me.
Yearning swelled within me.
Yearning swept through me.
Yearning swirled through me.
Yearning tightened inside me.
Yearning tightened my
features.
Yearning tightened my throat.
Yearning tugged at me.
Yearning wafted through me.
Yearning warmed my insides.
Yearning went through me.
My blood burned with
yearning.
My blood heated with
yearning.

My body burned with yearning.
My body drugged with yearning.
My body hardened with yearning.
My body heated with yearning.
My body hummed with yearning.
My body jangled with yearning.
My body shivered with yearning.
My body stirred with yearning.
My body throbbed with yearning.
My body thrummed with yearning.
My body twitched with yearning.
My body unfurled with yearning.
My chest clenched with yearning.
My ears shut in yearning.
My eyes blazed with yearning.
My eyes danced with yearning.
My eyes darkened with yearning.
My eyes flared with yearning.
My eyes flickered with yearning.
My eyes gleamed with yearning.
My eyes glittered with yearning.
My eyes glowed with yearning.
My eyes lit with yearning.

My eyes narrowed with yearning.
My eyes shimmered with yearning.
My face filled with yearning.
My face flushed with yearning.
My heart burned with yearning.
My heart filled with yearning.
My heart fluttered with yearning.
My heart swelled with yearning.
My pulse raced with yearning.
My skin flushed with yearning.
My voice slurred with yearning.
Yearning banked in my eyes.
Yearning combated in my brain.
Yearning danced in my belly.
Yearning flashed in my eyes.
Yearning flickered in my expression.
Yearning flickered in my eyes.
Yearning nipped at my skin.
Yearning swept through my body.
Yearning throbbed against my belly.
I felt a moment of yearning.
I felt a pang of yearning.
I felt a rush of yearning.
I felt a sense of yearning.
I felt a stab of yearning.
I felt a twinge of yearning.
I felt a wave of yearning.
I felt an ache of yearning.

My body was overwrought
with yearning.
My eyes went dark with
yearning.
My eyes were dark with
yearning.
My eyes were full of yearning.
My eyes were hazy with
yearning.
My eyes were heavy with
yearning.
My eyes were unclouded with
yearning.
My face glazed over with
yearning.
My throat was thick with
yearning.
My voice sounded rough with
yearning.
My voice was rough with
yearning.
My voice was thick with
yearning.
Yearning curled deep in my
belly.
Yearning pooled low in my
belly.

Z

ZEAL

Definition: Great energy or enthusiasm in pursuit of a cause or an objective.
See PASSION

Zeal boiled inside me.
Zeal bubbled through me.
Zeal caressed my mouth.
Zeal clawed at me.
Zeal clouded my mind.
Zeal coursed through me.
Zeal crowded my chest.
Zeal curled through me.
Zeal darkened my eyes.
Zeal darkened my irises.
Zeal dilated my eyes.
Zeal drifted through me.
Zeal entered my voice.
Zeal exploded inside me.
Zeal exploded within me.
Zeal filled my head.
Zeal flowed over me.
Zeal flowed through me.
Zeal fluttered inside me.
Zeal glowed inside me.
Zeal gushed through me.
Zeal heated my blood.
Zeal knifed through me.
Zeal laced my voice.
Zeal licked through me.
Zeal made me melt.

Zeal penetrated my heart.
Zeal poured through me.
Zeal pulsed through me.
Zeal pumped through me.
Zeal radiated from me.
Zeal ravaged my face.
Zeal rippled through me.
Zeal rose from me.
Zeal rose in me.
Zeal shattered within me.
Zeal slammed into me.
Zeal sluiced through me.
Zeal spiralled through me.
Zeal splintered through me.
Zeal surged through me.
Zeal swelled within me.
Zeal swept through me.
Zeal swirled through me.
Zeal thickened my voice.
Zeal tightened inside me.
Zeal tightened my features.
Zeal wafted through me.
Zeal warmed my insides.
Zeal washed through me.
Zeal went through me.
My blood burned with zeal.

My blood heated with zeal.
My body burned with zeal.
My body drugged with zeal.
My body hardened with zeal.
My body heated with zeal.
My body hummed with zeal.
My body jangled with zeal.
My body shivered with zeal.
My body stirred with zeal.
My body thrummed with zeal.
My body twitched with zeal.
My body unfurled with zeal.
My body vibrated with zeal.
My ears shut in zeal.
My eyes blazed with zeal.
My eyes burned with zeal.
My eyes danced with zeal.
My eyes darkened with zeal.
My eyes dilated with zeal.
My eyes filled with zeal.
My eyes flared with zeal.
My eyes flickered with zeal.
My eyes glazed with zeal.
My eyes gleamed with zeal.
My eyes glittered with zeal.
My eyes glowed with zeal.
My eyes hooded with zeal.
My eyes lit with zeal.
My eyes narrowed with zeal.
My eyes shimmered with zeal.
My eyes sparkled with zeal.
My face filled with zeal.
My face flushed with zeal.
My face mottled with zeal.
My heart burned with zeal.
My heart swelled with zeal.
My pulse raced with zeal.
My skin blushed with zeal.

My skin flushed with zeal.
My voice sang with zeal.
My voice shook with zeal.
My voice slurred with zeal.
Zeal banked in my eyes.
Zeal combated in my brain.
Zeal danced in my belly.
Zeal exploded in my chest.
Zeal flamed in my expression.
Zeal flared in my eyes.
Zeal flashed in my eyes.
Zeal flashed into my eyes.
Zeal flickered in my
expression.
Zeal flickered in my eyes.
Zeal gleamed in my eyes.
Zeal glittered in my eyes.
Zeal nipped at my skin.
Zeal shone in my eyes.
Zeal throbbed against my
belly.
My body was overwrought
with zeal.
My eyes grew hazy with zeal.
My eyes went dark with zeal.
My eyes were bloodshot with
zeal.
My eyes were bright with zeal.
My eyes were dark with zeal.
My eyes were full of zeal.
My eyes were hazy with zeal.
My eyes were heavy with zeal.
My face glazed over with zeal.
My throat was thick with zeal.
My voice was rough with zeal.
My voice was thick with zeal.
Zeal curled deep in my belly.
Zeal pooled low in my belly.

Printed in Great Britain
by Amazon